THIS BOOK HAS EVERYTHING YOU NEED

TO PREPARE FOR THE COAST GUARD

EXAM FROM THE BOTTOM UP

THIS BOOK DOES NOT TELL

YOU HOW TO PASS THE MODULES

IT TEACHES YOU HOW

IF YOU DOUBT THIS STATEMENT

ASK SOMEONE WHO ALREADY

HAS THE LICENSE.

CHANCES ARE VERY GOOD

THIS VOLUME WAS THEIR BIBLE.

THEN THUMB THROUGH THE INDEX

AND THE GLOSSARY.

THIS BOOK IS DEDICATED TO THOSE

WHO WENT BEFORE YOU.

TO THOSE WHO PURCHASED THE BOOK

WITH SERIOUS INTENT AND THEN...

studied for their respective licenses using only this text as a guide.

sat for their exams

took their licenses

and returned to talk

and to criticize

and to suggest

and from these talks the volume you now hold

was conceived.

THE COAST GUARD LICENSE

SIX PAC
TO
MASTER - 100 TONS

SAIL AND POWER

HOW TO PASS THE TEST
A SELF-TEACHING TEXT

14th EDITION

BY BUDD GONDER

Charters West

Publications

CHARTERS WEST

Library of Congress Cataloging in Publication Data

Gonder, Budd
    The Coast Guard License : From Six Pac To Master--100 Tons : sail
and power / by Budd Gonder. -- 14th ed.
        P.   cm.
    Includes index.
    ISBN 1-880093-03-0 : $29.95
    1. Navigation--Examinations, questions, etc. 2. Rules of the road
at sea--Examinations, questions, etc. 3. Ship captains--Licenses-
-United States. I. Title.
VK559.5.G66 1993
623.88'076--dc20   92-38247
                                                      CIP

FOR COROLLARY STUDY MATERIALS

PLEASE CONSULT THE BACK PAGES

OF THIS VOLUME

Charters West Publications
P.O. Box 597
Summerland, CA 93067

For License study support
TEL/FAX (805) 565-1050

READ THIS BEFORE YOU TURN ANOTHER PAGE

Here it is. The closest thing to truth on **the new licenses** you will find on the market today. However, since the license involves dealing with governmental bodies the reader should stand advised that anything herein is subject to change without notice and probably will. Currently, these are the most recent changes inaugurated by the Coast Guard and effective as of December 1, 1987.

License changes or not, it is the exams, appropriate information references and "How To" to which this book addresses itself. Readers should understand that Coast Guard test questions are devised at a central office then sent out to the Regional Exam Centers, (REC's). This relieves the CG personnel with whom you will come in contact of all test error responsibility. Furthermore, they are *under orders* not to reveal to you the questions missed in your exam, only **how many** you missed and whether or not you passed any given module. Regs state you may file a "protest", but this should be done **before** your exam is graded, indicating you have discovered a question with a possible error or several correct multiple choices. Thus, if the CG has erred, you may find ten days later that you actually *did* pass and are now the proud possessor of a license to carry passengers for hire.

Even after conquering this volume you are bound to have questions for your local office. Start your list now. See page 216. You will be glad you did, because no two offices are run exactly the same. The Great White Father in D.C. gives the local kids plenty of room to innovate. Thus, if you are undertaking this monumental task may we suggest you contact your local REC soon. The addresses and phones are on page 202. Aside from any personal questions you may have, you will receive a very interesting twenty-nine page pamphlet. Keep your letter short, but do it today. Three sentences tops. Tell them you are going to sit soon for your Masters Near Coastal Waters, or Great Lakes, or Inland, or perhaps the OUPV (Operator of Uninspected Passenger Vessels) more commonly referred to as the Six Pac.

Six Pac means you can carry as many as six passengers, but more on that later. Also, ask them to send along forms CG-866 and CG-719K as this will save you writing to them again after you get your pamphlet. An example of the CG-866 can be found on page 208-208. The physical form is on page 213-214 in the appendix, but more on health later.

And why isn't that little pamphlet published in this volume? That would be easy, but the basic items set forth in the pamphlet could change and the issue of this book you are reading might be several months or even several years old. On the other hand, the pamphlet you receive from the CG might be revised frequently due to the expected changes. This book is sometimes revised as frequently as six months. In short, if you keep it under 100 tons, this is your book.

They used to call the OUPV the Motorboat Operators License and you needed 365 days at sea, lakes or rivers to be eligible to sit for the exam. Now it's 360 days. But, we're getting ahead of the story. Documentation time and how to do it is found on pages 12-17.

Masters Near Coastal Waters, (Great Lakes and Inland also) are those operating **inspected** vessels carrying more that six passengers for hire. For this you need company letterheads accompanying those official sea time forms; unless you own your own vessel falling into that category.

In either case, it's not going to hurt to include in your letter one sentence asking for the latest requirements for whichever license you seek. You will receive a big packet. Read it carefully and if it doesn't show in two weeks, write for it again. Some of those REC's are real sloppy.

If you are going for a Western River

license, remember that a western river is anything that dumps into the Mississippi.

Turn to page 203 and glance down at item **V** on the application. This concerns nasty little things you might have committed during your roaring youth. If there was a conviction, the FBI has a copy and it is with this august office the Coast Guard turns to learn of your sordid past. Within the bounds of the Code of Federal Regulations (CFR) Title 46, Part IV, there is a paragraph in Subpart "B" #10.201. Within paragraph 10.201 is a sub-paragraph (b) which says: "No person is eligible for a license who has been convicted by a court of record of a violation of the dangerous drug laws of the United States, the District of Columbia, or any state or territory of the United States, within three years prior to the date of filing the application (this period may be extended up to ten years after conviction, if the gravity of the facts or circumstances of the case warrant) or who, **unless he or she furnishes satisfactory evidence of cure**, has ever been the user of or addicted to the use of a dangerous drug."

The bold emphasis are mine. So, let's narrow it down. You were busted for smoking pot last year, or maybe two years ago. Put it down on the application. You might as well. The FBI will turn it up anyway and if you lie you'll really be outside looking in-like forever. Each office can make its own decision on whether or not you're reformed and now a solid citizen. You might get hassled a little. Chances are good they'll overlook it unless it was a biggie. Now, what is satisfactory evidence of cure? I'm not sure myself, but again it depends on who you're talking to and perhaps even how that official person feels at that moment in time. Maybe you'd better get a hair cut, shave and dress up a little just to play it safe.

At the very least, the license should temper the cost of boat ownership. What a cottage industry! Talk about tax breaks. And on the upper echelons this is your first step to the bridge. Think about getting out of the galley, filleting fish, cutting bait or scrubbing down after the long voyage to the sport fishing grounds on a cattle boat. For the oil patch crowd it's a raise in pay and your job tenure takes on new meaning.

Take heart and look around you. If those idiots can do it so can you and chances are good this book had something to do with it. Always remember that anything worth having is worth fighting for.

First, razor blade out the fold-out chart in the back of the book and make lots of copies. **Always make your copies from this master** to prevent distortion found in 2nd and 3rd generation copies. This is the practice chart for all charting problems in the volume. Other examples on pages 204-207 come from the CG data banks using the three east coast charts you will be tested on no matter which exam center is nearest your port. You might want to become familiar with those three chart sets at our black and white price rather than the $13-$14 price Fed Gov price. Stop here for a moment and go read page 203 for a full explanation. Too big to reduce and fit in this volume. If you're going to order from Charters West, do it early on so you will have them when you need them. At this writing, the CG charting exams are given on three charts: 12221, 12354 or 13205. #18531 is used most often for the "Rivers" license.

Alternate chart work with memory cramming things such as the Rules of the Road so you won't forget what you've learned as you go along. Too much of one thing sublimates the others. Utilizing those answer sheets on pages 217-218 will discourage you from entering your answers on the test itself thereby giving yourself tips each time you take the quiz. The test should be clean and unmarked when you take it. And remember, the exam questions in this volume and the same ones appearing on current CG tests. This volume is reprinted approximately every six to eight months just to keep up with the CG question data banks.

Find the Fed Gov issue of your social security card. No fair using those metal or plastic things ordered from magazine ads. Only the real thing will do. Start ordering it now. Locate an official version of your birth certificate with the official seal stamped on it. A U.S. passport will do and sometimes even baptismal records, but check with the CG on any other documents. Not a citizen? That's okay as long as you stick to undocumented vessels and settle for having only the Six Pac ticket. In essence, that means you are limited to vessels of less than five net tons, **because any vessel of five net tons, or more, has to be documented for commercial work.** Don't argue, document it. Any big city telephone directory will list documentation agents. Use one. They know how to fill out the forms and can get action fast.

If it's close by, go visit your local REC. To some it's intimidating the first time around. Some like to go file their sea-time papers, application and medical forms in person rather than simply mailing them in. The physical is now good for a year, but must be on the CG form. A visit gives you a feel for the place and evaporates some of the mystery...and intimidation, if any. If the REC is hundreds of miles away write and ask if there is a "monitoring facility" near you. They do make these arrangements. Maybe everything can be done by mail and save you miles of travel and the expense of taking time off work and the test itself can be taken nearby. Now, let's consider your navigation and study equipment and don't start sweating. These two licenses do not require a celestial exam.

First examine our order form in the back of the book so you can compare prices in your area. At the very least you will need a course plotter and dividers. Ours are the most inexpensive found for the quality and everything is shipped out of Charters West on a one-day turn-around basis.

You will also need some felt pens; red, green, blue and yellow for pages 34-42. What a blast. When was the last time you shopped for school supplies?

Get a good automatic pencil. The Pentels are color coded. Try their Sharplet-2, #A129 which has a buff colored top and tip and has a dark brown cylinder with a lead diameter of 0.9 mm. It runs less than $2. Buy some extra lead and a big eraser. After all this, you're committed. Stick with this book two to three hours per day and you'll have that license in six weeks or less. No kidding. I know a lady in San Jose who bought this book on August 7 with no prior formal experience with the theoretical garbage found here. By September 12, thirty-six days later, *she had her license.* Okay, for all I know maybe she was at it eight hours a day and had an IQ of 180, but it's still a measure of the time it takes.

A continuous flow of complimentary letters arrives in our office. The classic was from a gent in Alaska who said, "Sitting down to that exam was like visiting an old friend. Passed the first time out after four weeks of evening study and I wasn't hurrying."

Think about that. They might have to call you Captain next month.

Budd Gonder
Summerland, CA.
January - 1993

**FOR LICENSE SUPPORT
TEL/FAX (805) 565-1050**

Our 1-800-SEA TEST
number is for ordering only.

‡

CONTENTS

Part I
GENERAL INFORMATION

Part II - RULES OF THE ROAD

Part III - NAVIGATION GENERAL

METRIC MEASURE	U.S.
1000 Meters (M)	3280.8 feet
500M	1640.4 feet
200M	656.2 feet
150M	492.1 feet
100M	328.1 feet
75M	246.1 feet
60M	196.8 feet
50M	164.0 feet
25M	82.0 feet
20M	65.6 feet
12M	39.4 feet
10M	32.8 feet
8M	26.2 feet
7M	23.0 feet
6M	19.7 feet
5M	16.4 feet

DISCLAIMER

This volume, and all prior editions, are **not** to be considered official Rules of The Road. This volume was published **solely** as a study guide for the acquisition of pertinent Coast Guard licenses to carry passengers for hire. The reader should be aware that the options and opinions contained herein are for license study purposes **only** and were not written and published as legal advice or advice on the practical operation of any vessel afloat.

A sincere effort has been made to present all of the examination ramifications, but in view of the widely divergent nature of the Coast Guard Regional Examination Centers' policies, variations are bound to occur.

The ability of a new boat owner to navigate his craft within the confines of a harbor is inversely proportionate to the size of his new toy.

Anyone carrying passengers for hire on the navigable waters of the United States needs the license. It doesn't matter where the waters are, be they inland, in the mountain lakes, down the Mississippi or out to sea. The next part makes hackles stand up on necks. What constitutes carrying passengers for hire?

Don't throw the book across the room. These are decisions handed down by the Coast Guard and the Federal Courts...not me.

1) Anyone accepting money or **gratuities** for taking someone else for a ride on their boat.

Take a friend out and he pays you - you're carrying passengers for hire and should have the license. Towing the neighbors kids water skiing and they never got into the boat because you were doing step starts off the lake front? If he pays you, you're carrying passengers for hire. Now get this; if he buys the gas, you're carrying passengers for hire.

2) You take a friend out fishing and he buys the beer. You're carrying passengers for hire.

3) You take a friend out fishing and he buys dinner that night after you return ashore. You're carrying passengers for hire. The Coast Guard could fine you and seize your vessel.

4) You are a harbor patrolman or a lifeguard working for a city, county or the state in some boat operating capacity. You tow someone in or rescue them with a boat and bring them in to shore. The person you carry does **not** pay you. But, the city does because this is in the course of your duties. You are carrying passengers for hire. Moreover, if you are engaged in towing, the Coast Guard wants you to have the towing endorsement on your license, which isn't a bad thing to have anyway. Most governmental bodies will deny this because recognizing past federal court decisions in the matter would put them out of business. However, just wait until a passenger aboard one of these vessels stubs his toe and sues. Take note: In Los Angeles County, and many other large municipalities, life guards operating boats offshore are required by the city to have the Coast Guard License.

5) You run the shore boat in a very small inland harbor. You take people out to their boats in a small outboard. You work only for tips. You are carrying passengers for hire.

6) You are a yacht salesman or broker. You demonstrate a boat with the client on board and he buys the boat. You collect a commission, either from the client or your broker. You are carrying passengers for hire.

7) You outboard kids around in a remote summer camp on a lake, river or isolated cove someplace. You only take them a few yards from dock to shore or to an activity. If you are a paid counselor, you're carrying passengers for hire.

‡

The Operator of Uninspected Passenger Vessels (OUPV) license used to be called the Motorboat Operators License. It's still called the Six-Pac. The old Ocean Operators License has been phased into what is now termed Master. This can be Master-Great Lakes, Master-Inland, or Master Near Coastal Waters. The coastal ticket is good for 200 miles offshore unless specified otherwise on the license. All licenses are to be carried on board when operating any of these craft for hire. More on this subject on pages 12-17

To date, there is no charge for the Coast Guard exams, but things are changing. At this printing the CG is hard at work attempting to append a stiff fee for the exams and licenses. Better check. There is a list of offices in the appendix. Call the closest one and keep up on it.

There are four or five modules, or sections, on the exam. You must complete them all within ninety days or start again. If you fail one part, you can try again, but three fails *on any part* and you start from scratch. If you fail three parts first time out, you must start all over, even if you did pass one or two of the remaining modules. An unlimited number of retakes is allowed. Most candidates do the whole bit in one day, others need two. It is very unlikely you will ever see the same exam twice. They have plenty of different forms, but retakes could get expensive if they start charging a fee.

Licenses must be renewed every five years with a year of grace to stretch it out, but no passenger carrying allowed during the grace period. The license **renewal** involves taking an open book test on the Rules of the Road and other general items *unless you can document a year of sea time.* Three hundred sixty days sea time **means no renewal exam!** Catch is with a the renewal exam you must get 90% correct. If you fail, they keep sending it back until you pass. If there is any limit, I am unaware of it. Most prefer to do it by mail; that's how open book it is. So, keep track of your sea time after you are licensed.

This publication is concerned with only two licenses. 1) **Operator of Uninspected Passenger Vessels (OUPV)** sometimes called the Six Pac and 2) **Master** up to "less than 100 tons." However, there are certain stipulations you must meet before the Coast Guard will even consider letting you sit for any exam.

THE SIX PAC LICENSE - OUPV.

The OUPV license means you can carry six or less passengers for hire on your own, or someone else's vessel if the vessel is less than 100 *gross* tons. This is more than the *net* tonnage quoted on any documentation papers. Don't call it Six Pac in front of the Coast Guard people. Some of them take offense, but I've never been able to figure out why. Most couldn't care less. Uninspected vessel means the CG isn't going to come running and examine your operation. Having the license means you're supposed to know what's legal and what isn't and abide accordingly. Still, there are some considerations.

While the license permits the holder to carry six or less passengers for hire on an uninspected vessel the keel **must have been laid in the United States.** You might get away with carrying a crew member as well as yourself and the six passengers, but it had better be a big boat and that crew member should not be among the paying guests.

The boat should also be up to current legal standards. As mentioned before, any vessel engaging in commercial activities must be documented if in excess of five net tons. It will need life jackets for everyone, a holding tank if it has a marine head, a special little sign by the engine room that states it's a "no-no" to discharge oily stuff into the waters, visual distress signals, etc. Basically, the same standards required aboard pleasure boats. One significant difference is the special type of life jacket required. Look carefully on most of the Personal Flotation Devices (PFD's) aboard pleasure craft and you will notice they are "approved" by the CG to be used on vessels **not carrying passengers for hire.** Carrying passengers means a special PFD I. Ask your chandler. They can show you a catalog. There are other requirements, but they are covered in the body of this text, mostly in the quiz sections. Watch for them.

Who do you have to be to get a Six Pac? Age, eighteen. Citizenship is not required unless you are operating a vessel of five net tons or more. You must prove 360 days at sea, twenty-five percent of which must have been within the last three years, (that's only ninety days). If you are going for the Near Coastal Waters license three months of that year at sea will have to be offshore-in the ocean. The rest can be inland. There is no longer a general area restriction on your license other than the distance offshore you will be allowed to operate, or an area assigned by the Officer In Charge (OinC) should he feel operational limits are warranted, say, due to the applicant's lack of experience. Such a restriction is rare.

There is also a provision for those running small passenger vessels for camps, yacht clubs and marinas. If acceptable to the OinC, your qualifying service can be limited to just four months on the Great Lakes and Inland, but your area of operation will be restricted to the area of experience. This limited license is also available in coastal waters with three months experience, but is also limited to uninspected vessels of less than 100 gross tons and the area of operation is limited. All applicants must supply evidence of having successfully completed a basic boating course with a boating organization such as the U.S. Power Squadron, the Coast Guard Auxiliary or the National Red Cross. This license is called a Limited Masters and could change at any time.

Three hundred sixty days at sea? How do you prove that? You can vouch for your own time if you've owned your own boat for a few years simply by filling out the appropriate sea time forms and filling in the blanks. Look at the blank squares on the form, page 205. A separate sheet should be used for each vessel, but note the squares only ask for "how many" days, not specifically which ones. Don't fill in the individual dates, just the *number* of days. If the vessel served on belonged to someone else you will need a letter attesting to your time from the owner or the licensed skipper who was in charge. Some offices want that signature notarized!! Such a letter will still not excuse you from filling out the usual sea time documents.

You will notice there are three separate forms from page 205-210. One is for

military service. Military service is acceptable if the vessel was close to same gross tonnage as the license for which you are applying. See page 211. Maybe you operated the captain's gig or a navy tourist boat in Pearl Harbor. If you have Coast Guard time you probably have it made as most CG discharges list the duty stations and vessels on the back and many are smaller air-sea rescue units. The Coast Guard assumes that about 60% of the time served on *all* military vessels was underway time unless you can document more.

The third is a Merchant Marine form. This form would more often be used for a Master's application than a Six Pac. Use it if you were working for someone else. The CG will also want a letter from the company attesting to your sea duty with them and it should be on the company letterhead. Be sure that secretary up front includes the following:
1) Name of vessel(s) and registration or documentation number(s) as well as the length of the vessel(s) and gross tonnage.
2) Dates of employment **aboard** when **underway**. This can be two inclusive dates but the exact number of days will have to be stated in no uncertain terms.
3) Be sure they include your area of operation and the number of hours per day you were on duty or standing watch. Currently, they are accepting four hour days for Six Pac but eight hour days for Masters. They love blue water time. Most OinC's will give you a day-and-a-half for twenty-four hour days underway. For Six Pac or Master's time aboard your own vessel, use the one entitled "Small Boat Experience".

The boats. Ah yes, the boats. Just about any old boat will do, but never mind the small outboard skiffs or daysailers unless it's a minimum of your time afloat. That might be all you get licensed for after passing the exam. Think about the size of the boat(s) you plan on using for declaring time. Maybe you have another question for the CG that should go on page 216.

Great Lakes licenses can be used on the Western Rivers but not vice versa. A

Great Lakes License makes the holder eligible to operate on any Inland waters. Great Lakes licenses mean extensive exams and include a test module on the COLREGS, otherwise known as the International Rules of The Road. However, any river license can be extended onto the Great Lakes with appropriate experience and re-examination. Coastal licenses can be used on the Great Lakes or any Inland waters. Great Lakes and Inland candidates might also investigate the concept of "mate" aboard inspected vessels. If allowed by the REC, you can take the exam with from three to six months experience, pass, serve aboard as a mate and then have your license issued when you complete your time afloat.

On the Western Rivers they call it a "Rivers" license. Like the Inland licenses there are some real on-going and ever-changing quirks to these River tickets. If you're thinking Inland or Rivers, call your local REC. There's an excellent chance you might have a very limited test on navigation and can ignore about the last fifty pages of this book. Again, a list of the REC's is listed on page 202.

Foreign vessel time is acceptable and time spent aboard vessels in foreign waters is also permissible if you can document it. Maybe now is the time to start contacting your friends vacationing in the Gobi Desert for their **notarized signatures** attesting to those six months you spent together cruising the Greek Isles. Get those letters in the mail today.

There is a space on the sea time forms for the Official Number. For most of us this means the state-issued numbers on the bow. If documented, the numbers are carved into the keel. Six digits for the latter. You say you've forgotten the state registration numbers on the boat you sold eighteen years back? Try the family photograph album.

How big can the boat be? If you are sitting for the Six Pac license your time should be on vessels less than one hundred gross tons and that's not demanding too much. A Sail Endorsement is required for Master's tickets, but not for Six Pacs. If you have done any sailing at all, the test is an insult to your intelligence. See page

157. You will need a year on sailing craft to have the endorsement on Great Lakes or Coastal Waters. Six months on Inland waters.

What if your own boat has a foreign laid keel? You're out of luck! It is illegal for a foreign laid keel vessel to engage in coast wise or inland trade. Besides, if it's over 5 net tons it must be documented to engage in trade and foreign vessels are hard to document as U.S. craft. This can be quite a shock for Taiwanese, Hong Kong and even Japanese made boat owners, but that's the breaks. Check it out with your local REC office. They'll be delighted to clarify it for you.

Ah, you're thinking, my boat can carry more than six passengers and do it safely. Well, at this writing the CG is thinking about extending the Six Pac to a Twelve Pac, but it's still in the works and the Rules are the Rules. Keep in touch with your local office, but be careful who you talk to. Some of those kids working in there will tell you anything to get you off the phone. If you want the knowledge for keeps, write them and get your answer in writing.

If your craft was originally built to CG specs you have another story and *maybe at one time* it was licensed to carry more than six passengers. In other words, it was an **inspected** vessel. If so, the boat once proudly carried, stapled to the pilot house bulkhead, a "certificate of inspection".
Maybe it can again and you're rich.

To *rebuild* a vessel to CG specs means literally tearing it apart. You would be better off buying a new one already built to CG specs. A naval architect can clue you in on the basic differences. Here, we're concerned more with licenses than the vessels.

Master To 100 Tons
Near Coastal Waters, Great Lakes and Inland Waters and Rivers.

You must be nineteen years old and have two years of service on vessels commensurate with the tonnage you want to work offshore. Only one year is required on Inland waters. The Master's license in this book is limited to 100 gross tons on Near Coastal Waters -less than 200 miles offshore-The Great Lakes and Western Rivers. If you skipped over the Six Pac License paragraphs above, go back and read them. Especially the part about documenting your sea time. If you are one of those who skips book introductions, stop here. Go back to page 5. There's important info there you need.

As indicated and will be discussed again later in this chapter, you must be a U.S. citizen and nineteen years of age. This license is issued in varying increments up to a point called "less than 100 gross tons". With this you can operate "inspected" vessels. By inspected it is meant that the CG has approved the original design, then watched carefully to make sure the builder conformed to the specs as the vessel was constructed. A Certificate of Inspection is then issued and tacked up in the pilot house. Even then, the CG makes periodic re-inspections. This certificate tells how many passengers the vessel can carry, required crew and the route permitted.

What if you had two years of good verifiable coastal sea time and you wanted to sit for the Master's exam instead of the Six-Pac? How much of that time should be aboard the heavier vessels and how heavy should they be? That's another REC decision, but read page 17 for a close description and remember that OinC's (Officer In Charge) do make decisions. Be nice and smile. The tests aren't all that different between Six Pac and Masters, so if you **can** go for the heavier Master's ticket, **do it.**

If a vessel is underway for more than twelve hours, **two** skippers are required or the presence of a "licensed mate." In some areas, they have what has come to be called a "Second Operator" to operate in place of a second fully licensed skipper. This second ticket man cannot operate the vessel without a licensed skipper aboard, but it saves the expense of hiring two licensed skippers. How do you get a second ticket? If there's a man on board who has ninety days of sea time with the boat and can pass the exam they will give him the second license. When the second ticket man has completed his sea time the

regular license will be issued to him.

Again, this book is mainly concerned with the exams and how to pass them. The license information is never free of change although lately things seem to have stabilized and become rather consistent from one REC to another. For example all of the modules, except Rules of The Road, are open book! Hey, all you need to know is which book has which info. Ah ha! The big catch. It's so complex that Charters West has a video with that info included. Shows you what the books look like and how the referencing works. Weird. That is, what books in the exam room contain which information. And note - when they say open book, they mean *their books,* not yours. You can't bring in your own and **never, never, never** walk into a REC carrying this volume. You could be shot.

Page 22 outlines some of the references and you **can buy your own set,** if indeed money is secondary to you. They are available from the Government Book Stores throughout the US as listed on page 215, but caution is advised. The CFR's (Codes of Federal Regulations) are extensive and expensive and often outdated on the shelves. If you purchase any of those described on page 215 keep in mind they should be dated *later than* January of 1988.

SEA TIME DOCUMENTATION AND OTHER GOOD STUFF

Time is allowed from training schools. Not more than two-thirds of the approved training courses can be substituted for the two years needed as time on deck, but that much would be unusual. They don't say so, but we're talking about major academy time such as the Annapolis Naval Academy, the New London Coast Guard Academy, or one of the maritime academies in Vallejo and at King's Point. If you are planning on attending an "approved" school make sure it is accredited with the Coast Guard. Ask the Coast Guard, not the school administrator. Service as an instructor at a bona fide school is creditable on a two for one basis; two months teaching is good for one month of sea time. Other experience in "marine related fields" is sometimes applicable. There's another question for page 216 if you think there is something in your history which might qualify.

What about your time from twenty years ago? What if you have only recently been dumb enough to go down to the sea again? Apparently, the only thing that matters is that 25% of your time must have been within the last three years. And how far back can you go as far as your own age is concerned? What about fishing out there with Daddy and Uncle Luke when you were twelve years old? The only mention made concerning ages in the Code of Federal Regulations revolves around how old you have to be to acquire various licenses. For example; you have to be eighteen for the Six Pac, nineteen for the Masters less than 200 tons and 21 years old for everything else. That gives rise to some interesting considerations.

If a nineteen-year-old applies for a Master's ticket verifying two years of time afloat, when did he get the time? It would have to be during the last year he was out of high school and maybe he really did go to sea for eight hours every day of that year. Now, we need one more year. Most public schools are in session for 180 days (six months) out of the year. If he took to the ocean the other six months he would have had to start doing so at the age of sixteen to make it and that means he hasn't had a day off in three years wherein he wasn't either at sea or in school. Okay, maybe he got smart and quit school, but theoretically doesn't this make your sea time eligibility go way back? And, of course, you'd need those registration numbers from the book you went out in with Daddy and Uncle Luke. Hey, anyone spending that much time out there is certifiable and shouldn't have the license anyway.

Military time. Kind of tricky so listen up. You can get credit for time on a craft up to 60% of the time spent on board. They *assume* you were at sea 60% of the time aboard, but there are other considerations. For example; what were your duties? Chief cook and bottle washer ain't gonna make it. Bos'n,

deckhand, radar operator, seaman, quartermaster and the like are considered *if you can prove the time aboard was applicable*. The burden of proof is on **you**. What they're looking for is deck hand experience. Back to page 216.

One would assume the closer you can come to 100 gross tons, the heavier a license you will receive. Most offices will issue the license in increments of 25 tons up to the max. They have a paragraph relevant to this. It states that on vessels not more than 200 gross tons, "the license will be limited to maximum tonnage on which at least 25% of the required experience was obtained, or 150% of the maximum tonnage on which at least 50% of the service was obtained, whichever is higher." So, get out your pencil and start calculating.

When the qualifying service is obtained upon vessels of five gross tons or less, the license will be limited to vessels of not more than 25 gross tons.

About time acquired before your license was granted. Ordinarily, any time acquired prior to the issuance of your original license is no longer valid. That is, if you had say, three months on a 150 ton vessel, but you did not declare it for your original license, don't plan on saving it to add to future time on another 150 ton or 200 ton craft. It's dead time. Not so with the sail endorsement qualifying time. Also, pre-license time can *sometimes* be used for "crossing-over" meaning the level of license. Often this is a decision left to individual REC's; again to page 216 if this might be applicable to your case. Also glance at page 159.

‡

Current CPR and Red Cross First Aid Certificates are required for all original licenses. Only CPR is required for renewals and must be earned within a year of your application. Also, start looking for a doctor *qualified* to give the dope test. Not all of them are. Very tricky.

The Coast Guard is continually revamping their requirements and test data banks. New sets of questions come up on a regular basis. While this book is reprinted about every six to eight months, there is no keeping up with this bureaucracy. So, take advantage of the situation and send us a self-addressed stamped envelope and we will mail you the latest updates...assuming there are any. This offer will be repeated several times in this volume.

As for the ever-changing data banks, well we try to keep on top of it and indicate additional test questions available to candidates. Even new rules are added, e.g., this recent thing about alternately flashing red and yellow lights for regattas. Yes! Regattas-sailboats racing and often monitored by committee boats or patrol vessels with flashing blue lights. The whole bit.

This particular new one is included with the Inland Rules quiz (all nineteen questions the CG is currently using) further on in this volume, so unlax for now. If you like to practice passing the tests, see the order form in the back of the book. Our prices are kept to a real minimum.

NEVER GIVE THE COAST GUARD ANY FORMS YOU HAVEN'T COPIED FOR YOUR OWN FILES. Take it from a pro. Someday you will need to access those records.

Always keep the land in sight, And never never sail at night.

GENERAL HEALTH REQUIREMENTS

1) No color blindness is allowed. I know one color blind captain, but he ran a long gamut of appeals to Washington, D.C. and his license restricts him to daytime operations. (Not that he lets that stop him). The red-green blindness is of particular concern to the CG. Even after your doctor has O.K.'ed your vision, they have a habit of screening applicants for color blindness right in the CG office. They even do this for renewals although it has been known for years that color blindness is a genetic birth defect and not progressively acquired; either you have it or you don't. They generally use the Ishihara psuedo-isochromatic plates, the one composed with little dots and shaded numbers.

2) Your corrected vision (glasses) should be at least 20/40 in each eye. Uncorrected vision should be at least 20/200 in each eye. If those numbers are as mysterious to you as they are to me, go check with your doctor.

3) Expect to be in fair physical condition. That ticker is going to get a check out. They check blood pressure, heart beat, turn your head and cough, depth of focus, color blindness and do a urinalysis for chemical dependency.

4) Any urine specimen will immediately show use of narcotics. If you're a user, either cure your habit or forget the license.

5) Your hearing will undergo a test, but many doctors are not equipped with an audiometer for accurate testing. They all have their own techniques for testing. Years ago one individual swore a nurse stood at the end of a long hallway and speaking in a low voice asked him to repeat his name. Sometimes, it's comical.

A copy of the current health form used by the Coast Guard is located in the appendix, but it isn't enough. As of December 21, 1990 the "periodic chemical testing" became effective as per 46 CFR (Title 46 Code of Federal Regulations) 16.220.

In other words, for renewals and original licenses a dope test is required. Sad part is, not all doctors, clinics and hospitals are set up to cope with this highly regulated and expensive test. It requires special handling with a chain of possession security. There is a list of Coast Guard Regional Exam Centers (REC's) in the appendix. Call the one nearest you for a list of available clinics, doctors and local labs.

If God had wanted man to learn to swim he would not have invented Cals, Valiants, Bertrams and the Cape Hatteras.

"If you can hear thunder, see lightning and eat mush, you're in."

CONSIDER

When you purchased this volume you became privy to some very special information and tips. Things from those who went before you. While reading remember that not all offices are the same. Some are drowning in a deluge of paperwork, stress and tension while others are dying for someone to drop by and talk. Mo bettah you learn it here than the hard way.

No one has ever accused the Coast Guard of being User Friendly. They don't care whether you get that license or not. You are dealing with an impersonal bureaucracy. Like all such "public servants" they are good at shrugging or pointing their fingers at someone else. You can buck it. In the long run you might even win, but it could get costly in time and travel. Running back and forth can be a real drag. So, go in smiling. Ask for help and look them right in the eye while you're smiling. **Oh God, keep smiling.**

Avoid taking your exam on a Monday, a Friday or just before a national holiday. When you commence a test module many offices will insist you finish by lunch, or if you start after lunch you will have to finish by closing time. Lunch can start at 1130. Quitting time can be as early as 1530. If you are in the examining room on Tuesday afternoon and still hard at it by 1530, they might let you stay until 1600, or even 1630 to finish while they clean up the day's mess. But, don't bet on it when Friday rolls around. What about Monday? Monday is the day everyone wants canceled. Do you think the CG personnel are any different? National holidays almost always come on Monday or Friday. Going in on a Thursday before a Friday or a national holiday might mean you are interfering with a few of the brass getting away early for that three day holiday. Wouldn't your chances be better on Tuesday, Wednesday or Thursday? When you call for your appointment try for one of those three.

Don't go in with a friend. Or, if you do, ignore the friend. Many CG officers are suspicious and don't like to see two people having lunch together and comparing notes before they come back in for the afternoon session. He travels fastest who travels alone.

If you can find one, get a waterfront doctor for your physical. Your own physician might put a check mark in the wrong place. If he does, the CG *could* send you back to have it done over. There's a waterfront doctor in every waterfront town. Ask around. For example, in San Pedro it's William R. Anderson, M.D. 593 West Sixth St. No appointment. Open at 0830 five days a week. Get there early and you'll be out by 0930 or sooner. Cheap. A good seaman's doctor has the medical exam forms on hand including the dope tests.

If you fail the exam, say the Rules of The Road part, and you know darn well you're right and they're wrong...**AND IT HAPPENS**...you will probably ask to see what you missed and the correct answer. Forget it. They won't show you missed answers. If you feel one of the questions was wrong and you wish to challenge it they have a "protest form" you can fill out, but do it **before you hand in your test.** There is a great deal of haggling going on between marine instructors and the U.S. Coast Guard. Heated correspondence and vigilant monitoring of the REC's actually led to two things; the license and exam changes of December 1, 1987 and the release under the Freedom of Information Act of all marine related exams by the Coast Guard. You will be taking some of those tests shortly, but all is not settled, nor are the tests flawless. One marine instructor on the Gulf Coast waltzed into a REC and took the AB maritime test to demonstrate the major faults and errors in their tests. Out of 175 questions he filed 35 protests! In Juneau they discovered the charting tests answers were based on the CG using a deviation chart incorrectly. How many failed before they chanced upon that flub?

You may not get an answer to your protest then and there, but your challenge will be investigated and you will be informed. In any case, they will not discuss the questions with you other than to give you general feed back on your weak areas and then only if they have time. CG logic is that they are not a training institution and therefore owe you nothing in the way of explanation or anything even faintly related to furthering your education. But, what do you care? You have (ahem!) this book.

I know what you're thinking. You're concerned about the Freedom of Information Act which would allow you to see your files. True, but the paper work would kill you. Recall also, that in any bureaucracy, dignity, false or otherwise, is all prevailing. Destroy that dignity, or challenge the authority and you could be making enemies. On the other hand, a bully slapped will generally tend to back off next time.

You should be aware of the CG chain of command in an examination center. First comes the Chief Petty Officer. Once he's put in a little time and gets his bearings he can be a wealth of information. Just above him is an officer with the rank of Lieutenant j.g. He's referred to as the "examining officer" or Inspector-Personnel. Just above him is a Commander -the SIP, (Senior Inspector Personnel) to whom you would make your first appeal. You might have to cool your heels in the outer office or return another day, so take a good book. After him is a four-striper, a captain with the title of MSO, or Marine Safety Officer. After that you move to the main district office where you find the District Commander. Generally, a captain or admiral. The next step is Washington, D.C. and by then their wagons are in a circle.

There's another side to the story. Junior grade officers don't care to have their decisions overturned. But more than that they detest having the commander down the hall stick a nose in their little bailiwick. Too many candidates do that and the commander **down** the hall starts wondering what's going on **up** the hall. Something he's supposed to do anyway.

Once in Long Beach's REC a friend of mine went in for an upgrade from 50 tons to 100 tons on the old Ocean Operator ticket. He got what he wanted, but when the j.g. went to stamp the little red ink CG seal on it he inadvertently stamped it right over the "100" in 100 tons. Buck had worked long and hard for his new tonnage and wasn't about to have it marred.

"Hey," he said. "You screwed it up. I want that to show. Can I have another license?"

Voiding a license and typing up another one is one big pain. The j.g. said something to the affect, "No way. We're busy here today. I can read that. It's okay the way it is."

"I want a new one."

"You're not getting a new one. Now beat it."

"Where's the C.O's office?"

"Down the hall, but he's a busy man."

"So am I, because I have to *make* my living instead of sitting around all day drinking coffee and contemplating my retirement."

Buck went down the hall, told the C.O's yeoman he was waiting to see the man and sat down. In about two minutes down came the j.g.

"Okay, I found a little time. Come on back and I'll see what I can do."

There are two important points here. 1) Buck already had his license. 2) He was dead right and knew it. Being right hangs pretty heavy here. Think about that, but anyone who thinks the Coast Guard or this book is flawless will not only believe Michael Jackson still has his original nose, but that Madonna is a shy and retiring virgin.

⚓

At this writing there are seventeen Regional Examination Centers (REC's) and several monitoring facilities. A complete list of the REC's can be found in the appendix. These "Centers" are charged with administering **all** the United States maritime exams; meaning everything from the OUPV to Master's unlimited oceans and tonnage not to mention the engineering bit. Most offices will require an appointment to take any exam. No two are alike.

The various test modules of the Six Pac (OUPV) and Masters less than 100 tons should not vary considerably from office to office. They all cover the same basic areas. Each office is bound by general guidelines when it comes to something as loose as assigning routes, but they must uphold the basic stipulations set forth in the mandates of Congress.

More about those four or five test modules mentioned earlier. Only the Rules of the Road module requires 90% to pass and is the only test **not** an open book exam requiring shifting into compound low. The other modules require 70% to pass and are open book. If you fail any modules you will be asked to wait at least ten days before attempting the exam again. When appointment time comes try asking if you can have two or three separate appointments maybe ten days apart. That way you could concentrate on one or two modules at a time. However, there are two problems here. It doesn't leave much room for failure and for anyone living far from the REC this can be very difficult and expensive.

The four modules are: **The Rules of The Road; Navigation/General; Deck/-General and Deck/Safety;** (both treated as one exam module) and **Chart Navigation.** Some will argue that Deck/General and Deck/Safety are different exams, but they are administered in the REC's as one exam. All modules are given in multiple choice format. Many candidates finish the entire ordeal in one day and exit with the license in hand. Nice goal. You won't be in the exam room for much more than two-three hour periods, i.e., six hours total, but don't let anyone tell you it's not a tough exam. Your success will be directly proportionate to how well and how consistently you study then how cool you are in the exam room. That is, you don't go bananas nervous when they lay that paper in front of you. Don't be discouraged by others who flay their arms and legs in the air telling you about the 99% failure rate. Bull. They're either the ones that haven't got the guts to try or they have their license and have little desire to see what they believe will become a flooded marketplace.

The exams don't always follow a particular sequence. The numbers below are merely a numerical guide.

1) **Rules of the Road.** There are two kinds of rules questions, but all on the same test and frequently mixed. Each question indicates that it is one of three types: Inland only, International only, or both. This particular body of marine law is referred to as the COLREGS (which means *Collision Regulations*). Our own U.S. Inland Rules of the Road are sometimes called the UNIFIED RULES, because they used to be so different from International. Our act is getting better, but there are still some sneaky differences we will point out. If you are after a coastal or Great Lakes route endorsement, you should know them all thoroughly. Relax, both are covered more than adequately in this book. It's the concept, or *why* the answer is what it is rather than simply *what* the answer might be. It was with this goal in mind that the questions in this volume were included. They all came from the Coast Guard data banks. In other words, the questions included herein were chosen as "teaching" test questions because they force you to learn the rules in an indirect manner not quite as boring as having to read and memorize the Rules themselves. In short, learning is better than memorizing any day. Your thirty will come from our *237 Rules* indicated on the order form, but never mind that now. Get the ones in the book straight first then the others will make more sense. **Getting right down to it, you don't really need anything more than this volume to make it as long as you have a current edition.** If you are sitting for the Inland license you

will take only the Inland Rules exam, but knowing both will help you see important differences. We will repeat this later, but finish your studies, then a week before your test appointment, sit down and read a copy of the Navigation Rules. They will make more sense than reading them now.

2) On the **Navigation/General** module you will need 70% passing. It will contain such questions as to the size, shape and color of buoys and where they belong in a channel. You will have chart symbols, weather, compass error, tides and government publications, to name a few. It is an open book exam. In this manual these groups are separated in both text and sample questions for easier mastering, but in the CG exams they will be well mixed.

3) **Chart/Navigation** is where you shine showing them how you can find your way from point "A" to point "B" without getting lost around "X" someplace. Ten problems with everything from simple dead reckoning to set and drift. Again, multiple choice. If you have trouble learning from a book like me, we have a video.

4) **Deck General** and **Deck/Safety** refers to seamanship in general along with rescue procedures, safety at sea, fire prevention and fire fighting, lifeboats, marlinspike seamanship, boat handling, minor main-tenance of engines, fueling, shipboard vocabulary -most of which belongs in the Merchant Marine- towing, anchoring, stability and certain subjects found referenced in the Codes of Federal Regulations (CFR's), some of which are indicated above and the subject of Pollution and the laws governing it.

The CFR's - No one could possibly memorize all the rules, regulations and safety demands written in the Code of Federal Regulations (CFR's). Reference is made to pollution as found in CFR Title 33 (Navigation & Navigable Waters) but mostly Title 46 (Shipping). These are certain federal rules and regulations relative to the operation of ships, large and small. Not everything on your Deck/Gen-

eral and Deck/Safety tests requires reference to the Codes, but there will be a few. The secret to getting through this test is being able to find the correct **Part** in any of these Titles when you need them. The Parts are numbered (as in **CFR Parts 166 to 199**) and seem infinite on the book shelf to anyone trying to find a simple answer. For example, Title 46 of the CFR's has nine volumes (numbered by **PART** on each spine) averaging over 300 pages each and we're talking small print and the index is not as simple as the one found in this volume. What you need is a guide to what **Parts** to seek out which also tells you which volume to pull down. Thus, once into the volume look at the Table of Contents in the front. This generally shows up around page 3, -as opposed to page iii- where the parts and pages are referenced. Go to the **Part** indicated by the page number. At the beginning page of each **Part** is a listing of **Sub-parts** and you're almost home free. Here's a list of the **Parts** (volumes) relative to the test you will take for the OUPV or Master to 100 tons. Put them on a list someplace and memorize them just before you stumble through the door. Our video entitled: "The Coast Guard License," spends about twenty minutes detailing these references, what they look like and the important indexes and table of contents therein.

33 CFR

Subchapter M - Marine Pollution Financial Responsibility and Compensation. **Parts 130-137.** Material for your oil pollution test.

Subchapter O - Pollution. **Parts 151-159.**

46 CFR

Subchapter C - Uninspected Vessels.
Parts 24-26. A biggee and most applicable for passenger carrying Six Pac vessels.
Subchapter H - **Parts 70-89.** This also includes passenger vessels *over* 100 gross tons, so watch your tonnage applications on your Master's ticket.
Subchapter T - **Parts 175 to 187.** Small passenger vessels *under* 100 gross tons. Most important to **your** cause.
Deck Safety has much more to it than simply the CFR's, but all of the other subjects are well covered in this volume.

WARNING

Perhaps this next part sounds like an apology, but you should know. No way does this volume have all the test questions. The questions were picked so you will learn from the answers. Still, a good sampling, but certainly not all there are. No way would they fit here and the CG keeps releasing new ones. So, Charters West published what we call **The Supplement** and **237 Rules**, both of which are easier to update than this volume. These are for candidates feeling they need more direct quiz work before taking on the CG, or perhaps if they should fail. (Ugh! - dirty four letter word).

We have extra quizzes are on all of the modules including Navigation. If you take the *Supplement,* with the *237 Rules,* and our *Chartlets* you will have almost 1100 questions and exercises taken directly from the CG data banks under the Freedom of Information Act. The CG bucked the decision and lost. Don't think they didn't say nasty things about that federal judge.

Charters West ships the next business day after receipt of the order. For east coast delivery plan on about six working days (UPS) and west coast about three working days. All costs are listed on the order form in the back of this book, but remember; all you're getting are hundreds of quiz questions and answers the CG has dreamed up and Charters West has re-published. No instructions as you will find in this book.

But, I gotta tell you before you spend any more money. We have a fat file of letters from lots of people who got their license from studying this book and nothing else.

‡

BRAG TIME

PRIVATE SEMINARS

At Charters West, I make arrangements to travel out for private seminars. These are held in four consecutive days from 0800 to 1100 and again from 1400 to **1700 each of the four consecutive days.** This means a great deal of hands-on classroom work involving plotting sessions, flashcards, gab festivities, instruction, reviews and scads of good memory crutches. I won't simply tell you how to pass that test, I'll **teach** you. This is not a hype class, it's a learning center. I get you over the big humps and after I'm gone all you have to do is absorb the memory units and practice the tests. You'll be amazed at how smart you really are.

"Cram" is a bad word. The process is an easy-easy thing with everything starting from the bottom up. I assume no one knows **anything.** Minimum- ten students, max is fifteen. Call up (1-800-SEA TEST) and I'll explain the details then send them in writing.

If you're the organizer in your squadron, flotilla, yacht or men's club send for details. If you're alone or there's only a few of you consider an ad in the newspaper under Job Training, Education, Personal or simply the Boats For Sale. Many experienced boaters crave this coveted scroll of expertise and will come storming out of their bilges in response to an offered class.

‡

RULES OF THE ROAD

When someone says "Rules of The Road" they're not just talking a list of specs you're suppose to memorize and spit out when told. The Rules come in several sections, all interrelated, yes, but individual within their own scopes. Consider the following arbitrary sub-divisions. It might help you keep things straight.

1) The correct maneuvering procedures based on which vessel has the right-of-way.
2) The correct signals when executing these maneuvers.
3) The signals in restricted visibility.
4) The visibility of lights. How far they should be seen on a dark and clear night.
5) The pecking order as regards rights-of-way.
6) The required lights and dayshapes to be shown on vessels underway, at anchor and aground.

Don't dwell continuously on the Rules. Take a break and move to the charting section to start honing your navigation skills. After a few days, go back to the Rules. Alternating these sections will keep you current on both.

‡

LAZY MAN'S VIDEO ANYONE?

We're not talking about a lot of flash and splash here, Just good hard information you need. We looked over the competition and it's rather sad, not to mention their exorbitant prices, so we went to work with model boats and a variety of examples. We mean lights, dayshapes, arcs of visibility, pecking order and maneuvering laws including the elusive restricted visibility signals. This isn't a series of second hand pictures from a book, nor is it simply a face talking at you. There is even a light and dayshape quiz at the end with immediate key recognition. Run it again and again until you have it straight. Nicely filmed and I betcha' we blow the rest of the CG license tapes right off the shelves. Since there are no middle men distributors we can sell it cheap. See the order form.

REQUIRED READING FOR VICTIMS OF DEATH AT SEA DUE TO COLLISION:

THE RULES OF THE ROAD.

RIGHTS OF WAY

Note the arcs of Vessel "A's" sidelights. Each side shines from dead ahead to 22.5° abaft the beam. Aft of this point the sidelights cannot be seen. Thus, if the sidelights disappear the sternlight shows up immediately. On this approach a vessel is overtaking. Forward of this mystical point called "22.5° abaft the beam" a vessel is either crossing or coming head-on. This makes vessels "D" and "E" overtaking "A", which gives "A" the right of way. Not even sailboat "D" has the right of way when overtaking! Crafts "F" and "G" are forward of 22.5° abaft the beam and, if at night, would see a green light. "F" and "G" have the right of way over "A". "B" has the right of way over "A" by virtue of being a sailboat. "C" must give way to "A".

When two vessels meet head-on there is no right of way conferred. Each should direct her course to starboard to pass port-to-port which is the **preferred** maneuver.

Passing in a narrow channel in International waters requires a special signal. There are no special signals in Inland waters for passing in a narrow channel. Some countries have no Inland rules and use International for everything. See "Maneuvering Signals" in this volume and note the signals are different when passing to port than passing to starboard. If "A" does not respond with the proper signal granting permission to pass try again. If "A" sounds five or more short blasts this indicates "doubt" or "danger". Wait. Try again later.

Both Inland and International require **all** vessels approaching a bend or **channel obstruction** to sound a prolonged blast. Coast Guard tests make a point of emphasizing one prolonged blast must be given **Inland** by vessels leaving a pier or berth. This includes, the CG insists, when **backing** away from berths or piers.

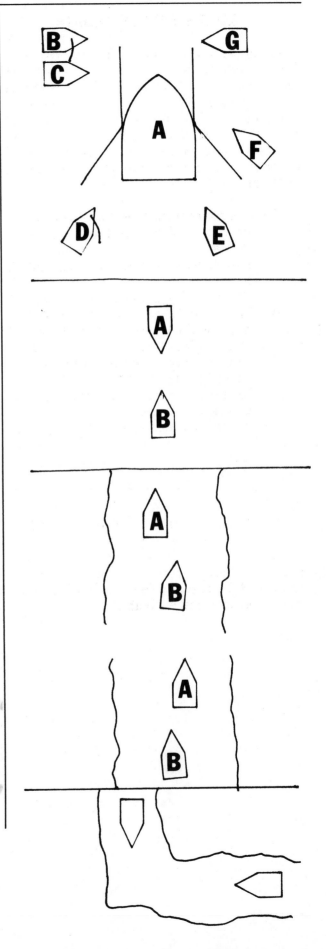

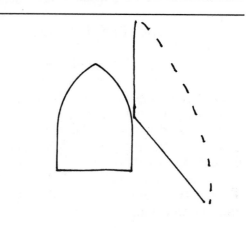

Vessels approaching from within the range of another's starboard sidelights have the right-of-way in any crossing situation. Thus, any power boat's starboard side, within this arc, is considered the "danger zone". Rules require a lookout in restricted visibility or when traffic is heavy. The helmsman **cannot** be considered a lookout. In International waters, a flashing one second white light visible for five miles can **supplement** the sound signals. Inland, the light can be white **or** yellow, visible for two miles. One flash equals a short blast, two are given for two blasts, etc. Inland rules allow maneuvering agreement via radio-telephone. International does not.

Sailboats have their own rights-of-way rules when encountering each other. First, a vessel on the starboard tack, (wind coming over starboard side-so mainboom is over port side) has the right of way over a sailboat on the port tack. Second: A sailboat on the same tack as another, but down wind of the other sailboat has the right-of-way. Also, if in doubt as to the other's tack-assume you are the give-way craft. In this diagram: "D" has the right-of-way over "A". "C" over "D", "B" over "A", "C" over "A", "E" over "A", "E" over "A" and "D" over "B".

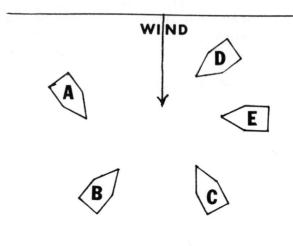

Definition of a sailboat's tack. A sailboat's tack is called on the basis of the **opposite** side over which the mainboom is extended. Mainboom over port side-starboard tack. Mainboom over starboard side-port tack.

Note the third diagram. "A" is on a port tack, "B" on a starboard tack. If "B" suddenly decided to come right, "A" would have to move...fast. And; "D" has the right of way over "C" as "D" is to the lee of "C"...downwind of "C". Then "B" has the right of way over "E" even through "E" is to the lee. Tack takes precedence as it is called out first in the Rules. But, "E" has the right-of-way over "A".

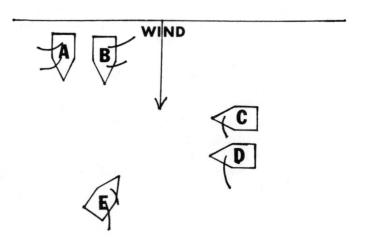

INTERNATIONAL

HEAD ON

One Short Blast - I **AM** altering my course to starboard to pass port side to.

Two Short Blasts - I **AM** altering my course to port.

Three Short Blasts - I **AM** operating in astern propulsion.

CROSSING

One Short Blast - Initiated by the give-way craft indicating she **IS** altering course to starboard to pass astern of the oncoming craft, or is slowing to allow other vessel to maintain course & speed **which is the duty of the stand-on craft.**

OVERTAKING

One Short Blast - Altering course to starboard to overtake vessel ahead. If "danger" signal is sounded, abort maneuver and try again later.

Two Short Blasts - Same as above but vessel overtaking is coming left to pass.

OVERTAKING
IN A NARROW CHANNEL

Two Prolonged - One Short. Given by the overtaking vessel in a narrow channel when the overtaking craft wishes to pass the vessel ahead by coming **right** and passing to the other vessel's starboard side.

Two Prolonged - Two Short. Same as above but coming **left** to pass.

**One Prolonged-One Short-
One Prolonged-One Short** - An agreement signal given by **stand-on** vessel in a narrow channel to vessel desiring to pass.

⚓

INLAND

HEAD ON

One Short Blast - I INTEND to leave you on my port side. Both craft must give this same signal **before** the maneuver.

Two Short Blasts - I INTEND to leave you on my starboard side. Both vessels signal **before** the maneuver.

Three Short Blasts - I am operating astern propulsion.

CROSSING

One Short Blast - Same as International except for one important difference. The signal is **returned** by the stand-on craft **BEFORE** the give-way craft can complete the maneuver.

OVERTAKING

One Short Blast - Same as International except the vessel ahead returns the signal indicating agreement for the maneuver.

Two Short Blasts - Same as International except the vessel ahead returns the signal indicating agreement for the maneuver.
There are no special "Narrow Channel" overtaking signals in Inland waters.

⚓

In both International and Inland Rules, a short blast has the duration of about 1 second. A prolonged blast runs between four and six seconds. They are called whistle signals; nothing else.

On International waters these signals are sounded when vessels are within sight of each other. On Inland waters they are sounded when vessels are within sight of each other **and** within a half-mile of each other. When the fog comes in, or other restricted visibility occurs, these maneuvering signals no longer apply.
Turn the page for the new set of rules.

SIGNALS WHICH ARE GIVEN AT LEAST ONCE EVERY TWO MINUTES BY VESSELS UNDERWAY.

One Prolonged Blast - Given by vessels underway "in or near" any area in which the visibility is restricted for any reason or in any way.

Two Prolonged Blasts - Underway, but stopped. No way on.

One Prolonged - Two Shorts - To be given **INLAND** in restricted visibility underway **or** at **anchor** by:
Fishing vessels fishing, or any craft restricted in ability to maneuver.
The same signal is also given **only** when underway by sailboats, vessels not under command and tugs pushing or towing. See flashcards and read p.49.

In **International** waters one prolonged and two shorts are sounded by any craft underway **or** at anchor when fishing or working vessels restricted in ability to maneuver. Also to be given by craft underway when: constrained by draft, restricted in ability to maneuver, not under command, sailboats, tugs pushing or towing and fishing vessels when fishing.

One Prolonged - Three Short - Signal to be given by any vessel when being towed IF MANNED; if more than one vessel, then the last vessel in tow sounds off, but only if MANNED.

Four Short Blasts - Identity signal for a pilot vessel. Pilot vessel must also give one prolonged blast when underway, and any other signals for a vessel of their respective size.

‡

SIGNALS WHICH ARE GIVEN AT LEAST ONCE EVERY MINUTE BY VESSELS ANCHORED OR AGROUND

One Short-One Prolonged-One Short Given by a vessel at anchor. This is an optional signal to give extra warning of one's position.

Five Second Ringing Of A Bell - Given by vessels at anchor. In Inland waters some vessels do not need to give this signal if anchored in special designated anchorage areas. This includes vessels less than 20 meters in length, barges, canal boats and scows plus other "non-descript" craft.

Five Second Bell - followed by - **Five Second Gong in Stern Area.** Given by vessels at anchor of 100 meters or more in length.

Three Distinct Strokes on the Bell followed by - **Five Second Ringing of the Bell** - followed by - **Three More Strokes on the Bell** - is the signal for a vessel aground. And if you think that's funny; if the vessel is 100 meters or more in length, the above signal must be followed by a **Five Second Ringing of the Gong** in the stern area.

VESSELS LESS THAN 12 METERS IN LENGTH: Not required to give the above bell signals but must have ready at hand some sound producing signal.

‡

Our **FLASHCARDS** include cards on sound signals above. Order form in back of the book

INTERVENING OBSTRUCTIONS OBSCURED CHANNELS AND FAIRWAYS

One Prolonged Blast - Given when approaching a blind bend or ANY obstruction making it difficult to observe on-coming traffic. The same signal is given in answer by any approaching vessel. **Inland Rules state** this signal must be given when leaving a dock or berth. Some CG tests have indicated this signal is valid even if **backing** out of the berth or dock.

Four Short Blasts - Optional signal for Pilot Boat on duty in restricted visibility. Rules call this an **identity signal**. Pilots must sound all the other required signals.

Five Short Blasts - Doubt or danger signal. The rule says "at least" five short blasts. Officially, the rules call it the "doubt" signal. Unsure of intention of other vessel. Used only when vessels are within sight of each other. Not used in restricted visibility.

MANEUVERING SIGNAL TIPS TO REMEMBER.

1) Except for #9 below, the maneuvering signals are always initiated by the "give-way" craft.

2) In Inland waters maneuvering signals can be agreed upon via radiotelephone between two vessels thus eliminating the necessity for sound signals. This is not the case in International waters.

3) In International waters signals are sounded when a change of course is necessary and only when vessels are within sight of each other.

This has an interesting implication that leads to tricky rules of the road questions. But, basically the Rules of The Road, the COLREGS, were codified solely as an effort to prevent collisions at sea.

4) In Inland waters signals are sounded when vessels are within sight of each other **and** when within one half-mile of each other.

5) If operating in restricted visibility when vessels were not within sight of each other, the maneuvering signals are not appropriate!

6) Special emphasis should be placed upon the fact that in International waters the maneuvering signals indicate **action**. You ARE coming right, coming left, or whatever. Again; if no change of course is necessary in International waters, no maneuvering signals are necessary.

7) On Inland waters the signals indicate you **intend** to come right, left, etc. The object being to await agreement of the stand-on craft before executing the maneuver.

8) Any river emptying into the Mississippi is considered a Western River. Simply because there are no navigable rivers in your district does not necessarily mean there will be an absence of river questions on your quiz.

9) When a vessel is operating on the Great Lakes or Western Rivers or any inland waters specified by the Sec. of the Navy, and the vessel is proceeding **"down-bound" with a following current**, this vessel shall initiate the maneuvering signals, propose the manner and place of passage and have the right-of-way.

10) Vessels 100 meters or more in length at anchor should illuminate their deck areas

⚓

THE ARCS AND VISIBILITIES OF LIGHTS

The following is a one page condensation of the distance lights are required to be seen on various power and sailing craft. While initially the memorization appears impossible, please bear with it while we establish some memory crutches enabling you to answer the questions encountered in the Coast Guard exam. In the entire Rules quizzes you might get one on visibility. The questions is; which one? As you read this page, glance at the diagrams on the next page as well as the graph below.

Upon close scrutiny of the arcs of visibility one notices first that:

1) All sidelights show an arc from dead ahead to 22.5° abaft the beam. For **each** sidelight that's 112.5°. Total arc of both sidelights is therefore 225° which is the same **total** arc required on masthead lights.

2) All masthead lights show an arc of 225°.

3) All stern lights show an arc of 135°. Add the masthead arcs and the sternlight arcs together and you have 360°. Now, let's study patterns.

Vessel	Sidelights	Sternlight	Masthead Lights
Less than 12 meters...	1 mile........	2 miles........	2 miles.
Greater than 12.......... but **less than** 20 meters.	2 miles..........	2 miles........	3 miles.
20 meters, but.......... **less than** 50 meters.	2 miles........	2 miles..........	5 miles.
50 meters or greater..	3 miles..........	3 miles..........	6 miles.

Side and sternlights on vessels are seen the same distance except for the first one above and that's the only time a "1" shows up. One mile, five miles and six miles only show up once each. Three miles shows three times! Four never shows. Read across the 50 meter line; 3 + 3 = 6! All the rest are 2's and there are six of them.

The simple number grouping below is like the one above only without the names. Memorize those numbers and you've got 'em cold.

1-2-2
2-2-3
2-2-5
3-3-6

‡

Sidelights are always 112.5° of arc on each side.

Combined side-lights are allowed on craft less than 20 meters in length.

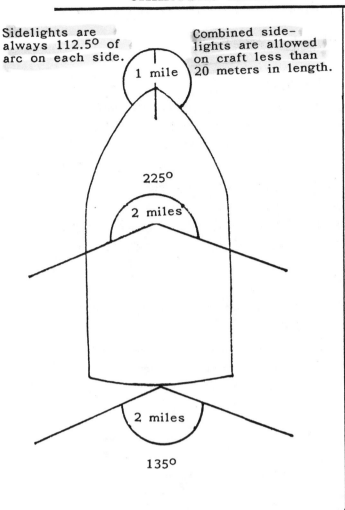

VESSEL LESS THAN 12 METERS

All sidelights show 112.5° of arc.
All sternlights show 135° of arc.
All masthead lights show 225°.

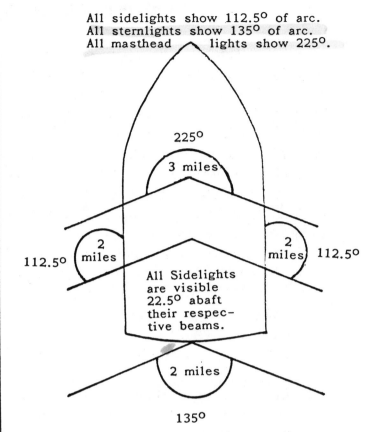

All Sidelights are visible 22.5° abaft their respective beams.

VESSEL GREATER THAN 12 METERS
BUT LESS THAN 20 METERS

VESSEL 20 METERS OR GREATER
BUT LESS THAN 50 METERS

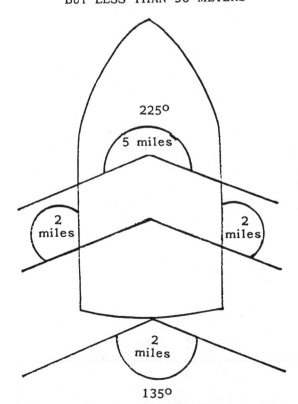

VESSEL 50 METERS OR GREATER
IN LENGTH.

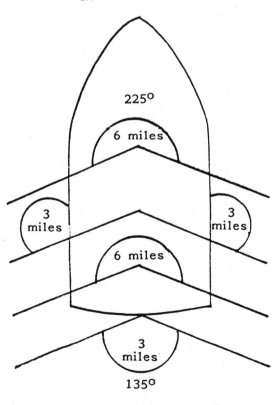

THE INTERNATIONAL PECKING ORDER

Below, in matching columns, is a simplified version of the so-called "pecking order". The farther down the pole the less right-of-way is conferred. Top man is Not Under Command. The Unified rules (read Inland) and International are very much alike with one glaring exception in #3. However, the Unified rules are very clear as regards craft travelling in traffic patterns or rivers, fairways and channels. Note: the lights below are "all-round" lights visible for 360º.

VESSEL

NIGHT SIGNALS | **DAYSHAPES**

1) Not Under Command: No steerage , no power or perhaps underway with no way on. "Red over red, the captain's dead."

2) Restricted In Ability To Maneuver: Underwater operations, surveying, fueling at sea, recovering aircraft, transferring cargo, fuel or personnel, servicing aids to navigation, dredging.

Towing-severely restricted in maneuverability. Note:this requires TWO separate signals: One indicating towing, + restricted maneuver-ability.

Minesweeper. No other restricted in ability signal required, but needs masthead light(s).

3) Vessel Constrained By Draft: A deep draft vessel in a narrow or shallow channel. No such signal Inland.

4) Fishing or Trawling: Fishing is using "lines, nets or trawls" but NOT trolling. Note separate signals for "fishing" vs. "trawling".

5) Sailing: Sailboat under sail. Red over green masthead lights optional. Sailboats must display inverted cone when under sail with engines running.

6) Powerboats: Low end of totem pole. Only lights required are those specified in regular rules section on lights and dayshapes. Note that towing is included here unless the skipper indicates otherwise by hoisting signals indicated in #2 above.

Dayshape if tow 200 meters or more astern

DISTRESS SIGNALS

DYE
MARKER
(ANY COLOR)

CODE FLAGS
NOVEMBER
CHARLIE

SQUARE FLAG
AND BALL

WAVE
ARMS

RADIO-
TELEGRAPH
ALARM

RADIO-
TELEPHONE
ALARM

POSITION
INDICATING
RADIO
BEACON

SMOKE

RED STAR
SHELLS

CONTINUOUS
SOUNDING

FLAMES ON
A VESSEL

GUN
FIRED AT
INTERVALS
OF 1 MIN.

SOS

SOS

"MAYDAY"
BY RADIO

PARACHUTE
RED FLARE

ORANGE
BACKGROUND
BLACK BALL
& SQUARE

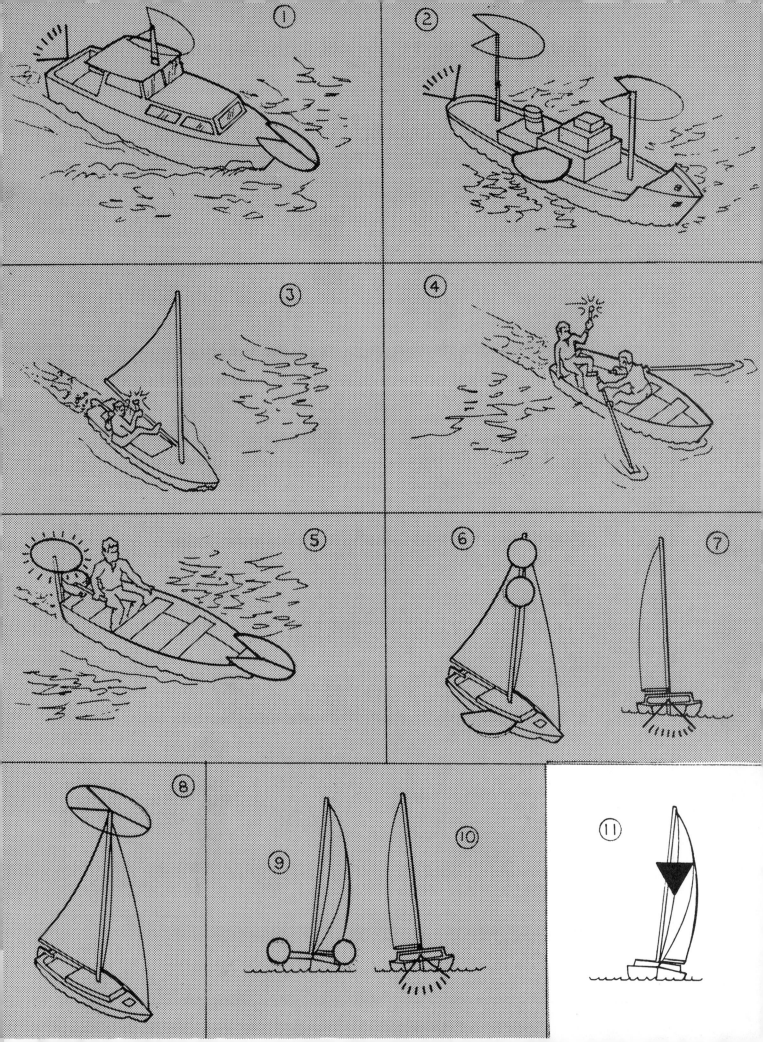

1) **INTERNATIONAL** - Power vessel less than 50 meters in length. Needs one 225º masthead light forward. If less than 12 meters **may** exhibit an all-round (360º) white light & sidelights. **All** sternlights are 135º of arc.

INLAND - If less than 12 meters can use 360º light in lieu of masthead light, (See #5 below) and combined sidelights can be used as it is less than 20 meters.

3) **INTERNATIONAL** - If less than 7 meters in length sailboats can use electric torch (flashlight) or lantern to show in time to prevent collision...if sidelights are impractical.

INLAND - Same.

5) **INTERNATIONAL** - If less than 7 meters and making less than 7 knots the 360º light aft can be used in lieu of the masthead light forward. Sidelights to be used if practicable. If less than 12 meters, the 360º light can be used, but the combined sidelights **must be** used.

INLAND - If less than 12 meters the 360º light can be used in lieu of the masthead lights. The sidelights **must be** used.

8) **INTERNATIONAL** - A Special arrangement for running lights on sailboats less than 20 meters in length.

INLAND - Same.

2) **INTERNATIONAL** - Example of power vessel 50 meters or greater in length. The after masthead light is added and must be higher than the one forward. Both are 225º arcs. Due to length, sidelights are now split and the usual sternlight is required. The after masthead light is optional for vessels less than 50 meters in length.

INLAND - Almost the same. On the Great Lakes, any craft can opt for a 360º light aft to replace the after masthead light and sternlight.

4) **INTERNATIONAL** - Rowboats can light up like sailboats. The white "lantern" (flashlight) is required when sidelights are not available or impractical. Collision prevention is the whole key. Or, as Thucydides put it: "A collision at sea can ruin your entire day."

INLAND - Same.

6) **INTERNATIONAL** - Sailboats *less than 20 meters* have a special option. They can exhibit 360º red over green lights at the masthead. When this option is used the combined sidelights and sternlight mast-top combination shown in #8 cannot be used.

INLAND - Same.

9) A sailboat shown head-on. Note that no white light can be seen. **Number 10** is the sternview showing the required 135º sternlight. This is the case both **International** and **Inland**.

11) **INTERNATIONAL** - Dayshape for sailboat with sails up but also with engine running. She is no longer considered a sailboat, but a power vessel.

INLAND - Not required on sailboats under sail with engines running if less than 12 meters in length.

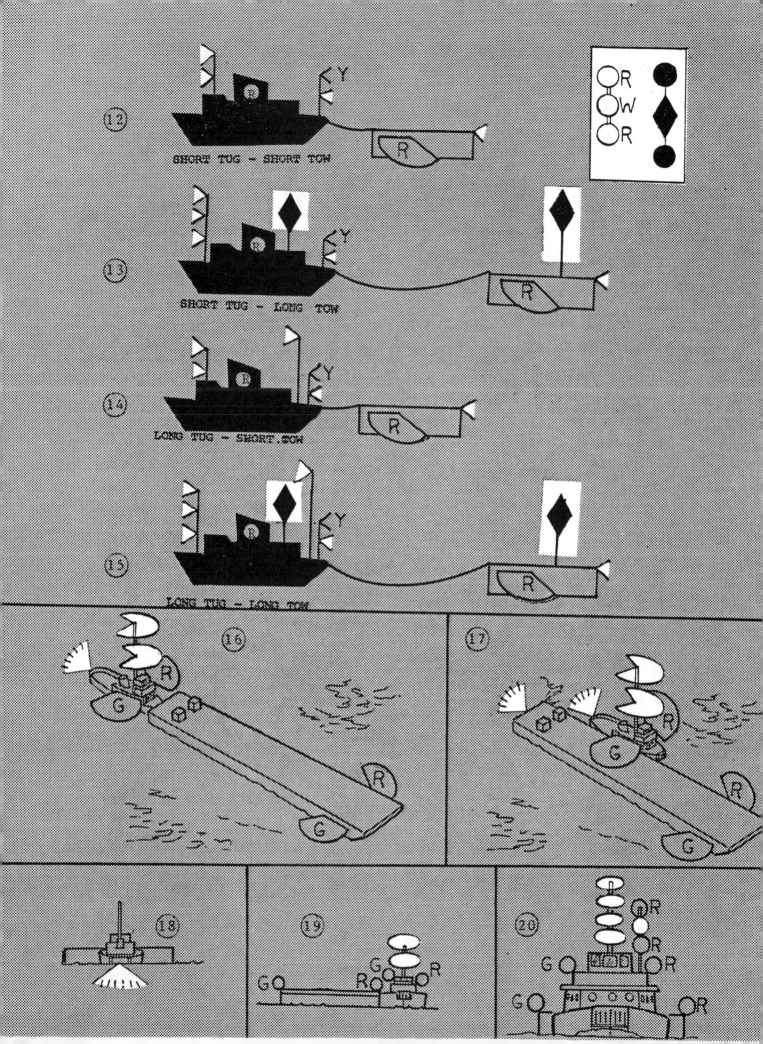

SHORT TUG – SHORT TOW

SHORT TUG – LONG TOW

LONG TUG – SHORT TOW

LONG TUG – LONG TOW

INTERNATIONAL TUGS

Develop this memory crutch for the International Tugs:

If the tug is less than 50 meters in length it's a "short tug".

If the tug is 50 meters or greater in length it's a "long tug".

NOW THE BARGES
THEY ARE TOWING BEHIND.

If the barge is less than 200 meters astern it's a "short tow".

If the barge is 200 meters or farther, it's a "long tow".

Now read the next column on your right.

COMPARE THE DESCRIPTIONS
BELOW WITH THE TUGS
ON THE FACING PAGE

12) Short tug-short tow. Two 225° masthead lights forward.

13) Short tug-long tow. Three 225° masthead lights forward. The diamond dayshape for the daytime.

14) Long tug-short tow. Same as #12 above but add a 225° after masthead light. Thus, viewed head-on you would see three white lights coming right at you.

15) Long tug-long tow. Same as #13 above but add a 225° after masthead light.
And don't forget the diamond dayshape. It's only needed when the tow is more than 200 meters astern. Required on both tug and tow.

Did you notice the sternlights? Yellow over white. Both 135° arc. But careful here. The yellow one is called a "**towing** light", but the white is still a "**stern**light".

16) This is a short tug pushing her barge. Note the yellow towing light is eliminated- she is not "towing", she's "pushing". This is the one rare occasion when the barge does not need a sternlight. Note that tug and barges **ALWAYS** need sidelights. All vessels or barges towed behind or alongside always need stern & sidelights. In #16, if the tug were a "long tug" she would need an after masthead light.

18) Tug pushing her tow as seen from astern. No yellow towing light necessary.

17) Short tug with her barge alongside. Note that now sternlight is required on barge.

19) Short tug with barge alongside.

20) Long tug with her barge and coming right at you! Also note the dayshape for "restricted in ability to maneuver". The barge's sidelights should be visible on each side of the tug.

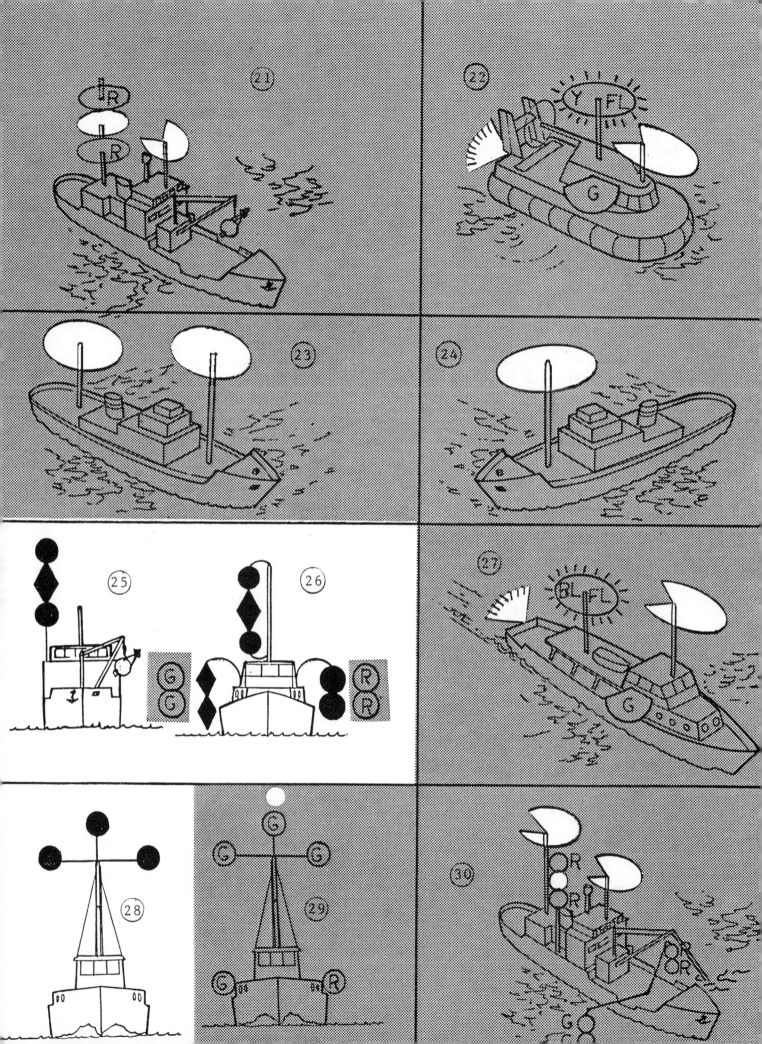

21) **INTERNATIONAL** - Coast Guard Buoy Tender. The 360° vertically arranged red-white-red -offset from centerline- indicates restricted in ability to maneuver. Since the vessel is not actually making way the sidelights are extinguished. Anchor lights are not required as technically, she is not anchored.

INLAND - Same.

23) **INTERNATIONAL** - Vessel 50 meters or more in length and at anchor. Note that both lights are 360°, **atop** masts and are reversed in position from those viewed on a vessel underway. Not like masthead lights which are lower than tips of masts. The stern anchor light is LOWER than the forward one. Vessels 100 meters or more in length must **also** illuminate their decks at night. Black ball is the dayshape for being at anchor. All dayhapes are black, except flags.

INLAND - Same.

25 & 26) **INTERNATIONAL** - Number 25 is the dayshape for a vessel restricted in her ability to maneuver.
Number 26 is engaged in some form of underwater work. Passing side is denoted by the black diamonds over the side. The night counterpart is #30 below. Note: Underwater work is anything from telephone cable to having a hardhat diver down.

INLAND - Same, except vessels less than 12 meters need not signal unless diving operations are in progress.

28 & 29) **INTERNATIONAL** - Minesweeper. Considered restricted in ability to maneuver without having to use the signal. The three black balls or three green lights are reserved for minesweepers only. You must stay clear of the vessel by 1,000 meters.

INLAND - Same, except stay clear of sides 500 meters, stern by 1,000 meters.

22) **INTERNATIONAL** - A "non-displacement" craft. Here, a hovercraft. Needs all the usual lights PLUS a "flashing light". A flashing light on a vessel is one which always flashes at 120 fpm.

INLAND -Same.

24) **INTERNATIONAL** - Vessel less than 50 meters in length and at anchor. Only one 360° white light required. Vessels less than 7 meters in length need not show the light if not anchored in area normally used by other vessels.

INLAND - Same except vessels less than 20 meters are exempt in approved anchorage areas.

27) **INTERNATIONAL** - No special law enforcement lights are indicated under International Rules of The Road.

INLAND - Flashing Blue Light. Law enforcement. Federal or local.

30) **INTERNATIONAL** - Underwater operation. For example, dredging. Favorite on CG exams. Red 360° lights mark the non-passing side. Stay away. Pass on the green light side. Excusing the perspective of the sketch, these lights are always higher than the sidelights.

Note absence of side and sternlights. He is not making way. "Underway" is defined as not at anchor, not aground and/or not tied to a pier or dock.

INLAND - Same.

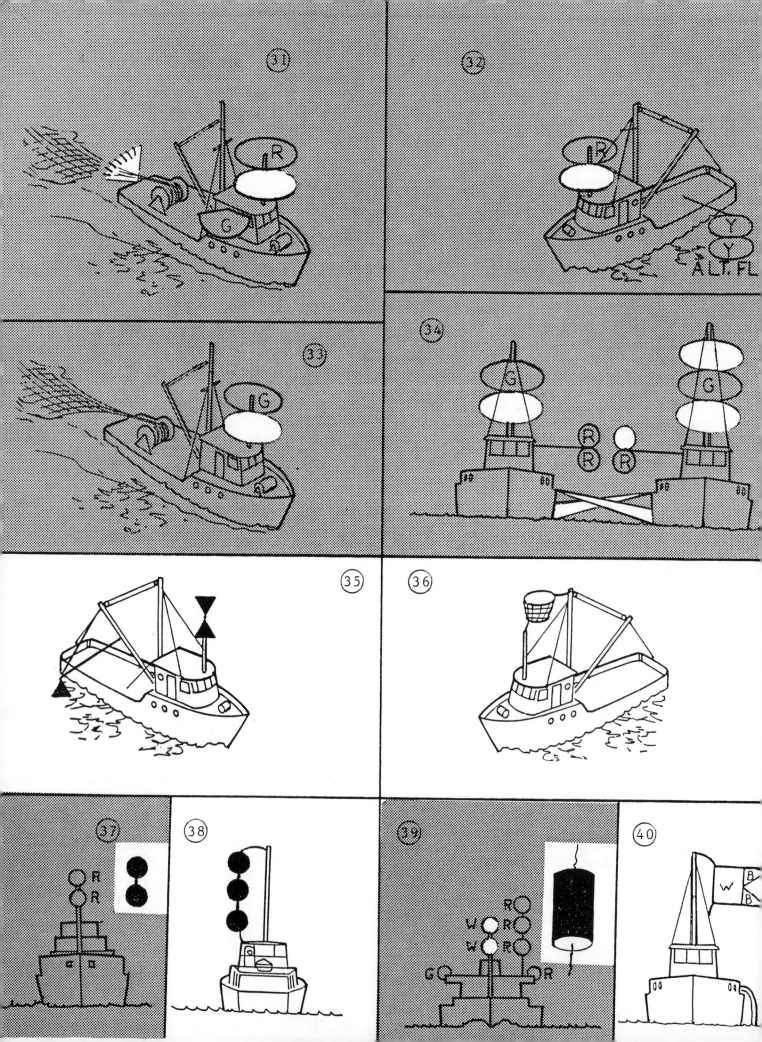

31) **INTERNATIONAL** - A fishing vessel is considered fishing only when using lines, nets or trawls. Trolling is not considered fishing! "Red-over-white, Fishing Tonight." Side and sternlights displayed only when underway. Special lights and dayshapes for fishing shown only when actually engaged in fishing. Fishing in navigable channels or fairways is illegal.

INLAND - Same.

33) **INTERNATIONAL** - A trawler has different lights than the other fishing vessels. Green over white. Frequent test question. Trawling means she is dragging the bottom as opposed to the fishing vessel above with nets or lines. The net shown here is weighted and on the way to the bottom.

INLAND - Same.

35) **INTERNATIONAL** - Dayshapes for fishing vessels. Two cones apex to apex and up high. Small cone over side -should be higher than sidelights- indicates nets on that side horizontally out 150 meters or more. At night this is a white 360° light in the direction of the gear. Cone over side is NOT used by trawlers...nor is the 360° light.

INLAND -Same.

37 & 38) **INTERNATIONAL** - Not under command. Two red lights, each 360° arranged vertically. "red-over-red," the captain's dead." Engine down, prop fell off, drifting. If a vessel is aground this same signal is used but a white anchor light is added, or two if the vessel is 50meters or greater in length. Three black balls is aground. Popular test question.

INLAND - Same.

32) **INTERNATIONAL** - Purse seiners can show a special signal of two 360° vertically arranged flashing yellow lights when hampered by their fishing gear. They flash alternately every second.

INLAND - Same.

34) **INTERNATIONAL** - Special lights for trawlers when fishing in fleet or as a team. They can shine searchlights on each other's hull. Separate signals to indicate current maneuver: Vertically arrange two white lights=shooting the nets; white-over-red=pulling the nets; red-over-red=nets hung up on obstruction below. Special masthead lights green over white. If less than 50 meters in length the top white masthead light is optional. Only when actually underway would the sidelights and sternlight be lighted.

INLAND - Same.

36) **INTERNATIONAL** - The only standard dayshape not black is the basket for fishing vessels less than 20 meters in length. The two cones in #35 can be used instead.

INLAND - Same.

39) **INTERNATIONAL** - The cylinder shape describes a deep draft vessel in a shallow channel. Cargo vessels, freighters or very large craft unable to deviate from course. At night, three vertically arranged 360° red lights.

INLAND - At this writing, no such signal inland. However, no vessel may restrict the passage of another craft which is in a traffic zone by crossing the zone or fairway.

40) **SPECIAL NOTE: - The Alfa Flag** is for divers down. Rigid construction to show all around.

41) INTERNATIONAL - See pp. 36-37.

INLAND - Note the big difference between Inland and International is two towing lights when towing alongside or pushing ahead as on the next panel. BOTH are yellow and recall they are called "towing lights"...not sternlights. The mast-head light arrangement is same as International.

43) INTERNATIONAL - Note the **solid** attachment of the tug to the dredge. This is an example of a **composite unit.** Thus, both are treated as one vessel. In this case the dredge shows the masthead and sidelights while the tug fills in with the sternlight. Also restricted in ability to maneuver.

INLAND - Same.

45) INTERNATIONAL - See numbers 12-15.

INLAND - The Inland tug shows the same as the International tug **when towing astern**. Since tow is less than 200 meters astern only two 225° masthead lights forward. The tug shows an after masthead light as she is 50 meters or greater in length. If barges are towed in tandem or abreast the entire tow is lighted as one barge.

47) INTERNATIONAL - Submerged or partially submerged tows require special lights and dayshapes. The rectangles in the next column represent the lights on tows at various lengths and breadths. A black diamond dayshape -like numbers 13 and 15- is required on the tow. If 200 meters astern, a shape at each end is required.

INLAND - Same lighting arrangement for various sizes of tows, but only one dayshape is required and should be near the stern of the tow.

42) INTERNATIONAL - See International Tugs - this section.

INLAND - Tug is less than 50 meters in length. Only a pushed barge shows that "special flashing light." Light is yellow and flashes 50-70 fpm. Arc of that light can be anything from 180° to 225°. **Used Inland and only when pushing.**
And note the tug still has two yellow "towing" lights instead of merely the stern light as used when pushing or towing alongside in International waters.

44) INTERNATIONAL - A dredge under her own power. In this case she is actually underway and moving...see the sidelights? If she becomes stationary the sidelights are extinguished. Restricted in ability to maneuver. She can show two 360° red lights over the bow, stern or either side to indicate side **not** to pass. Similarly placed dual green lights for side to pass. See #'s 26 & 30.

INLAND - Same.

46) INTERNATIONAL - "White-over-red, pilot ahead." He uses these lights ONLY when on duty which could include being at anchor. If at anchor this would add another 360° white light to his array but would extinguish his sidelights and sternlight.

INLAND - Same.

48) INTERNATIONAL - No dredgepipe signals in the International Rules.

INLAND - The yellow lights mark the pipeline. The vertical red lights mark the navigable opening. All 360° lights.

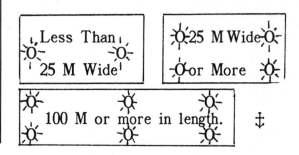

Marina del Rey is where the big boats live in California when they can't find room in Newport. It's a very sterile environment where condos surround pristine boats, sparkling docks and the crafts are mainly for cocktail parties and sea stories. I know a charter skipper down there with the ultimate in working convenience. He monitors the local classified and the *L.A. Times*.

When someone has a beautiful vessel for sale that doesn't seem to be moving Arch - a fictitious name to protect the guilty- invites the eager seller out to lunch. Archie flashes his license and says, "Let me charter that boat for you." Oblivious to the owner's disappointment in not having a hot buyer in hand, Archie continues.

"If you let me try it maybe we can cut a deal. You've got $50,000 tied up there and the money's not working for you." This is a terrible sin in the rarefied air of stratified society. "Try depreciating that over five years and tell me how much income tax you're not going to pay. You'll have a cottage industry that won't quit and I'll be doing all the work. All you have to do is buy a wheel barrow to cart it off to the bank. Ask your tax man about this kind of a deal and watch him smile."

"Keep talking," says the mark, sitting back down and ordering another martini.

Archie continues. "You go get a dba - doing business as- from the county. Call it something cute, like Pau Hana Charters. You plunk the money in for advertising, fuel, and upkeep, which is about what you're doing now anyway, and I'll run the boat for half the net. Now explain to me how you're going to lose."

The last time I saw Arch, he had a real class act. Three sailboats ranging in length from 25 feet to 72 feet and four power boats. He seldom goes out

himself. He goes windsurfing or lies on the beach with those sandy bottomed beach bunnies while making marks in the sand to keep track of his skippers coming and going. His skippers go fishing with the big boys from Tokyo, Munich, Rio and New York.

Arch has never owned a boat.

Why bother? ‡

Rule 9(b): A vessel less than 20 meters in length or a sailing vessel shall not impede the passage of a vessel which can safely navigate only within a narrow channel or fairway.

A GUIDE TO THE TEST TIPS

So far you have covered the Rules of The Road, Lights and Dayshapes, Maneuvering Signals, Signals In Restricted Visibility, not to mention a small dissertation on the license requirements. Now let's go through a general overall view of the types of questions the CG will ask you on the Rules. This is a tip sheet indicating CG emphases on the tests. Remember, this is the closed book exam requiring 90% accuracy seeming to make it the toughest of all the modules.

CAUTION HERE. If you are planning on working offshore each test question indicates one of three things: Inland, International or Inland **and** International. If you're not watching carefully the change could escape you and down the tubes goes your first attempt. Above all else, **READ THE DIRECTIONS.** Take along a 3 x 5 card. Each question will be multiple choice. Cover up the choices and read the question. Decide on an answer then move the card and look for the answer you want. If the answer isn't there, **pick the best answer**, which is what the directions will say anyway. Try this technique with the first test in this book. You will surprise yourself to discover you didn't really **read** a good many of the questions. Without a clue? Pick the one that first hits you as being correct, or pick the longest one. That old ploy might work as the CG hasn't really mastered test construction.

DON'T MUCK UP THE TESTS.

Don't make marks in your book indicating your choice of answer. Make some copies of the blank answer sheets in the appendix and use those. That way the next time you take the same test, the answers won't be automatic or influence your decision.

Careful of the tests in the CG office. You will receive a test booklet and told not to write in it. The test booklet might be covered in loose plastic. You will also receive an IBM answer sheet to indicate choices A,B,C, or D. If the test booklet appears to have some choices indicated beneath the plastic cover...ignore them. Use your own brain, not someone else's suggestions.

Now let's run through these test tips. Read them carefully before taking the next two tests. These are the outstanding facts upon which the CG basis many questions.

TEST TIPS

1) If you are reading this book more than a year after publication, be advised there **could have been some changes.** Up-to-date lists of questions are available. We call one of them "237 Rules," meaning, as of this printing, these are the latest and it is from these 237 questions your thirty will be taken. We also publish our own "Rules of The Road." This is a book like the official rules, but each facing page to a rule explains how the CG uses that particular rule in their tests and what they want emphasized. Illustrations like this volume so you don't have to keep switching back and forth. See the order form in the back of the book. In any case, be sure to read some form of the Rules of The Road before going in for your exam, but don't read it until after you've finished this book. Say, about a week before going in for the exam. I promise it will be a real eye-opener.

2) The Western Rivers are rivers which empty into the Mississippi River. There is no mention, in the new Rules of The Road, of the Red River of The North.

3) Many Western Rivers have their own "Vessel Traffic Control" centers. The VTC rules differ by the area. You should check with the local CG in the area of your operation to determine how they differ from the regular Rules.

4) **An Inland Rule (Unified)** permits Western River vessels to operate **without masthead lights** due to low bridges.

They use a short staffed 360° light on the stern to replace the masthead and stern lights.

5) A vessel bound down-river *with a following current* has the right of way over a vessel bound up-river.

6) A tug with tow, bound up-river, does not have the right of way over a non-towing vessel coming down-river. However, if the up-bound tug displayed the signals for being "restricted in ability to maneuver" and the down-bound does not, then the up-bound tug would **seem** to have right of way. The down-bound vessel has the right of way **with a following current**. Watch out! Unless a tug has hoisted the "restricted in maneuverability" signal he is considered nothing more than an ordinary, up and coming, young red-blooded American powerboat with only the rights accorded thereto. He can have fifty barges back there, but with no "restricted" signals the little sailboat has the right-of-way.

7) But, any vessel crossing the river, channel or fairway or traffic lane must give way to any vessels ascending or descending said river, channel or fairway or traffic lane.

8) Keep to the right.

9) Keep a proper lookout. The helmsman is NOT considered a valid lookout!

10) The Rule of Good Seamanship says: a) Keep proper lookout, b) Use the Rules to avoid collision, c) Use the proper lights and dayshapes, d) Use radar properly.

11) When navigating by radar, especially in restricted visibility, any change of course necessary for safety should be a "substantial" change of course. Easier to detect on radar by other nearby vessels.

12) The radiotelephone can be used Inland to designate maneuvering intentions. There is no such mention of this in the International Rules.

13) There is controversy as to whether sailboats should sound maneuvering signals on Inland waters. Compare the wording in International vs. Inland Rules in Rule 34(a).

14) Maneuvering signals can be *supplemented* by flashing lights. One flash, of about one second duration supplements a short blast. There is no supplemental light signal for a prolonged blast! Inland you can use a yellow OR white 360° light visible for at least two miles. International permits only the use of a white light visible for at least five miles. Man, do they use that one.

15) You may not determine if a risk of collision does or does not exist based on scanty information...especially scanty radar information.

16) If, in restricted visibility, you detect a vessel forward of your beam you should slow, but *maintain steerage way*.

17) All vessels, Inland and International, shall travel at a **safe speed**. And just what is a "safe speed"? That is, what constitutes "safe"? Read the conditions outlined in Rule 6. If you include operating with radar, there are twelve conditions to consider. The CG will give you a question asking, "Which does **not** apply to safe speed."

18) If a collision situation exists and you are in "extremis" you should make any move necessary to avoid the collision. To hell with the Rules. The term "extremis" still shows up in some REC tests, but the term is no longer used in the Official Rules.

19) The duty and requirement of the stand-on vessel is to maintain course and speed.

20) In Inland waters, signals are given when vessels are within sight of each other *and* within a half mile of each other.

21) Giving signals and maneuvering your vessel upon the approach of another, infers that unless you did maneuver, there would be a collision. If no maneuvering is necessary in International waters, the inference is that there is no need for a signal. If a signal needs to be given in International waters it is because the vessels are within sight of each other and a course change is necessary. Be sure you know the difference between Inland and International on this. See again page

27 and learn it.

22) Inland Rules insists that there be **agreement** before a maneuver is made. You are supposed to wait until the other vessel returns the signal before commencing your maneuver.

23) Note the difference in the technical meanings of blasts given Inland and International.

Inland: one blast; I *intend* to leave you on my port side.

International: one blast; I *am* altering my course to starboard.

24) Maneuvering signals are instigated by the give-way craft.

25) In Inland waters, maneuvering signals are returned by the stand-on craft when meeting, crossing or overtaking.

26) Maneuvering signals in International Waters are not returned by the stand- on craft when crossing, or overtaking unless overtaking in a narrow channel.

27) Be sure you know and understand the signals for *International Narrow Channels* when one vessel is overtaking another. There is a return signal. *See page 27.*

28) The traditional "danger signal" of at least five short blasts infers *doubt* when maneuvering. The danger-doubt signal is never used in restricted visibility.

29) One prolonged blast, Inland or International, is given when approaching an obstruction which might inhibit visibility of on-coming vessels. Also given by sailboats. There is an Inland Rule (#34g) stating you must sound one prolonged blast when leaving a dock or berth. While the rule doesn't exist in International Rules the CG tests insist that this is the case when leaving a berth, pier or dock due to the *obstructed visibility* caused by the dock, pier or berth!

30) A vessel is underway when NOT tied to a dock, at anchor or aground. And keep in mind that you could be "underway", but with no way on. Drifting.

31) ANY vessel overtaking another vessel is considered the give way craft. Even a sailboat passing a powerboat is burdened to give way.

32) A minesweeper, by the nature of her duty, is considered "restricted in ability to maneuver". The three green lights indicate this. No other lights or dayshapes are necessary to indicate this impairment.

33) Avoid speeding up to avoid collision. Slow down. Instead, if possible, change course and make it "substantial".

34) There are no special signals for "passing in narrow channels" in Inland waters.

35) What is the difference between overtaking and crossing? If a vessel is more than 22 1/2° abaft the beam of another vessel, it's an overtaking situation. **Forward** of 22 1/2° abaft the beam of another vessel is considered crossing. Obviously, the third alternative is head on.

36) If, upon approaching another vessel at night, and you see the sternlight, it's an overtaking situation. If you see either of the sidelights, it's a crossing situation. Theoretically, it's impossible to see both the sternlight and the sidelights simultaneously.

37) One seen on a test asked who had the right-of-way when a sailboat approached a fishing vessel fishing in a fairway. Ans: Sailboat. It's illegal to fish in a fairway when you obstruct traffic! Does this mean if the other guy is doing something illegal, you have the right-of-way?

38) The preferred course change to avoid collision when meeting head on is to change course to the right.

39) Ordinarily a fishing vessel, engaged in fishing, has the right of way over a sailboat, but he has to be engaged in fishing at the time.

40) All **OUPV** and **Master** candidates should know the rules for sailboats vs. sailboats whether they plan on doing sail charters or not.

41) Sailboats under sail do not use white masthead lights. Recall, there is a special 360° red over green mast top light indicating a sailboat underway at night, but no white masthead light...when sailing with no engine running.

42) **Fog Signals** are required when

operating within a half-mile of an area of restricted visibility...e.g., a fog bank.

43) Every vessel is required to have some form of sound producing device aboard to indicate position in restricted visibility. Even when at anchor if not anchored in an "approved anchorage".

44) There is no such thing as a *fog horn* on a vessel. Sail or power. Now they're called whistles, "fog signals", or "sound producing appliances". Foghorns are situated ashore in lighthouses, or such. Beware of the question using the term "foghorn" when referring to a ship at sea.

45) The Old Rules used to make repeated reference to the "points" of the compass. A point is 11 1/4° of the compass. There are 32 points. Divide 32 points into 360 degrees to get the 11 1/4°.

46) Concerning weird lights with funny names.

    a) Flashing yellow lights are found on Inland on dredge pipelines and mark the dredge pipe.

    b) "Flashing light" means 120 fpm, or more. Could be any color. Good example is a hovercraft or law enforcement craft.

    c) "Special flashing light" means a yellow light flashing at 50-70 fpm. This is found only on the bow of a barge being pushed ahead by a tug in Inland waters. It has an arc ranging from 180° to 225° meaning it could be mounted on the bow below the deckline.

    d) A "towing light" is a yellow stern light on a tug -International and Inland- which is towing astern. This towing light is vertically above the usual white stern light and has the same arc of visibility; 135°. Only Inland tugs when pushing their tows, or towing alongside, are required to show two vertically arranged "towing" lights on their sterns.

    e) There are alternately flashing yellow lights on purse seiners. See #32 on page 40.

    f) Submarine. Careful here. This is dictated by the Sec. of the Navy and seems to change every other national holiday. At this writing, three one second

yellow flashes, dark for three seconds, then a repeat cycle. Yellow 360° lights. You see a lot of those.

47) Catch question: What vessel displays a blue light? Ans: None. Law enforcement displays a "flashing" blue light.

FOG SIGNALS-A SUMMARY

Technically, the term "restricted visibility" is used. This means **any** kind of visibility restriction: fog, haze, rain, hail, sleet, snow or a bad hangover. The Rules indicate these signals should commence when you are within a half-mile of any fog bank or area of restricted visibility. Some signals are sounded underway, some when at anchor and even special ones when aground. Some are sounded every minute, some every two minutes. The CG loves these, so get them straight. See page 28. They are so bad we put them on our flash cards along with the lights and dayshapes.

48) Powerboats underway, every two minutes...one prolonged blast.

49) Powerboats underway, but stopped, every two minutes, **two** prolonged blasts.

50) There are some special **Inland** restricted visibility signals. Study this next part carefully. One prolonged and two short are given every two minutes in restricted visibility by the following vessels **whether underway or at anchor**. And careful here. If at anchor-signal is given every **minute**.

INLAND

    a) Any vessel restricted in ability to maneuver,

    b) All fishing vessels...when fishing.

The following sound one prolonged and two short **when underway:**

    a) Vessels not under command,
    b) Sailboats under sail.
    c) Tugs pushing or towing.

51) Now let's look at the International counterpart to the above. One prolonged and two short are given every two minutes in restricted visibility by:

INTERNATIONAL

a) Any vessel not under command,
b) Any vessel restricted in ability to maneuver, **also when working at anchor.**
c) A vessel constrained by her draft,
d) Sailboats,
e) Fishing vessels, **also when at anchor, fishing.**
f) Tugs pushing or towing.

52) The one prolonged and two short signal is also given by **Inland and International** tugs, when pushing or towing in restricted visibility. If the barge being towed, (or the last one in the tow if there are more than just one) gives one prolonged and **three short,** but only if said barge is **manned.**

53) Bells and gongs are never used when underway. What **are** bells and gongs used for? Glad you asked. Listen up 'cause this applies to both Inland and International.

a) A five second bell is sounded **every minute** by vessels at anchor in restricted visibility.

b) If vessel is 100 meters or greater the five second bell is rung in the forward part then a gong for another five seconds near the stern.

c) If aground, an additional bell signal is given: Three "distinct" strokes, the usual five second ringing, then another "distinct" three strokes. And if you are unfortunate enough to be 100 meters or greater, don't forget the gong right after the last three "distinct" strokes. If you're the only man on watch you have a lot of jogging to do on a vessel over 100 meters in length.

d) You don't think that's enough? Still afraid of getting run over? Tell ya what's ya do. Sound one short, one prolonged, one short. It's an optional signal anyone can give when at anchor. Frequently on CG tests.

e) The above are all **one minute** interval signals...Inland and International. There's one exception. Any vessel less than 12 meters can, instead, "make some other efficient sound signal at intervals of not more than **two minutes".**

f) Then, of course, there's the pilot vessel when engaged in duty who **may** sound four short as an identity signal. However, Pilot still has to abide by all of the others above.

g) Inland waters permit the use of an adjunct to the maneuvering signals in the form of a white **or** yellow light. The light is used in conjunction with the maneuvering signals...one flash, one blast, etc. International allows only a white light...no yellow.

h) We save one of the most important for last because it leads to trick questions on exams. The usual maneuvering signals are given "when vessels are within sight of each other". Thus, **regular** maneuvering signals **are not used in restricted visibility!**

54) Nobody, but nobody, anchors in a fairway, channel, shipping lane or traffic pattern.
55) Small craft, under 20 meters, do not have to sound fog signals all night if anchored in an "approved anchorage," but that exception is only stated in the Inland Rules!!
56) Fishing means fishing with lines, nets or trawls. If you have trolling lines stringing from astern, you're not considered fishing and have no special rights of way.
57) Trawling is "green over white".

Regular fishing boats show "red over white". If you don't know what that means, go back to the boat pictures and look up the fishing boats and trawlers on page 40 again. Very important.

58) "Notice To Mariners," is published by the Secretary of The Department of Transportation in Washington, D.C.

59) **"Local** Notice to Mariners," is published by the CG in each district.

60) A man standing on the beach, with his hands straight out at his sides is signaling the semaphore letter "R". This means "affirmative" and nothing more.

61) Take out your copy of Rules of The Road and compare Inland and International Rule 9(d). The International Rule says sounding the danger signal is optional in this situation. The Inland Rule states it is mandatory. Nit-picky? You betcha' and the CG has questions on this very point. Get it straight.

62) A man on a vessel moving those outstretched arms up and down is not drunk trying to keep his balance. He is signaling for help. See "Distress Signals" on page 33.
You knew that.

63) A new biggie on Inland Rules. Now they have alternately flashing yellow and red lights to indicate a regatta. The CG has nineteen questions all rigged up for this new one. They are reprinted following the Inland Rules test herein. It would be most unusual if your Rules tests did not contain one of these.

Charters West Publishing Company now has on the market a copy of the Official Rules of The Road. As mentioned, the difference from the Fed Gov's edition is that our manual comes with facing pages on each Rule indicating the areas of interest as regards the tests. Don't even think about sitting for your ticket without first reading **some copy** of the Rules of The Road, preferably after you have completed your studies.

The final test is at sea.

The port side is where the wine is kept.

WARNING-READ THIS

1) Most of the questions on all of the modules came directly from CG exams. They were acquired through the Freedom of Information Act. These are not all of the questions available from the CG, but it would take several books this size to print them all; even those used on the Six Pac and Master-100 Tons. And sometimes we think **all the answers are not correct. Therein lies the dilemma.** Do we print the correct answer or the answer the Coast Guard currently wants? One instructor in Alaska (a retired Coast Guard officer, academy instructor who also once commanded a REC) reviewed one of our Rules tests a few years back and pronounced 16 wrong answers. And he was right! When the CG changes the answers, or more often revamps the entire questions, we change ours, but there is a lapse. Okay, what are we driving at. Well, how about the latest we have and **FREE?** Get our address off page 4 and send us a stamped self-addressed envelope and **IF** there are changes, you get the latest in the return mail. If none are available, you might have to wait. If after working with all the test questions herein you still feel a bit queasy, see our order form in the back of this book. We have a whole volume of questions on all the modules. Cheap.

2) Do not mark up the tests. Use the blank numbered test sheets on pages 217-218. If you haven't done so already, get some copies. You'll need them. No sense in giving yourself tips next time you take the exam. Go it cold each time. You need to understand the concept, not memorize a bunch of answers.

3) Take the entire test before checking the answers which are at the end of each test. You'll be glad you did. If you get better than 60% the first time, you're genius material and shouldn't even waste your money on silly books like this.

4) Use a 3 x 5 card. Cover up the multiple choice answers and try to figure YOUR answer before looking at the choices offered. You might think about doing this on the real CG quiz when your day comes. Makes you really **read** the questions. Too often students complain they missed questions because they didn't really *read* the question. They only *thought* they read it. Never accept ANY answer until you have read all of the choices.

5) While grading your answers, don't memorize them. Try to grasp the concept of **why** that was the correct answer.

6) Don't waste your time, temper and attitude arguing with the answer. Instead, consider trying to find why the answer was so strange. Look for a tricky word or phrase. Better you get caught herein than in the exam room.

7) If it's a boat vs. boat question regarding right-of-way, sketch the question before trying to answer it. We have excellent video displays of this on our own Rules video tape. Cheap! Order form is on the last page.

8) Your first test in this volume is on the "Unified" or Inland Rules. The next will be on the International. Don't plan on any particular sequence when the CG administers the various modules. There is no sequence, but nothing to stop them from arranging one for you if you catch them at a slow time and ask politely.

9) Many feel the Rules of The Road make more sense *after* a thorough study of something like this book and the tests. One thing is for sure; you really should read a copy before sitting for the exam. You will discover and learn the nature of terms such as: "a vessel through which some exceptional circumstance" and "a vessel which from the nature of her work" which constantly show up in the Rules exam.

Besides, if the general public hears about a book called *The Rules of The Road*, drug companies will lose money on their sleeping pills.

‡

1) You are navigating in a narrow channel and must remain in the channel for safe operation. Another vessel is crossing the channel ahead of you from your starboard and you are doubtful as to whether your vessel will pass safely if she continues on her present course. Which statement is true?

a) You must stop your vessel, since the other vessel has the right of way. b) You must sound one short blast of the whistle, and turn to starboard, c) You must sound the danger signal, d) You must stop your engines, and the sounding of the danger signal is optional.

2) What is the required whistle signal for a vessel leaving dock or berth?

a) One short blast, b) One prolonged blast, c) Two short blasts, d) One long blast.

3) In a narrow channel, you are underway on vessel "A" and desire to overtake vessel "B". After you sound two short blasts on your whistle vessel "B" sounds five short blasts on the whistle. You should:

a) Pass with caution on the port side of vessel "B", b) Hold your relative position, and then initiate another signal after the situation has stabilized, c) Answer the five short blast signal then stop your vessel until the other vessel initiates a signal, d) Slow or stop and expect radical maneuvers from "B".

4) A vessel is proceeding downstream in a narrow channel on the Western Rivers when another vessel is sighted moving upstream. Which vessel has the right of way?

a) The vessel moving upstream against the current, b) The vessel moving downstream with a following current, c) The vessel located more towards the channel centerline, d) The vessel sounding the first whistle signal.

5) You are overtaking a vessel in a narrow channel and wish to leave her on your starboard side. You may:

a) Attempt to contact her on a radiotelephone to arrange for the passage, b) Proceed to overtake her without sounding whistle signals, c) Sound five short blasts, d) Any of the above.

6) A vessel displaying a flashing blue light is:

a) Transferring dangerous cargo, b) A law enforcement vessel, c) A work boat, d) Engaged in a race.

7) When power-driven vessels are in a crossing situation, a signal of one short blast by either vessel would mean:

a) "I intend to leave you on my port side", b) "I intend to hold course and speed", c) "I intend to change course to starboard", d) "I request a departure from the Rules".

8) If you were coming up on another vessel from dead astern and desired to overtake along the other vessel's starboard side, what whistle signal would you sound?

a) One short blast, b) One prolonged blast, c) Two short blasts, d) two prolonged blasts.

9) Which statement is true concerning narrow channels?

a) You should keep to that side of the channel which is on your port side, b) You should avoid anchoring in a narrow channel, c) A vessel having a following current will propose the manner of passage in any case where two vessels are meeting, d) All of the above.

10) Which term is NOT defined in the Inland Navigation Rules?

a) Seaplane, b) Restricted visibility, c) Underway, d) Vessel constrained by her draft.

11) When you are overtaking another vessel and desire to pass on the left or port hand of the vessel, you should sound:

a) One short blast, b) One long blast, c) Two short blasts, d) two prolonged blasts.

12) You have made your vessel up to a tow and are moving from a pier out into the main channel. If your engines are turning ahead, what whistle signal should you sound?

a) One prolonged and two short blasts, b) Three long blasts, c) One prolonged blast, d) Five or more short rapid blasts.

13) Under the Inland Navigational Rules, what is the meaning of a two short blast signal used in a meeting situation with another vessel?

a) "I am turning to starboard", b) "I am turning to port", c) "I intend to leave you on my starboard side", d) "I intend to leave you on my port side".

14) For the purpose of the Inland Navigation Rules, the term "Inland Waters" includes:

a) The Western Rivers, b) The Great Lakes on the United States side of the International Boundary, c) Harbors and rivers shoreward of the COLREGS demarcation lines, d) All of the above.

15) A vessel crossing a river on the Western Rivers has the right of way over:

a) Vessels ascending the river, b) Vessels descending the river, c) All vessels ascending and descending the river, d) None of the above.

16) What lights are required for a barge, not part of a composite unit, being pushed ahead?

a) Sidelights and a sternlight, b) Sidelights, a special flashing light, and a sternlight, c) Sidelights and a special flashing light, d) Sidelights, a towing light, and a sternlight.

17) A power-driven vessel operating in a narrow channel with a following current on the Great Lakes or Western Rivers is meeting an upbound vessel. Which statement is true?

a) The downbound vessel has the right-of-way, b) The downbound vessel must initiate the required maneuvering signals, c) The down-bound vessel must propose the manner and place of passage, d) All of the above.

18) Your vessel is proceeding down a channel, and can safely navigate only within the channel. Another vessel is crossing your bow from port to starboard, and you are in doubt as to his intentions. Which statement is true?

a) The sounding of the danger signal is optional, b) The sounding of the danger signal is mandatory, c) You should sound two short blasts, d) You should sound one prolonged and two short blasts.

19) The stand-on vessel in a crossing situation sounds one short blast of the whistle. This means that the vessel:

a) Intends to hold course and speed, b) Is changing course to starboard, c) Is changing course to port, d) Intends to leave the other on her port side.

20) You are crossing the course of another vessel which is to your starboard. You have reached an agreement by radiotelephone to pass astern of the other vessel. You must:

a) Sound one short blast, b) Sound two short blasts, c) Change course to starboard, d) None of the above.

21) Passing signals shall be blown on inland waters:

a) Upon sighting another vessel rounding a bend in the channel, b) When in a meeting situation with another vessel on a clear day, c) When crossing the track of another vessel less than one half mile away with both vessels in sight of each other, d) All of the above.

22) You are proceeding up a channel in Chesapeake Bay and are meeting an outbound vessel. Responsibilities include:

a) Keeping to that side of the channel which is on your vessel's port side, b) Stopping your vessel and letting the outbound vessel initiate the signals for meeting and passing, c) Appropriately answering any whistle signals given by the other vessel, d) Giving the outbound vessel the right of way.

23) When overtaking another power-driven vessel in a narrow channel a vessel desiring to overtake on the other vessel's starboard side would sound a whistle signal of:

a) One short blast, b) Two short blasts, c) Two prolonged blasts followed by one short blast, d) Two prolonged blasts followed by two short blasts.

24) A law enforcement boat may display a:

a) Blue flag, b) Flashing blue light, c) Flashing red light, d) Flashing amber light.

25) Your vessel is meeting another vessel head to head. To comply with the steering and sailing rules you should:

a) Exchange one short blast, alter course to the left and pass starboard to starboard, b) Exchange one short blast, alter course to the right and pass port to port, c) Exchange two short blasts, alter course to the left and pass starboard to starboard, d) Exchange two short blasts, alter course to the right and pass port to port.

26) A vessel overtaking another in a narrow channel, and wishing to pass on the other vessel's port side, would sound a whistle signal of:

a) One short blast, b) Two short blasts, c) Two prolonged blasts followed by one short blast, d) Two prolonged blasts followed by two short blasts.

27) A fleet of moored barges extends into a navigable channel. What is the color of the lights on the barges?

a) Red, b) Amber, c) White, d) None of the above.

28) What signal must a power driven vessel give, in addition to one prolonged blast, when backing out of a berth with another vessel in sight?

a) 2 short blasts, b) 1 blast, c) 3 short blasts, d) 4 blasts.

29) At night, a light signal consisting of two flashes by a vessel indicates:

a) An intention to communicate over radiotelephone, b) That the vessel is in distress, c) An intention to leave another vessel to port, d) An intention to leave another vessel to starboard.

30) You are overtaking a vessel in a narrow channel and wish to leave her on a starboard side. You may:

a) Attempt to contact her on the radiotelephone to arrange for the passage, b) Proceed to overtake her without sounding whistle signals, c) Sound four short blasts, d) Any of the above.

31) For the purpose of the Inland Navigation Rules, the term "inland waters" includes:

a) The Great Lakes on the United States side of the International boundary, b) The water surrounding any islands of the United States, c) The coastline of the United States, out to one mile offshore, d) Any lakes within state boundaries.

32) When two vessels are meeting on the Hudson River, which vessel shall sound the first passing signal?

a) The vessel going upstream, b) The vessel coming downstream, c) A vessel that is towing, d) Either vessel.

33) You are on vessel "B" leading vessel "A" which desires to overtake you on the starboard side. After exchanging one blast signals, you should:

a) Alter course to the left, b) Slow your vessel until vessel B has passed, c) Hold course and speed, d) Alter course to the left or right to give vessel B more sea room.

34) Which of the following is not contained in the Inland Navigational Rules?

a) An inconspicuous, partly submerged vessel, b) A seaplane, c) An air-cushion vessel, d) A vessel constrained by her draft.

35) You are operating a vessel through a narrow channel and your vessel must stay within the channel to be navigated safely. Another vessel is crossing your course from starboard to port, and you are in doubt as to his intentions. You:

a) May sound the danger signal, b) Must sound the danger signal, c) Should sound one short blast to show that you are holding course and speed, d) Are required to back down.

36) Your vessel is meeting another vessel head to head. To comply with the rules, you should:

a) Exchange one short blast alter course to the left and pass starboard to starboard, b) Exchange one short blast, alter course to the right and pass port to port, c) Exchange two short blasts, alter course to the left and pass starboard to starboard, d) Exchange two short blasts, alter course to the right and pass port to port.

37) Which of the following may be used to indicate the presence of a partly submerged object being towed?

a) A diamond shape on the towed object, b) An all-round light at each end of the towed object, c) A searchlight from the towing vessel in the direction of the tow, d) All of the above.

38) What type of light is required if a vessel uses this light to signal passing intentions?

a) All-round white light only, b) All-round yellow light only, c) Either an all-round white or yellow light, d) Any colored light is acceptable.

39) Two vessels in a crossing situation have reached agreement as to the intentions of each other over the radiotelephone. In this situation whistle signals:

a) Are required, b) Are optional, c) Are required if crossing within one half mile, d) Are required when crossing within one mile.

40) You are underway in a narrow channel and you are being overtaken by a vessel astern. After the overtaking vessel sounds the proper signal indicating his intention to pass your vessel on your starboard side, you signal your agreement by sounding:

a) One short blast, b) Two prolonged blasts, c) Two prolonged followed by two short blasts, d) One prolonged, one short, one prolonged and one short blast in that order.

41) You are in a meeting situation with another vessel and blow a one blast passing signal. The other vessel answers with two blasts. What should be your next action?

a) Pass on the other vessel's starboard side, b) Blow the danger signal, c) Pass astern of the other vessel, d) Hold course and speed.

42) What lights are required for a barge being pushed ahead, not being part of a composite unit?

a) Sidelights and a sternlight, b) Sidelights, a special flashing light, and sternlight, c) Sidelights and a special flashing light, d) Sidelights, a towing light, and a sternlight.

43) When overtaking another power-driven vessel in a narrow channel, a vessel desiring to overtake on the other vessel's port side, would sound a whistle signal of:

a) One short blast, b) Two short blasts, c) Two prolonged blasts followed by one short blast, d) Two prolonged blasts followed by two short blasts.

44) At night a barge moored in a silo used primarily for mooring purposes shall:

a) Not be required to be lighted, b) Show a white light at each corner, c) Show a red light at the bow and stern, d) Show a flashing yellow light at each corner

45) You are underway and desire to overtake another vessel ahead. After you sound two short blasts on your whistle, vessel "B" sounds five short blasts on the whistle. You should:

a) Pass with caution on the port side of vessel "B", b) Not attempt to pass vessel B until that vessel sounds and you answer a passing signal, c) Answer the five short blast signal then pass on the port side, d) Keep sounding passing signals until the same signal is received from vessel "B".

46) Which statement is true concerning the fog signal of a vessel 15-meters in length anchored in a "special anchored area" approved by the Secretary of Transportation?

a) The vessel is not required to sound a fog signal, b) The vessel shall ring a bell for 5 seconds every minute, c) The vessel shall sound one blast of the foghorn every 2 minutes, d) The vessel shall sound three blasts on the whistle every 2 minutes.

47) A power-driven vessel, when leaving a dock or berth, is required to sound:

a) Two short blasts, b) One long blast, c) One prolonged blast, d) No signal.

48) While underway during the day you signal a small motorboat showing a flashing blue light. The blue light indicates a:

a) A workboat, b) Boat involved in a race, c) A law enforcement craft, d) Rescue boat.

49) Which is true of a down-bound power-driven vessel, when meeting an up-bound vessel on the Western Rivers?

a) She has the right of way, b) She shall propose the manner of passage, c) She shall propose the place of passage, d) All of the above.

50) Whistle signals shall be exchanged by vessels when:

a) They are passing within one-half mile of each other, b) Passing agreements have not been made by radio, c) Course changes are necessary to pass, d) Doubt exists as to which side the vessels will pass on.

51) A barge more than 50-meters long would be required to show how many white anchor lights when anchored in a Secretary of Transportation approved "special anchorage area?"

a) 1, b) 2, c) 3, d) 4.

52) You are navigating in a narrow channel and must remain in the channel for safe operation. Another vessel is crossing the channel ahead of you from your starboard and you are doubtful as to the intention of the crossing vessel. You must:

a) Stop your vessel, since the other vessel has the right of way, b) Sound one short blast of the whistle, and turn to starboard, c) Sound the danger signal, d) Stop your engines, and the sounding of the danger signal is optional.

53) While underway during the day you signal a small motorboat showing a flashing blue light. The blue light indicates a:

a) Law enforcement boat, b) Boat involved in a race, c) Workboat, d) Rescue boat.

54) Which vessel underway need not show a white masthead light at night?

a) A powercraft 10 meters in length, b) A sailboat under sail, c) A dredge, d) A law enforcement craft.

55) One short blast from a stand-on powercraft in a crossing approach means:

a) I am altering my course to port, b) I intend to alter my course to port, c) I intend to alter my course to starboard, d) I will maintain course and speed.

56) Referring to the sketch at right, which should vessel "A" not attempt?

a) To come right, b) To come left, c) To stop, d) All of these.

57) A vessel approaches you from your starboard side. You should first:

a) Wait for him to signal intent, b) Blow one short blast, c) Maintain course and speed, d) Come right slowly.

58) The weather is restricted in visibility and you detect a vessel forward of your beam. You should:

a) Come to a full stop until a bearing on the other vessel is substantiated, b) Keep sufficient headway to maintain steerage way, c) Increase the frequency of your fog signal, d) Post two lookouts, one on each bow.

59) On which of the vessels below would you not find a yellow navigation light?

a) A barge, b) A law enforcement craft, c) A submarine, d) A tug.

60) Which vessel is considered underway?

a) Aground, b) Not under command, c) Anchored, d) Secured to a mooring buoy.

61) Which of the following is not considered restricted visibility?

a) Darkness, b) Sandstorm, c) Smoke, d) Mist or fog.

62) Your engine is jammed in neutral, but you are drifting astern. You should signal:

a) Three short blasts, b) Five or more short blasts, c) A rapid ringing of the ship's bell, d) None of these.

63) The night is foggy and you detect another vessel closing fast with no sound signals, You should sound:

a) Five short blasts, b) One short blast every two minutes, c) One short blast every minute, d) One prolonged blast every two minutes.

64) As regards underway signals in restricted visibility; which vessel below does not belong in the group?

a) Tug with tow, b) Sailboat, c) Fishing vessel, d) Powerboat.

65) A 30 meter tug is pushing her tow. On a dark and clear night approaching her starboard beam forward of 22.5° abaft her beam, which light would you see first?

A flashing yellow light, b) Masthead light, c) Sternlight, d) Green sidelight.

66) A white 360° light would be seen in what position on a powercraft underway?

a) Aft, b) Forward, c) Midships, d) Cabin top.

67) A potential collision situation is deemed to exist when:

a) The relative bearing of an on-coming craft does not vary, b) When the other craft displays the November-Charlie flags, c) When a stand-on vessel fails to return a maneuvering signal, d) When the other vessel makes a radical change of course.

68) Which of the following lights is not authorized?

a) Steering light, b) Towing light, c) Sternlight, d) Sidelights

69) Annex I of the Rules of the Road is concerned with:

a) Technical details of signals for fishing vessels, b) Technical details of sound signal appliances, c) Distress signals, d) Technical details of positioning of lights and shapes.

70) Annex II, of the Rules of the Road is concerned with:

a) Technical details of signals for fishing vessels, b) Technical details of sound signal appliances, c) Distress signals, d) Technical details of positioning of lights and shapes.

71) Annex III of the Rules of the Road is concerned with:

a) Technical details of signals for fishing vessels, b) Technical details of sound signal appliances, c) Distress signals, d) Technical details of positioning of lights and shapes.

72) Annex IV of the Rules of the Road is concerned with:

a) Technical details of signals for fishing vessels, b) Technical details of sound signal appliances, c) Distress signals, d) Technical details of positioning of lights and shapes.

73) Navigation lights are required to be lighted:

a) Between sunrise and sunset, b) Twenty minutes before sunset, c) In any restricted visibility & from sunset to sunrise, d) Only at night or when foggy.

74) The arc of visibility of lights aboard vessels is measured:

a) By points of the compass, b) From dead ahead to two points abaft the beam, c) In a variety of ways, d) In degrees only.

75) In which case does the sailboat not have the right-of-way over the powerboat?

a) When overtaking, b) When crossing a fairway, channel or river, c) When approaching a fishing vessel, fishing, d) All of these.

76) Four vessels meet in a narrow channel. Which has the right-of-way?

a) Minesweeper on duty, b) A vessel not under command, c) A vessel aground, d) None of these-this is a special circumstance.

77) Four sailboats meet. Which has the right-of-way?

a) Close hauled on a port tack, b) Running down wind, c) Sailing on a starboard tack, d) Sailing to the windward of the other three.

78) A sailboat is approaching the port bow of your powerboat. The sailboat is flying an inverted black conical shape, apex down. You should:

a) Stand-on, b) Slow down, c) Blow one blast, d) Come left.

79) An 18 meter power vessel should have a masthead light visible for a minimum of:

a) 1 mile, b) 2 miles, c) 3 miles, d) 5 miles.

80) The Pilot Rules are found in:

a) The Coast Pilot, b) Annex V, c) The Light List, d) The Pilot's Handbook.

81) Which statement regarding signals in restricted visibility is true?

a) Underway signals are sounded every two minutes, b) Anchored vessels sound the signal once every minute, c) Vessels aground sound their signal every minute, d) All statements are true.

82) Which of the following would be considered operating in restricted visibility?

a) Dark moonless night, b) A very cloudy day, c) Within a half-mile of a fog bank, d) On a winding river with heavy traffic.

83) Three masthead lights on a tug means:

a) The tow is over 200 meters astern, b) The tug is 50 meters or more in length, c) a & b, d) a or b.

84) Upon approaching a vessel with a black conical shape, apex up, and extended over the side, you should conclude it is:

a) A dredge, pass on the side opposite the cone, b) a purse seiner with a net over the cone's side, c) A fishing vessel with nets out on the cone side over 150 meters, d) A minesweeper maneuvering.

85) Which vessel underway would never show a ball-diamond-ball dayshape?

a) Fishing vessel, b) Tug, c) Harbor patrol, d) Minesweeper.

86) A vessel displays a basket from one of her yards. She is:

a) Greater than 50 meters, b) Greater than 20 meters, c) Less than 20 meters, d) Less than 50 meters, but greater than 20 meters.

87) Which of the following dayshapes would you see on a working dredge not underway?

a) One black ball, b) Two cones, apex to apex, c) A black diamond, d) Two black balls.

88) Which of the following is a distress signal?

a) The alfa flag, b) The November-Charlie flags, c) The ensign flown upside down, d) A green flare.

89) How many degrees of arc of light are visible on each side of a sternlight?

a) 67.5^o, b) 135°, c) 112.5^o, d) 225°.

90) Visibility is restricted and you hear a whistle signal of one short-one prolonged-one short. The vessel sounding this signal is:

a) Anchored, b) Underway, c) Aground, d) In distress.

91) A vessel over 20 meters in length, anchored in fog, would sound:

a) A fog horn, b) Whistle, c) Bell, d) Gong

92) A barge being towed shall give one prolonged and three short blasts on the whistle in restricted visibility when:

a) Entering congested waterways, b) When manned, c) When two or more barges are towing from the same tug, d) All of the above.

93) A vessel making a stern approach with intent to pass another vessel need not sound a signal when:

a) No change of course is necessary to pass, b) Overtaking is already in progress, c) The passing vessel is over 1,000 yards astern, d) The lead vessel is approaching a wide harbor mouth.

94) Maneuvering signal lights can be:

a) White, b) Or yellow, c) Visible for two miles, d) Any of these.

95) An acceptable substitute for maneuvering signals is:

a) Radio telephone communications, b) Visual hand signals, c) Semaphore communications, d) None of these are permitted as substitutes.

96) Your radar indicates you are in a close-quarter situation with another vessel and the fog is very dense. You should sound:

a) One prolonged blast every two minutes, b) Three short blasts and back down, c) Five short blasts every minute, d) A siren or other radical sound to attract attention.

97) A strong northerly is blowing offshore. Sailboat "A" is close-hauled and both vessels are on starboard tacks. "B" is south of "A":

a) "B" has the right-of-way, b) "B" is to the lee of "A", c) "A" must give-way, d) All of these.

98) Two sailboats are approaching each other under sail and at risk of collision. Vessel "X" is sailing downwind with her mainboom over the port side and her jib over the starboard side. Vessel "Y" is close-hauled with her mainboom over the starboard side and her jib parallel with the main:

a) "X" is on a port tack and must give way, b) "X" is on a starboard tack and has the right-of-way, c) "Y" is to the lee of "X" and has the right-of-way, d) "Y" is on a starboard tack and has the right-of-way.

99) A pilot boat on duty in restricted visibility:

a) **Must** sound only four short blasts, b) **Must** sound regular signals, but **may** sound her own four short as well, c) **Can** substitute the four short blasts for any underway signals in restricted visibility, d) **Can** opt for any combination of the above.

100) Which vessels listed below shall not impede the passage of vessels operating in a traffic pattern?

a) A vessel less than 20 meters in length, b) A fishing vessel fishing with lines nets or trawls, c) A sailboat, d) All of these.

101) Yellow lights are not used to identify:
a) A dredge pipe, b) The heads of tows being pushed ahead by towboats, c) Purse seiners, d) A seaplane on the water.

102) Yellow lights are not used to identify:
a) U.S. Submarines, b) Vessels towing by pushing ahead, c) Law enforcement vessels, d) Dredge pipelines on trestles.

103) A flashing blue light is used to identify:
a) Law enforcement vessels, b) U.S. Submarines, c) Air-cushion vessels in the nondisplacement mode, d) Dredge pipelines on trestles.

104) A vessel is displaying an alternating red and yellow light. This indicates that the vessel is:
a) In distress, b) Fishing with lines extending out over 500 feet, c) Engaged in public safety activities, d) Restricted in ability to maneuver.

105) A law enforcement vessel patrolling a marine regatta may show either a flashing blue light or:

a) Two amber lights in a horizontal line, b) An alternately flashing red and yellow light, c) A high intensity flashing light (strobe), d) A fixed green light over a red flashing light.

106) The special light assigned for a vessel engaged in public safety activities must be located:
a) On top of the mast or highest structure on the vessel, b) So as not to interfere with the visibility of the navigation lights, c) As far forward as possible, d) So that it is not visible more than 22 1/2° abaft the beam.

107) A vessel engaged in public safety activities may display a special light. Which of the following is not considered a public safety activity?
a) Search and rescue, b) Patrolling a regatta, c) Fire-fighting, d) Setting a buoy.

108) You are the stand-on vessel in a crossing situation. The other vessel is showing an alternating red and yellow light. What action should you take?
a) Stand on, b) Heave to, c) Alter course to assist, d) Yield the right of way.

109) You are the stand-on vessel in an overtaking situation. The other vessel is showing an alternately flashing red and yellow light. What action should you take:
a) Alter course to assist, b) Yield right of way, c) Stand on, d) Heave to.

110) Yellow lights are not used to identify:
a) Towing vessels pushing ahead, b) Air cushion vessels in a nondis-placement mode, d) Purse seiners, d) U.S. Submarines.

‡

1) C	28) C	55) D	82) C	110) C
2) B	29) D	56) D	83) D	
3) B	30) A	57) B	84) C	
4) B	31) A	58) B	85) D	
5) A	32) D	59) B	86) C	
6) B	33) C	60) B	87) D	
7) A	34) D	61) A	88) B	
8) A	35) B	62) D	89) A	
9) B	36) B	63) D	90) A	
10 D	37) D	64) D	91) C	
11) C	38) C	65) B	92) B	
12) C	39) B	66) A	93) C	
13) C	40) A	67) A	94) D	
14) D	41) B	68) A	95) A	
15) D	42) C	69) D	96) A	
16) C	43) B	70) A	97) D	
17) D	44) A	71) B	98) B	
18) B	45) D	72) C	99) B	
19) D	46) A	73) C	100) D	
20) D	47) C	74) D	101) D	
21) D	48) C	75) D	102) C	
22) C	49) D	76) D	103) A	
23) A	50) A	77) C	104) C	
24) B	51) D	78) A	105) B	
25) B	52) C	79) C	106) B	
26) B	53) A	80) B	107) D	
27) C	54) B	81) D	109) A	

Fishing vessels, when fishing, have the right of way over sailboats and certain powercraft. Fishing means fishing with lines, nets or trawls.

1) To indicate that a vessel is constrained by her draft, a vessel may display:

a) Three 360 degree red lights, b) Two 225 degree red lights, c) Three 360 degree blue lights, d) Two 225 degree blue lights.

2) A power-driven vessel pushing ahead or towing alongside will display:

a) A single white light forward, b) Two forward masthead lights in a vertical line, c) Two towing lights in a vertical line, d) Two all-round red lights where they can best be seen.

3) Which statement is true concerning a vessel "constrained by her draft?"

a) It must be a power-driven vessel, b) It is not under command, c) It may be a vessel being towed, d) She is hampered because of her work.

4) A vessel using a traffic separation scheme shall:

a) Only anchor in the separation zone, b) If obliged to cross a traffic lane, do so at as small an angle as is practicable, c) Avoid anchoring in areas near the termination of the scheme, d) Utilize the separation zone for navigating through the scheme if she is impeding other traffic due to her slower speed.

5) When moving from a berth in international waters, a vessel must sound:

a) A prolonged blast, b) Three short blasts, c) A long blast, d) None of the above.

6) You are in charge of a 250-meter freight vessel proceeding down a narrow channel. There is a vessel engaged in fishing on your starboard bow one-half mile away. Which statement is true?

a) You are not to impede the fishing vessel, b) If you are in doubt as to the fishing vessel's movement, you may sound the danger signal, c) You are to slow to bare x until clear of the fishing vessel, d) You must sound the danger signal.

7) The International Rules of the Road apply:

a) To all waters which are not inland waters, b) Only to waters outside the territorial waters of the United States, c) Only to waters where foreign vessels travel, d) Upon the high seas and connecting waters navigable by seagoing vessels.

8) A towing light is:

a) Shown at the bow, b) White in color, c) Shown in addition to the sternlight, d) An all-round light.

9) In a narrow channel, an overtaking vessel which intends to PASS on the other vessel's port side would sound:

a) One prolonged followed by two short blasts, b) One short blast, c) Two short blasts, d) Two prolonged followed by two short blasts.

10) While underway on the high seas in restricted visibility, you hear a fog signal of one prolonged and two short blasts. It could be any of the following EXCEPT a vessel:

a) Minesweeping, b) Engaged in fishing, c) Constrained by her draft, d) Being towed.

11) A vessel displaying three red lights in a vertical line is:

a) Not under command, b) Aground, c) Dredging, d) Constrained by her draft.

12) At night, a power-driven vessel of less than 7-meters in length where its maximum speed does not exceed seven knots must show when underway:

a) Sidelights and a sternlight, b) The lights required for a vessel more than seven meters in length, c) Sidelights only, d) One all-round white light.

13) A signal of intent, which must be answered by another vessel, may be sounded in international waters by

a) A vessel meeting another head and head, b) A vessel crossing the course of another, c) A vessel overtaking another, d) Any of the above.

14) When two vessels are in sight of one another, all of the following signals may be given EXCEPT:

a) A light signal of at least five short and rapid flashes, b) Four short whistle blasts, c) One prolonged, one short, one prolonged and one short, d) Two short whistle blasts.

15) A vessel engaged in mineclearing shall show special identity lights:

a) Instead of the masthead lights, b) Which mean that other vessels should not approach within 1000-meters, c) That are 225 degree green lights, d) All of the above.

16) Lighting requirements in inland waters are different from those for international waters for:

a) Barges being pushed ahead, b) Vessels constrained by their draft, c) A vessel towing by pushing ahead, d) All of the above.

17) What whistle signal, if any, would be sounded when two vessels are meeting, but will pass clear starboard to starboard?

a) One short blast, b) Two short blasts, c) Five or more short blasts, d) No signal is required.

18) In a narrow channel, a vessel trying to overtake another on the other vessel's port side, would sound a whistle signal of:

a) One short blast, b) Two short blasts, c) Two prolonged blasts followed by one short blast, d) Two prolonged blasts followed by two short blasts.

19) On open water, a power-driven vessel coming up dead astern of another vessel and altering course to starboard so as to pass on the starboard side of the vessel ahead would sound:

a) Two short blasts, b) One short blast, c) Two prolonged blasts followed by one short blast, d) One long and one short blast.

20) If at night a vessel displays three all-round red lights in a vertical line, during the day she may show:

a) Three balls in a vertical line, b) A cylinder, c) Two diamonds in a vertical line, d) Two cones, points together.

21) A vessel not under command sounds the same fog signal as a vessel:

a) Towing, b) Constrained by her draft, c) Under sail, d) All of the above.

22) Your vessel is crossing a narrow channel and a vessel to port is within the channel and crossing your course. He is showing a black cylinder. What is your responsibility?

a) Hold course and speed, b) Sound the danger signal, c) Begin an exchange of passing signals, d) Do not cross the channel if you might hinder the other vessel.

23) You are approaching another vessel and will pass starboard to starboard without danger if no course changes are made. You should:

a) Hold course and sound a two blast whistle signal, b) Hold course and sound no whistle signal, c) Change course to the right and sound one blast, d) Hold course and sound one blast.

24) Which of the following statements is correct concerning a situation involving a fishing vessel and a vessel not under command?

a) The fishing vessel must keep clear of the vessel not under command, b) If the vessel not under command is a power-driven vessel, it must keep clear of the fishing vessel, c) They must exchange whistle signals, d) Both vessels are required to take action to stay clear of each other.

25) Which signal is only sounded by a power-driven vessel?

a) A signal meaning "I am altering my course to starboard.", b) A signal meaning "I intend to overtake you on your starboard side.", c) A signal meaning that the vessel sounding it is in doubt as to the other vessel's actions, d) A signal sounded when approaching a bend.

26) The light which may be used with a vessel's whistle is to be:

a) Used when the whistle is broken, b) Used prior to sounding the whistle, c) Used only at night, d) A white light

27) While underway in fog, you hear a prolonged blast from another vessel. This signal indicates a:

a) Sailboat underway, b) Vessel underway, towing, c) Vessel underway, making way, d) Vessel being towed.

28) Which of the following may be used to show the presence of a partly submerged object being towed?

a) An diamond shape on the towed object, b) An all-round light at each end of the towed object, c) A searchlight from the towing vessel in the direction of the tow, d) All of the above.

29) At night, a barge being towed astern must display:

a) Red and green sidelights only, b) A white sternlight only, c) Sidelights and a sternlight, d) One all-round white light.

30) Which of the following may be used as a distress signal?

a) Directing the beam of a searchlight at another vessel, b) A smoke signal giving off orange colored smoke, c) A whistle signal of one prolonged and three short blasts, d) International Code Signal PAN.

31) If your vessel is approaching a bend and you hear a prolonged blast from around the bend, you should:

a) Back your engines, b) Stop your engines and drift, c) Answer with one prolonged blast, d) Sound the danger signal.

32) Failure to understand the course or intention of an approaching vessel should be indicated by:

a) One short blast, b) One prolonged blast, c) No less than five short blasts, d) Not less than five prolonged blasts.

33) If you are the stand-on vessel in a crossing situation, you may take action to avoid collision by your maneuver alone. When may this action be taken?

a) At any time you feel it is appropriate, b) Only when you have reached extremis, c) When you determine that your present course will cross ahead of the other vessel, d) When it becomes apparent to you that the give-way vessel is not taking appropriate action.

34) If your vessel is underway in fog and you hear one prolonged and three short blasts, this is a:

a) Vessel not under command, b) Sailing vessel, c) Vessel in distress, d) Vessel being towed.

35) A pilot vessel on pilotage duty at night will show sidelights and a stern light:

a) When at anchor, b) Only when making way, c) At any time when underway, d) Only when the identifying lights are not being shown.

36) A power-driven vessel underway in fog making NO way must sound what blast (s) on the whistle?

a) One long, b) Two prolonged, c) One prolonged, d) One prolonged and two short

37) A 95-meter vessel aground shall sound which fog signal?

a) A rapid ringing of a bell for 5 seconds every two minutes, b) A whistle signal of one short, one prolonged, and one short blast, c) A long blast of the whistle at intervals not to exceed one minute, d) A rapid ringing of a bell for 5 seconds, preceded and followed by three separate and distinct strokes on the bell.

38) A 200-meter vessel is aground in fog. Which signal is optional?

a) A bell signal, b) A gong signal, c) A whistle signal, d) All of the above.

39) Which of the following is a distress signal?

a) A triangular flag above or below a ball, b) The International Code Signal of distress indicated by JV, c) A green smoke signal, d) Flames on the vessel as from a burning tar barrel.

40) Which vessel must show forward and after masthead lights when making way?

a) A 75-meter vessel restricted in her ability to maneuver, b) A 100-meter sailing vessel, c) A 150-meter vessel engaged in fishing, d) a 45-meter vessel engaged in towing.

41) A vessel must proceed at a safe speed:

a) In restricted visibility, b) In congested waters, c) During darkness, d) At all times.

42) A sailing vessel underway may exhibit:

a) A red light over a green light at the masthead, b) A green light over a red light at the masthead, c) Two white lights in a vertical line at the stern, d) An all-round white light at the bow.

43) The word "vessel", in the Rules, includes:

a) Sailing ships, b) Nondisplacement craft, c) Seaplanes, d) All of the above.

44) A sailing vessel with the wind abaft the beam is navigating in fog. She should sound:

a) Three short blasts, b) One prolonged blast, c) One prolonged and two short blasts, d) Two prolonged blasts.

45) If a towing vessel and her tow are severely restricted in their ability to change course, they may show lights in addition to their towing identification light. These additional lights may be shown if the tow is:

a) Pushed ahead, b) Towed alongside, c) Towed astern, d) Any of the above.

46) If two sailing vessels are running free with the wind on the same side, which one must keep clear of the other?

a) The one with the wind closest abeam, b) The one with the wind closest astern, c) The one to leeward, d) The one to windward.

47) Define a "vessel not under command" as a vessel which:

a) From the nature of her work is unable to keep out of the way of another vessel, b) Through some exceptional circumstances is unable to maneuver as required by the rules, c) By taking action contrary to the rules has created a special circumstance situation, d) Is moored, aground or anchored in a fairway.

48) Additional light signals are provided in the Annexes to the Rules for vessels:

a) Engaged in fishing, b) Not under command, c) Engaged in towing, d) Under sail.

49) Which vessel may combine her sidelights in one lantern on the fore and aft centerline of the vessel?

a) A 16-meter sail vessel, b) A 25-meter power-driven vessel, c) A 28-meter sail vessel, d) Any non-self-propelled vessel.

50) The duration of a prolonged blast of the whistle is:

a) 2 to 4 seconds, b) 4 to 6 seconds, c) 6 to 8 seconds, d) 8 to 10 seconds.

51) A vessel "restricted in her ability to maneuver" is one which:

a) From the nature of her work is unable to maneuver as required by the rules, b) Through some exceptional circumstance is unable to maneuver as required by the rules, c) Due to adverse weather conditions is unable to maneuver as required by the rules, d) Has lost steering and is unable to maneuver.

52) When underway in restricted visibility, you might hear, at intervals of two minutes, any of the following fog signals EXCEPT:

a) One prolonged blast, b) Two prolonged blasts, c) One prolonged and two short blasts, d) Ringing of a bell for five seconds.

53) What is the identity fog signal which may be sounded by a vessel engaged on pilotage duty?

a) 2 short blasts, b) 3 short blasts, c) 4 short blasts, d) 5 short blasts.

54) A vessel of less than 20-meters in length may display a basket as a dayshape when she is engaged in:

a) Trawling, b) Diving operations, c) Trolling, d) All of the above.

55) A bell is used to sound a fog signal for a:

a) Power-driven vessel underway, b) Sailing vessel at anchor, c) Vessel engaged in fishing, d) Vessel not under command.

56) You are seeing another vessel and its compass bearing does not significantly change. This would indicate that:

a) You are the stand-on vessel, b) Risk of collision exits, c) A special circumstances situation exists, d) The other vessel is dead in the water.

57) What lights are required for a barge being towed alongside?

a) Sidelights and a sternlight, b) Sidelights, a special flashing light, and a sternlight, c) Sidelights and a special flashing light, d) Sidelights, a towing light, and a sternlight.

58) A towing vessel pushing a barge ahead which is rigidly connected in composite unit shall show the lights of:

a) A vessel towing by pushing ahead, b) A power-driven vessel, not towing, c) A barge being pushed ahead, d) Either answer A or answer C.

59) You are the watch officer on a power-driven vessel and notice a large sail vessel approaching from astern. You should:

a) Slow down, b) Sound one short blast and change course to the starboard, c) Sound two short blasts and change course to port, d) Hold course and speed.

60) You see a vessel's green sidelight bearing due east from you. The vessel might be heading:

a) East, b) Northeast, c) Northwest, d) Southwest.

61) A vessel shall be deemed to be overtaking when she is in such a position with reference to the vessel she is approaching that she can see, at night:

a) Only the sternlight of the vessel, b) The sternlight and one sidelight of the vessel, c) Only a sidelight of the vessel, d) Any lights except the masthead lights of the vessel.

62) A vessel trawling will display a:

a) Red light over a white light, b) Green light over a white light, c) White light over a red light, d) White light over a green light.

63) If it becomes necessary for a stand-on vessel to take action to avoid collision, she shall, if possible:

a) Not decrease speed, b) Not increase speed, c) Not turn to port for a vessel on her own port side, d) Not turn to starboard for a vessel on her own port side.

64) Your vessel is NOT making way, but is not in any way disabled. Another vessel is approaching you on your starboard beam. Which statement is true?

a) The other vessel must give way since your vessel is stopped, b) Your vessel is the give-way vessel in a crossing situation, c) You should be showing the lights or shapes for a vessel not under command, d) You should be showing the lights or shapes for a vessel restricted in her ability to maneuver.

65) A sailing vessel which is also propelled by machinery shall show during daylight hours:

a) A black diamond, b) A black cone, c) A black ball, d) A basket.

66) The rules concerning lights shall be complied with in all weathers from sunset to sunrise. The lights:

a) Shall be displayed in restricted visibility during daylight hours, b) Need not be displayed when no other vessels are in the area, c) Shall be set at low power when used during daylight hours, d) Need not be displayed by unmanned vessels.

67) The masthead light of a 25 meter sailboat would become visible within:

a) 1 mile, b) 2 miles, c) 3 miles, d) None of these.

68) Masthead lights on a tug showing four white lights from dead ahead would have masthead lights which are visible at least:

a) 6 miles, b) 5 miles, c) 4 miles, d) 3 miles.

69) Approaching from aft of 22 1/2° abaft the beam of a 19 meter craft the light you see should be visible for:

a) 1 miles, b) 2 miles, c) 3 miles, d) 4 miles.

70) A six meter outboard making 6.5 knots must show at least:

a) Sidelights, b) A sternlight, c) A 360° white light aft, d) An electric torch.

71) Air cushion vessels underway show a special 360° light which is:

a) Yellow, b) Blue, c) Flashing yellow, d) Red.

72) A black cylinder at the forestay of a vessel indicates:

a) Not under command, b) Deep draft in shallow channel, c) Aground, d) A sailboat underway with engines running.

73) A black cone, apex up, means the vessel is:

a) Towing, b) Sailing, c) Fishing, d) Tending buoys.

74) A rapid ringing of the gong is a type of restricted visibility signal required:

a) On small craft, b) On vessels of 100 meters or more, c) On all buoy tenders, d) On some large vessels when aground.

75) To which of the following vessels would a sailboat not be obligated to give way?

a) Trawler, b) Purse seiner, c) A vessel trolling, d) Buoy tender on duty.

76) A vessel laying a submarine cable would show the dayshapes of:

a) Black balls, b) Black diamonds, c) Black cone(s) d) Both a & b.

77) Visibility is restricted and you hear two prolonged blasts. This could be:

a) A trawler, b) A dredge, c) A Buoy Tender, d) Any of these.

78) A heavy fog closes in. You should travel:

a) At a safe speed, b) At a moderate speed, c) At a speed enabling you to stop in half the distance of visibility, d) With lookouts posted fore and aft.

79) A fishing vessel is anchored and fishing in a fog. She sounds the same signal as what other anchored vessel:

a) A sailboat, b) A vessel restricted in ability to maneuver, c) A vessel not under command, d) All of these.

80) Which two vessels sound one prolonged and two short when working at anchor.

a) Fishing and restricted in ability to maneuver, b) Restricted in ability to maneuver and not under command, c) Not under command and fishing, d) Any of these.

81) Restricted visibility and you detect a vessel forward of your beam:

a) Maintain course and speed, b) Slow down, but maintain steerage way, c) Stop and wait until your intended path is clear, d) Back down.

82) One prolonged and two short blasts in a fog would indicate:

a) A minesweeper, b) A vessel aground, c) Pilot vessel on station and on duty, d) Power vessel underway with way on.

83) Which vessel can use combined sidelights?

a) A 25 meter sailboat, b) A 20 meter power boat fishing, c) A 5 meter rowboat, d) A 28 meter powerboat.

84) Flown from the forward mast or stay, which code flags indicate distress?

a) Alfa-bravo, b) November-Charlie, c) Delta-Tango, d) Hotel-Lima.

85) In clear visibility you hear four short blasts. This is:

a) A wrong signal, b) A manned vessel under tow, c) A vessel backing out of or departing a slip or dock, d) A pilot vessel.

86) Visibility is severely restricted. You can see only the lower deck of a vessel ahead which has two vertically arranged 360° white lights over the side. You infer:

a) A trawler shooting her nets, b) A mooring buoy, c) A vessel 50 meters or more aground, d) A vessel, less than 12 meters, underway.

87) A ten meter powerboat may show which minimum lights when operating at night?

a) Anchor light, b) Sidelights, c) 360° light aft & sidelights when available, d) 360° white light aft and sidelights.

88) A 10 meter sailboat must show which of the following?

a) A sternlight, b) A 360° masthead light, c) A range light, d) A flare-up light.

89) You detect a vessel on your radar during a heavy rain storm. You should:

a) Sound one prolonged blast, b) Stop until the way is clear, c) Make a distinct change of course and/or speed immediately, d) Sound five short blasts.

90) A give-way vessel overtaking a stand-on vessel sounds two short blasts then passes the vessel ahead:

a) Port side to, b) Starboard to starboard, c) Port to port, d) starboard side to.

91) You sight a vessel's lights, all of which are 360°. One high white light is forward, two red vertically arranged lights amidships and a lower white light aft. This vessel is:

a) Towing a submerged object, b) Aground, c) Servicing buoys, d) Moored over a wreck.

92) A vessel trolling would avoid which type of craft?

a) Sailboat, b) A tug restricted in ability to maneuver, c) Trawler with nets down, d) All of these.

93) A vessel approaching you at a relative angle of 210° evidences which of the following situations?

a) Overtaking, b) Crossing, c) Head-on, d) Collision.

94) Certain vessels are encouraged to use inshore traffic zones at all times. These are:

a) All small craft, b) Sailboats and vessels less than 20 meters in length, c) Only sailboats, d) Only vessels less than 20 meters.

95) A vessel approaching you at a relative bearing of 115°:

a) Is a stand-on vessel, b) Is a give-way craft, c) Could see your green sidelight at night, d) Could not see your sternlight at night.

96) Vessels pushing or towing alongside could show a maximum of how many masthead lights?

a) one, b) two, c) three, d) four.

97) The dayshape for a submerged or partially submerged vessel being towed greater than 200 meters astern is:

a) None, b) A black diamond, c) Two black diamonds, d) The Bravo flag.

98) How far should a vessel on approach stand clear of a minesweeper?

a) 500 meters, b) 1,000 meters, c) 1500 meters, d) 1 mile.

99) Diveboats less than how many meters are exempt from displaying the dive flag?

a) 12 meters, b) 16 meters, c) 20 meters, d) None are exempt.

100) All vessels aground are required to display proper signals indicating this except those less than:

a) 12 meters, b) 20 meters, c) 50 meters, d) All must show the signal.

101) You are about to cross a narrow channel when you see an approaching vessel that can only be navigated safely within the channel. You should:
a) Cross the channel as you have the right of way, b) Cross only if the vessel in the channel is approaching on your port side, c) Not cross the channel if you might impede the other vessel, d) Sound the danger signal.

102) A vessel engaged in mineclearing shows special identity lights:
a) In addition to the lights required for a power-driven vessel, b) Which means that other vessels should not approach within 1000 meters of the mineclearing vessel, c) Which are green and show all-round, d) All of the above.

103) What equipment for fog signals is required for a vessel 20 meters in length?
a) Whistle and bell only, b) Whistle only, c) Bell only, d) Whistle, bell and gong.

104) What is the minimum sound signaling quipment required aboard a vessel 14 meters in length?
a) Any means of making an efficient sound signal, b) A bell only, c) A whistle only, d) A bell and a whistle.

105) A tug is towing three unmanned barges in line in fog. The third vessel of the tow should sound:
a) No fog signal, b) One short blast, c) One prolonged and three short blasts, d) One prolonged, one short, and one prolonged blast.

106) A tug is towing three manned barges in line in fog. The first vessel of the tow should sound:
a) No fog signal, b) One short blast, c) One prolonged and three short blasts, d) One prolonged, one short, and one prolonged blast.

107) When should the fog signal of a vessel being towed be sounded?
a) When the vessel being towed is unmanned. b) When the vessel being towed is manned, c) All towed vessels, manned or unmanned, must sound fog signals, d) Towed vessels are never required to sound fog signals.

1) A	26) D	51) A	76) D	101) C
2) B	27) C	52) D	77) D	102) D
3) A	28) D	53) C	78) A	103) A
4) C	29) C	54) A	79) B	104) D
5) D	30) B	55) B	80) A	105) A
6) B	31) C	56) B	81) B	106) A
7) D	32) C	57) A	82) A	107) B
8) C	33) D	58) B	83) C	
9) D	34) D	59) D	84) B	
10 D	35) C	60) D	85) A	
11) D	36) B	61) A	86) A	
12) D	37) D	62) B	87) C	
13) C	38) C	63) C	88) A	
14) B	39) D	64) B	89) A	
15) B	40) A	65) B	90) D	
16) D	41) D	66) A	91) B	
17) D	42) A	67) D	92) D	
18) D	43) D	68) A	93) A	
19) B	44) C	69) B	94) B	
20) B	45) D	70) C	95) B	
21) D	46) D	71) C	96) C	
22) D	47) B	72) B	97) C	
23) B	48) A	73) C	98) B	
24) A	49) A	74) B	99) D	
25) A	50) B	75) C	100) A	

Vessels are considered "underway" when not at anchor, not made fast to shore and not aground.

NAVIGATION GENERAL

This section is somewhat like an air training ground school. It is studied and mastered before they let you near the plane. In this case, it's before you pick up a course plotter, dividers and calculator. These are basic skills you need to tackle the CG questions on **both** the chart plotting problems and those problems found in the quiz at the end of this section. In short, it's time to start learning the techniques of correcting compass error, learning to calculate speed-distance-time and ivory tower stuff like doubling the angle on the bow and computing deviation by utilizing a range. Also included is the U.S. buoyage system, tides, charts, publications, and a little on weather, plus just enough for you to squeak through on gyro compasses and instruments.

As indicated earlier, this is a 70% quiz and while this is a "How To" book it is not a complete text. If so, it would be the size of Chapman's, Bowditch and Knight's Modern Seamanship combined. The object here is to tell you *what* you need to know, show you 90% of it, tell you where to find the rest then show you a good sampling of the exams. Incidentally, the CG admits freely that the above three volumes are used heavily as resource material for the exams. Don't bother with everything in Chapman's, but **certain parts** will put you on top. For example, perusing Chapman's latest edition on chapters 13, 14, 16, 18, and maybe even 23 will answer a lot of "why" questions one has upon finishing the following section and related quiz. Using common sense means you might learn more from the quiz than from any text. A great deal depends on the individual's experience.

Aids to Navigation, Weather, Tides, Navigation, Instruments and Charts. The divisions are ours, not the CG's, but that's where the questions are. So you skip ahead and read some of those Instrument

questions and come apart. "What do I know about the theory of Loran?" you scream. "Especially that kind of Loran." You throw the book across the room and stomp out tripping over your lower lip. Peace, brothers and sisters; there are ways and one is reading chapter 23 in Chapman.

Of course, if you are really concerned that you can deduce nothing from the questions themselves then you should give serious consideration to reading up on the subject. Complaining about it isn't going to take any of those questions off the exams. For example, go to Chapman's on Radionavigation Systems. Find LORAN in the index. In just **two pages** of reading you will know where the CG got their test questions. You will be informed of such esoteric qualities of Loran-C as the facts that it is a lower radio frequency carrier of about 100 kHz with ground-wave range, along with its secondary stations, of about 1200 miles and 3,000 miles on the sky-waves and accurate to within 0.1 to 0.25 of a mile. Those statements alone will cover about ten questions.

The written material and tests are handled separately herein, but stand advised you will face a well-mixed forty questions on the CG exam. Forty questions? Can't be too bad.

‡

Tides are vertical movements of large bodies of water which in turn cause currents to flow. The terms *ebb tide* and *flood tide* are incorrect. It's flood current and ebb current, i.e. the horizontal motion of water. There is no *slack* tide. It's slack *water*. Think how many boats have been misnamed. You need to know this.

The Coast Guard's idea of weather is rather idealistic. Right out of an academy classroom. The weather in general is based on some general principles which are cited herein and while they are obviously not always true, in CG exams, it's the way to bet. And our apologies if some of this is old hat to you.

PRESSURE-CYCLONES and ANTICYCLONES

The overleaf holds several diagrams relative to our opening salvos on this involved subject upon which we are going to touch just enough. Keep in mind we are dealing with the situation as it exists in the northern hemisphere. First the high and low pressure areas.

A **high pressure area** is generally one of **clear calm weather** and can have a diameter of several hundred miles as in figure #1. The wind from a high circulates out from the center in a **clockwise direction**. The wind from the high pressure area is "dumping" into the low pressure area. The low pressure area wind is much less stable, gustier, stronger and is spiraling into the low's center in a **counter-clockwise** direction. Winds are strongest in the center. Not a nice place to be. How does one locate the center of a low? It's called **BUYS BALLOT'S LAW** (a Dutchman) and involves facing into the wind in a low pressure area. As you do, the center of the low is to your right and a shade behind you, or, if you like, about 120° relative to your heading. Put yourself on one of those little boats in the figure #1 low and see how it fits.

Isobars are lines of equal pressure. Something like fathom curves in the ocean. Some examples are shown in figure #6 and in this case they are measured in the weather map standard of millibars. The lower the number, the lower the pressure. The isobars are not always symmetrical or evenly spaced or made up of flowing lines. However, if the isobars are grouped closely together on one edge, as they are in figure #3, it is called a steep gradient indicating where the winds are the strongest. Closely grouped isobars equal strong winds.

How do you remember all of this clockwise and counter-clockwise bit? Simple. Grab a piece of scrap paper and a pencil then look at figure #2. Draw a large sprawling backward letter "S". Now, make the top of the "S" spiral inward to the center and do the same with the bottom to complete the figure. Now, start at the top of the "S" where the high's center is located and spiral outwards and keep right on going-following the lines-until you spiral inwards at the bottom where the low is situated. Aha! You had to spiral clockwise to get out of the high and counter-clockwise to get into the center of the low. And that's the way the winds blow in the highs and the lows. Another word for a low pressure area is a "cyclone". Highs are called "anti-cyclones."

Here, the high is on the top and the low is on the bottom. While that isn't always the way they position themselves on the face of this planet, it's a good memory crutch.

Even without a pronounced high or low pressure area the diurnal (daily) pressure varies a little just with the time of day. The lowest pressure spots are at 0400 and 1600. The highest occur at 1000 and 2200.

How about a few symbols? A front line inscribed with small triangles is a cold front. On a weather map it is colored blue. A front line colored red and with small semi-circles is a warm front. Combinations produce occluded fronts, figure #4, and stationary fronts, figure #5. The line representing the occluded front is purple on a weather map.

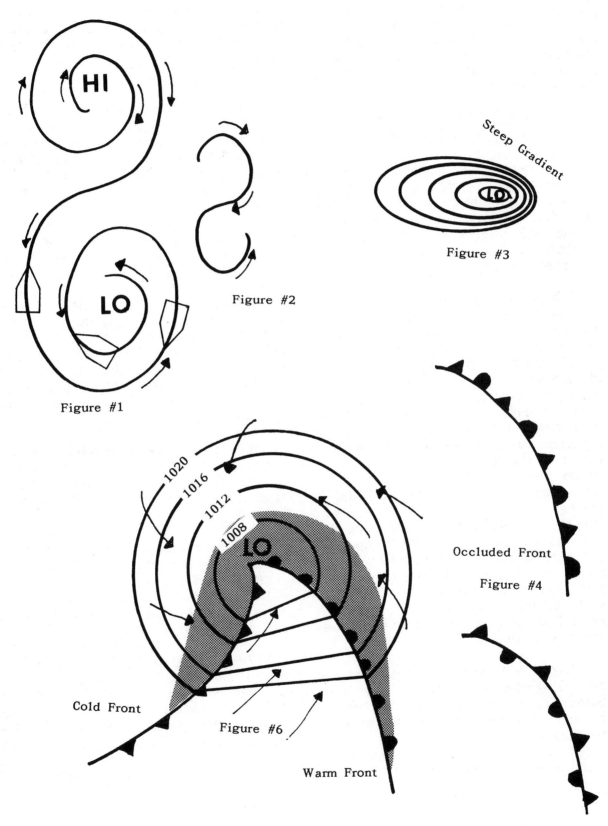

HI

LO

Figure #1

Figure #2

Steep Gradient

LO

Figure #3

1020
1016
1012
1008
LO

Cold Front

Figure #6

Warm Front

Occluded Front

Figure #4

Stationary Front

Figure #5

FRONTS

Low pressure areas often generate or are tied in with warm and cold fronts. On figure #6 on the last page both fronts are shown emanating from the center of the low. Both fronts are moving east. The warm front, dense with water vapor, is more to the east and moves slower than a dry cold front. If the cold front catches the warm front there is rain. The overtaking is called an occlusion. Now you need to know what's happening on the ground or sea when these fronts go by. The cloud names and abbreviations are on the next page along with their expected altitudes. *You need this.*

An **approaching warm front** is heralded by specific clouds. First, far to the east of the warm front one finds cirrus, then closer to the front, cirrostratus and finally altostratus and perhaps even fog or rain from nimbostratus right at the front. Precipitation starts and can continue for up to eighteen hours. Wind from E to SE and the barometer is dropping steadily. Sketch in the cloud **abbreviations** from the next page.

As the warm front passes clouds dissipate, partial clearing, warmer air, rain stops, wind veers (moves clockwise in direction) to S or SW. Note the small arrows on diagram #6 indicating the direction from which the wind is coming in each area. Pressure is still falling, but nothing like before. Starting to level off. More cloud abbreviations to sketch in as when the warm front is finally past, the clouds are back. Stratus, strato-cumulus. Drizzles at best. Temp up, pressure steady. Humidity up due to moisture laden warm air mass. Fair visibility. See if you can't carefully insert these facts into #6 your own way. This would make a terrific study guide once complete and would cover much more than half the test questions on weather.

As the cold front hits, unstable air. Vertically developing cumulus or cumulonimbus. Heavy showers and/or thunderstorms if this air mass is warm and unstable. Pressure up. Temp down.

Behind the cold front it is decidedly colder. Cumulus clouds. Showers for a few hours. Wind W to NW, gusty, still veering. Pressure continues to rise, temp drops. Colder dryer air takes over so dew point drops. Excellent visibility.

SUMMARY ON FRONTS

Stationary front is when a warm and cold front meet head-on or nearly so and the air mass is at a standstill, figure #5. Example would be a warm Gulf air mass coming ashore to meet a cold front in the southern states. Cold air holds less moisture than warm air. Think sweaty bodies in the tropics. Warm air is turbulent and unstable. A colder air mass aloft with a warmer (hence rising) air mass below makes for unstable weather. The opposite would be a cold ground air mass below with a warmer air mass above making for very stable conditions. It is warm air rising and becoming turbulent which causes instability. Remember that. Remember all of this.

A cold front advances faster than a warm front. When a cold front goes by, the pressure rises and the temp drops. If a cold front overtakes a warm front an occlusion occurs and the warm air is pushed aloft and there is rain.

Cold fronts can produce thunderstorms which come from cumulonimbus clouds. Big vertical guys to 20,000 ft. Strong winds coming from the base. When fronts pass, winds veer. North of the low the winds back and come in from the east.

Now let's go for that cloud I.D.

HIGH CLOUDS ABOVE 20,000 FT	CIRRUS Ci CIRROSTRATUS Cs CIRROCUMULUS Cc
MIDDLE CLOUDS 20,000 FT TO 6,500 FT	ALTOSTRATUS As ALTOCUMULUS Ac
LOW CLOUDS BELOW 6,500 FT	STRATUS St NIMBOSTRATUS Ns STRATOCUMULUS Sc

VERTICAL DEVELOPMENT CLOUDS

| CUMULUS Cu From a base 1500 ft topping off at 16,000 ft. | CUMULONIMBUS Cb Bases range from 1/2 Mi to 12 miles high |

CLOUD TYPES

High up above 20,000 feet are the cirrus (Ci) clouds. Cirrus is cob webby and transparent. Pure ice. If it thickens it becomes cirrostratus (Cs) and puts halos around the sun and moon. Then comes cirrocumulus (Cc) so called because things are getting lumpy. Arranged globular masses and sometimes called "mackerel skies."

In the middle are clouds thick enough to have water droplets. Altocumulus are in globs with edges barely touching. Inconsistent thickness. Altostratus is often a rain cloud. Thick lower altostratus can produce long-lasting precipitation.

Down below 6500 feet are the thick and wavy clouds. Twisted wool. Stratus clouds are very low sometimes hitting the ground to become fog. A cloud to produce drizzle. Covers the tops of high hills and buildings.

Good thing to remember is the generalization that true rain comes only from altostratus or nimbostratus clouds.

VERTICAL DEVELOPMENT CLOUDS

Cumulus means piled up. Vertical development from small to large with massive upwards growth. Cumulus clouds are the types billowing up and forming over mountains, islands and atolls.

Cumulonimbus. Heavy with very high development. Cauliflowers. Often with an anvil top being blown around up in the high winds. Near the base; rain, snow, hail or thunderstorms. Sailing towards this base the first thing you feel is a violent change of wind direction so the strong wind comes from the direction of the cloud base.

DEW POINT

Condensation and evaporation are opposites. To evaporate obviously the water must reach a certain temperature. Likewise, to condense back into some form of water, such as fog or rain, the air containing the water vapor must be cooled to a certain temperature while maintaining the same pressure. When condensation occurs the "dew point" has been reached.

Weather people quote two temperatures at weather stations. One is temperature and one is "dew point." For example, the temperature might be 68° and the dew point 64°. When both temps are the same, condensation occurs and they say the dew point has been reach. They can even plot the rise of the dew point and the decline of the temperature and predict when fog will occur. Everyone knows how temperature is measured, but how do they measure dew point?

They use an instrument called a psychrometer. It consists of two thermometers mounted side by side. One is the ordinary kind, the other has the tip wrapped in wet muslin. By swinging the psychrometer overhead, or exposing it to wind or a fan, the moisture in the wet muslin in evaporated. The evaporation of this moisture in the muslin forces the temperature of this "wet bulb" down. Reading the wet bulb gives the "wet bulb depression" and is used to calculate the dew point on a special chart, the likes of which you needn't be bothered. Dew Point is that temperature to which a body of air must be cooled to reach saturation, create visible moisture in the air. An example would be warm moisture laden air blowing out over a cooler ocean. The air cools by being in contact with the colder water. The air cools to the dew point and you have fog.

Now you know what a dew point and a psychrometer are, what's a hygrometer? A hygrometer is an instrument used to calculate relative humidity. That's a nice way of asking what percentage of the surrounding atmosphere is moisture. An anemometer is an instrument used for measure wind speed and a barometer measure atmospheric pressure.

MISCELLANY

Miscellany means there's no place else to stuff this information without making a bigger thing out of it than we have already. A katabatic wind is a wind rolling down an incline and cooling as it does so. Not one meteorologist interviewed seemed to know where one would find such a wind at sea or over any great body of water in the U.S., but there it is.

Sea breezes occur in the daytime and blow from the sea onshore. This is cooler air blowing onshore due to different temperatures ashore.

Land cools quickly; in one evening. Water changes temperature very slowly; sometimes over months the temperature will differ by only a few degrees. Since land cools quickly, by around midnight a land breeze has developed. That is, an offshore breeze is blowing. However, remember that if that warm land breeze (mountains cooling off after a hot day) blows out over a cooler water, you will often get fog.

Weather "systems" in Canada and the U.S. move easterly having been pushed there by the prevailing westerlies. They are often "steered" by the polar jet streams which also move predominantly easterly.

Wind directions are frequently cited in direction names rather than degrees of the compass. If boxing a compass is unclear now is the time to learn the main sixteen points. Draw a circle with eight equally spaced diameters through it then fill in these points in a clockwise fashion. It gives one perspective.

North: north-north-east; north-east; east-north-east;
East; east-south-east; south-east; south-south-east;
South; south-south-west; south-west; west-south-west;
West; west-north-west; north-west; north-north-west; and back to north.

☩

TIME

That's right...**time**. Everything goes by the 24 hour clock. You know, military time...navy time, or whatever. This means the clock doesn't start over again at noon. Each one of the 24 hours in the days has its' own special number. Compare these.

First These   Then these

0200 = 2:00 A.M.   1235 = 12:35 P.M.
0230 = 2:30 A.M.   1259 = 12:59 P.M.
0615 = 6:15 A.M.   and one minute later
0900 = 9:00 A.M.   1300 = 1:00 P.M. which
1159 = 11:59 A.M.   is correct because
and two minutes   that's the 13th hour
later it's 1201 =   of the day.
12:01 P.M. Don't   2000 = 8:00 P.M.
forget that   2359 = 11:59 P.M.
1200 = 12:00 A.M.   2400 or 0000 =
or noon.   12:00 P.M.
                    or midnight.

All of which leads to a thing called elapsed time. How long it takes to get from point "A" to point "B". Here are a few for practice. First whip out your trusty 3 x 5 card and cover up the answers in the right column and try to figure how much time has gone by from Column #1 to Column #2.

Col #1 DEPARTURE	Col #2 ARRIVAL	Col #3 ELAPSED TIME
0400	0700	3h
0230	0530	3h
0315	0545	2h 30m
0345	0515	1h 30m

Right! That last one is still a subtraction problem, but you have to borrow. Watch.

The catch is to be aware that the first two columns on the left are reserved for hours only. The two columns on the right are for minutes. If you do any borrowing, you must borrow one of the hours on the left and convert it to sixty minutes. Then add the sixty minutes you borrowed to the minutes you already have on the right. Regarding the last example above. From 0345 to 0515 means you line them up like this:

    0515
    0345

However, you can't take 45 minutes from 15 minutes. So, you borrow one hour from the five hours on the **top left**. Take that hour, convert it to 60 minutes, then add it to the 15 minutes you already have on the top in the minutes column. That makes for 4h 75m. Now you can subtract.

    0475
    0345

0130, or more appropriately, 1h 30m = length of time which has elapsed since you got underway.

Before going any farther, try these. **And forget your calculator on this.** The calculator goes by tenths, hundredths, thousandths, etc. Time goes in units of 60. Again, cover up column 3.

#1	#2	#3
0630	0728	58m
0630	0732	1h 02m
1130	1330	2h
1159	1442	2h 43m
1000	1658	6h 58m
2300	0100	2h
2250	0210	3h 20m
2009	0308	6h 59m

‡

DISTANCE ON A CHART

This is the simple one. Pull out the big book chart and grab your dividers. On the **right** side of the chart near the bottom is 34° of latitude. From 34° to 34° 10' is ten nautical miles. (Remember - 10' is pronounced 10 minutes.) **Be sure to measure only on the right or left side of the chart.**

Go ahead and count them. Ten spaces. Ten miles. What's the catch, you ask? Well, so maybe there's a couple. 1) You have to be able to measure the distance to the nearest **tenth** of a mile. Something like using an old fashioned slide rule. With a little practice you'll be surprised at how adept you can become. 2) On a regular large chart you must be sure to use what is called the "mid-lat" to take your measurements. This means you should use that part of the chart closest to the distances you are measuring. On a regular small scale chart ten miles at the top is shorter than ten miles at the bottom of the chart. Not much on most, but enough to throw off a CG answer.

In other words, if you're going to measure from the Anacapa Light to the Bunny Isle Light, use the measurements in that general area. Don't go to the top of the chart to measure this particular distance. Spread the dividers so they stretch from Anacapa to Bunny. Put the points of your dividers right on the dots beneath the tear drops. Without opening or closing the dividers, slide them gently over to the right side. Place one point on the 34° mark and notice where the other point falls on the small grid. How many miles? Would you buy 12.2 miles? Try another one.

How about Cavern Point to Anacapa Light? Spread the dividers between them then make your comparison on the side of the chart. Either side-just so you don't budge the dividers and keep in the general area of the bottom of the chart when you take these measurements. Did you get 10.4 miles? You don't have to indicate "nautical" miles. If you are measuring on a **chart** everyone assumes you are talking about nautical miles. On a **map** it's statute miles. Curious? OK, a statute mile is 5,280 feet. A nautical mile is 6,076 feet.

Here's some more for limbering up. The answers are in the shaded area on the next page. Do them **all** before you check your answers. Takes guts, but do it. And don't get sore because you have to look for most of these fictitious places. You will have to become acquainted with this chart and know it as well as your own. Might as well start now.

One more thing. If you haven't already discovered it, always measure from the center of the dot which indicates the light, to the center of the next light's dot. Lights ashore are marked by teardrops. Buoys with a triangle. With the buoys, again it's the **dot** beneath the triangle which is **supposed** to indicate the exact location of the buoy.

1) Try a long one first. Use your course plotter to draw a line from Santa Barbara Point Light to the West Point Light on Santa Cruz Island. Then spread your dividers on the **side** of the chart to equal ten miles. Walk off the ten mile increments, counting them as you go. Then measure the remaining small distance and add everything together.

Special Note: Some prefer to measure distances on a chart to the nearest millimeter using a metric ruler then compare this to the latitude scale on the side of the chart. This will also work on a regular large NOS chart as very long plastic metric rulers are available at almost any stationery store.

Others feel this is sacrilege and that dividers are the only way to go. For example, I get 16.2 cm from the S.B. Light to the West Pt. Light. This converts on the latitude scale to 21.4 miles, which is the same answer. Try both and see which you prefer.

2) Try from Spa Rock Light to Brockway Point Light on Santa Rosa.

Don't come to Santa Barbara looking for these exotic islands of Spa Rock and Bunny Isle. Now that I think about it, those lights out there on those islands don't exist either, but they should. Well, okay, there is a light on Anacapa Island and one on the southern tip of Santa Rosa which isn't shown.

3) Go from Brockway Point Light to West Point Light.

4) Santa Barbara Bell Buoy (Fl G) to Bunny Isle Light, thence to West Point Light. State the total distance.

5) Go from Spa Rock Light to the Anacapa Light.

ANSWERS

1) 21.4 M, 2) 19.8 M, 3) 11.9, 4) 44.1, 5) 43.8

⌐HOW TO SAVE EXAM TIME⌐
♡   ♡
WITH THE COAST PILOT

Some exams have little curves thrown in. Some would call them trick questions, but that's a bit much for one like this, because what the Coast Guard is trying to do is measure your ability to use the *Coast Pilot*. For example, for some time there was a well known question on the piloting exams asking for the distance from the Chesapeake Light to Baltimore, Maryland. That can be measured, but only if Baltimore is on the chart and it wasn't! Go frantically looking for a chart with Baltimore on it? Where do you look? They gave you only one chart when you went into the exam room and that's it. Where you do go is the back pages of the local *Coast Pilot*. Back there someplace is one of those distance charts like you find on road maps. Look for the one detailing the Chesapeake and find Baltimore on it. It explains that from the Chesapeake **entrance** to Baltimore is 150 miles. And sure enough, one of the choices on your test says, c) 150 miles and you pick it and move on with a smug smile. You blew it!
Look at the question again. The distance you were looking for was from the **Chesapeake Light**, and there is an additional 19 miles from the light to the Chesapeake Entrance. You should have picked, d) 169 miles.
So, don't sit there squinty-eyed and grinning. Go get familiar with the *Coast Pilot* and check out the rest of those tables and the information available in both the front and the back. Don't expect to find Dutton's and Chapman's in the exam room, but the Coast Pilot will be there. And, no, you can't take your own reference books. You have to know how to use the government ones, but when you do it's almost sexual. We have the Coast Guard License Video that even shows them to you.

SPEED, DISTANCE AND TIME

How accurate should answers be in the CG exam as regards speed, distance and time? The traditional standard of accuracy says you should have speed to the nearest tenth of a knot, distance to the nearest tenth of a nautical mile and time to the nearest minute.

Don't hesitate to use your trusty hand-held calculator, but make sure you don't show up for the test with weak batteries.

If you are to know the **speed** the boat is going and assuming no fancy electronic gear is aboard to give you an automatic read-out, then you must first know the distance covered and the length of time taken to cover said distance.

For example: if your boat makes 6 miles in 30 minutes, then you're travelling at a **speed** of 12 knots. Or: Speed = 60 x the distance divided by time. The 60 is used to make things come out to the nearest minute of time. As a formula it looks like this:

$$S = \frac{60 \times D}{T}$$

Then, we replace the letters with numbers which apply to this particular case:

$$S = \frac{60 \times 6 \ (\text{miles})}{30 \ (\text{minutes})}$$

The rest is arithmetic which is where your calculator comes in:

$$S = \frac{360}{30} = 12 \ (\text{knots})$$

If this is so simple it's insulting please keep in mind we're starting from the bottom here and not all of us remember everything learned in eighth grade math. Besides, we're using whole numbers. Let's mix it up a little.

Here is the same problem, only this time assume that "time" is the missing factor. The equation for **time** is:

$$T = \frac{60 \times D}{S}$$

Again, we replace the formula letters:

$$T = \frac{60 \times 6 \ (\text{miles again})}{12}$$

The last step looks like this:

$$T = \frac{360}{12} = 30 \ (\text{minutes})$$

That takes care of finding **time** which assumes you know the distance travelled and the speed of your craft.

We have also covered **speed**-which assumes you know the distance covered and the time underway.

There's only one left. This time assume we know how long underway and the speed of the boat. Now, we're looking for **distance**.

Formula looks like this:

$$D = \frac{S \times T}{60} \ (\text{speed times time})$$

Using the same problem the numbers replace the letters:

$$D = \frac{12 \times 30}{60}$$

$$D = \frac{360 \quad (12 \text{ times } 30)}{60} \qquad D = 6 \text{ (miles)}$$

We now have three formulas. All you have to do is remember the formulas.

Not easy? Like you might get "tied up" in the exam room and pull a big fat blank? Try this:

Suppose you were missing...say, "time". Put a finger over the "T" in the diagram left and look  what's left. 60D is written **over** the "S", right? The term 60D means multiply 60 by the distance. Since the 60D is "over" the "S" that means multiply sixty times the distance **then** divide by the speed of your craft. Your answer will come out in minutes. You need to express the answer in hours and minutes, so divide the answer (the minutes) by 60. Don't divide it on your calculator. Do it on paper. Your answer will be in hours. The remainder is the minutes left over.

Maybe you will have to measure the distance on your chart first, but the assumption is that you know your departure point and your destination.

If you need to find speed, cover up the "S". What's left? 60D **over** "T". Multiply the two factors 60 and your distance, then divide by the time. **Before you divide by time, make sure time is expressed in minutes...**not hours and minutes.

What if the "distance" was missing? Just cover up the upper portion of the circle leaving "S" and "T" next to each other. Letters next to each other infer multiplication. After you have multiplied the value given for "S" and "T" **don't forget to divide by 60.** Then round off

your answer to the nearest tenth. In other words, if your final answer came out: 45.67, you would round off to 45.7, because the numeral in the hundredths column (7) is more than 4. If the final answer was, say 45.64, then drop the four to get 45.6

Don't scoff at using the numeral "60" all the time. If you try reducing hours to fractions or decimals without using the 60, sooner or later one of your rounding off items wouldn't jibe with the "pure" answer and the Coast Guard will be waiting for you.

Time for the big trial. Try this one: Assume your boat speed to be 10 knots. You have been underway for 2 hrs. and 15 minutes (after this time will read like 2h 15m) so the question is how **far** have you travelled? Now, don't look any further down the page until you have at least tried.

Multiply speed (10) by the time-135 (minutes), then divide by 60.
22.5 nautical miles, right?

Now try one when you're trying to find the speed of your boat. The assumption is you know how far you have travelled and how long it took. Make the distance 78.6 miles and the elapsed time 6h 14m.

That makes for something like this: 60 x 78.6, (4716) then divide by your time underway which was 374 minutes. 4716 divided by 374 = 12.61. Since the last numeral, the one in the hundredths column is less than 4, you drop it, rounding off to 12.6 knots.

Getting kind of tiresome, eh? Don't let it get to you. Take another swig and believe that it's going to get easier every time. Remember learning to ride a bike and to drive a car? Remember junior high school?

Go for one on time. Assume underway at a speed of 13.6 knots having travelled a distance of 34.6 nautical miles.

That means you must multiply that distance of 34.6 miles by 60, which yields 2076. That number gets divided by your speed of 13.6, producing an answer stating 152.65. Now what?

That 152.65 is an answer in minutes. Your answer has to be to the nearest minute. So round off. You should get 153 minutes. Now break it down into hours and minutes. **Not on your calculator.** Do it the long hard way...you know, with one of those things called a pencil. Dividing 60 into 153 yields an answer of 2 hours with a remainder of 33. The 33 is the minutes remaining. Hence, a final answer of 2h 33m. Not too tough, eh?

Here's three of each kind. All mixed up. The answers are in the shaded area again in the next column. **AH—DON'T LOOK.** Do them all first.

1) Distance is 15.2 miles on your chart and the time to make the run is 2hr 10m. How fast were you going?
2) The distance covered is 47.9 miles and you're making 13.2 knots. How long did it take you?
3) You have 3h 2m to cover 55.8 miles. How fast must you go?
4) You're hauling it out at 18.6 knots for a distance of 74.8 miles. How long did it take you to make the trip?
5) Underway for 4h 19m at a speed of 12.5 knots. How far?
6) Travelling at 14.6 knots for 3h 47m. How far?

⚓

Vessels engaged in underwater work display the dayshape of two black balls over the working side of the craft to indicate oncoming craft should not pass on that side.

The REC will not expect you to define the physics of tidal forces such as the interactions of the sun, moon and earth. You *will* be expected to know the basic vocabulary and be able to read tide tables and compute simple high and low tides at various ports. We're not talking those wispy little commercial pamphlets from your local bait stand. The references will in the Fed Gov publications.

The U.S. coasts have four tides about every 24 hours; two highs and two lows. On the east coast one high or low is about equal to the next one in height, but not so on the west coast. The west coast enjoys what is termed **mixed tides**. One high and low cycle will be radically different from the following one. The diagrams on the next two pages will stick in your memory better than mere words.

The term **Datum Level** is the depth you find written on the charts. The tide doesn't get much lower than this. That's handy to know. The depth indication on a chart means anything dangerous will be indicated at what is almost the lowest tide. When the tide does get lower than the **Charted Depth** it's called a "minus" tide. Therefore, **Datum Level** and **Charted Depth** basically mean the same. Again, study the diagrams. The term **Datum Level** is the term used in the Chart's Tidal Block. Pick one from your own area and study the descriptions in the Tidal Block or your chart Title Block.

On both east and west coasts datum levels are computed from Mean Lower Low Water. Mean is a fancy word for average. Thus, the lows are computed from the *lowest* of the two radically different lows. They were added up for the year then divided by 365 days to get the mean, or average. Not just for one year, mind you, but for the last **nineteen** years. The same was done on the east coast except the lows were virtually the same.

The few low tides falling below the Datum Level are indicated by a "-" sign. If higher than the Datum Level, a "+" sign is **sometimes** used. If there is no sign, assume a positive (+) one.

The **range** of any tide is the difference in feet from one high to the next low or vice-versa. All tide measurements are expressed in tenths of a foot, not in inches.

When tides are at their extremes, that is higher highs and lower lows, they are termed **Spring Tides**. When the tides are minimal, that is higher lows and lower highs, they are called **Neap Tides**. Imagine the multiple choice question possibilities in that one. Now go back and read the shaded box on page 73.

To publish tide tables along a given coast for all the ports would be too much. Instead, an official Tide Table is published by the NOS showing **Reference Stations** and **Subordinate Stations**. The first is a major port listing the times and heights of high and low tides each day. The subordinate stations are those situated up and down the coast from the Reference Station. Pick the applicable Reference Station to your locale and apply the time and height differences. For practice, try the samples on page 88.

CAUTION

A CG quiz question concerning "depths" was brought to light by one of our spies. The question asked for the maximum depth of water at the Cape Henry approach channel. Up in one corner the **Chart Notes** revealed the maximum depth. However, the Coast Pilot for the area revealed an entirely different maximum depth. A protest was filed even though the test answer choices indicated one answer found on the Chart Notes. Never hesitate to protest questions if you possibly can.

⚓

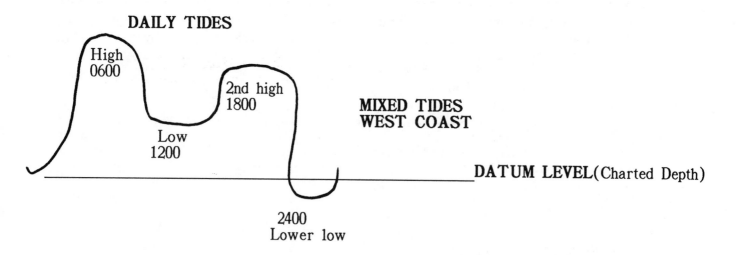

DAILY TIDES

High
0600

2nd high
1800

Low
1200

MIXED TIDES
WEST COAST

DATUM LEVEL (Charted Depth)

2400
Lower low

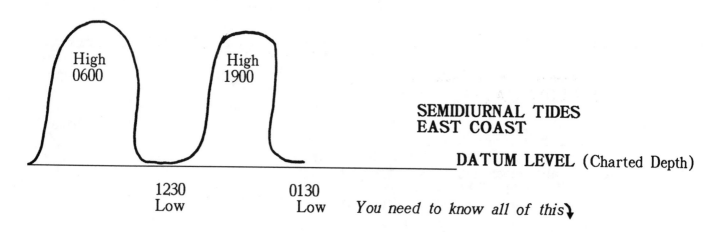

High
0600

High
1900

SEMIDIURNAL TIDES
EAST COAST

DATUM LEVEL (Charted Depth)

1230
Low

0130
Low   *You need to know all of this*↘

The west and east coasts both have two complete tide cycles approximately every 24 hours 50 minutes. The west coast is simply more radical. (That figures). West coast is all **mixed** up. The two highs and lows are different. On most of the east coast they are almost identical. Also keep is mind tidal movement is vertical in nature caused by the gravitational pull of the sun and moon. This in turn causes ebb and flood **currents**. When tidal movement pauses between ebb and flood currents it is called a **stand**. The rise or fall between a high and low tide is called the **range**. The most rapid rate of current flow occurs approximately half-way between low and high tides then the rate tapers off as either the high or low is reached. Higher highs and lowers lows are **spring tides** which occur during new and full moons and most often during the first and third weeks of the month. **Neap tides** are more moderate tides. Higher lows and lower highs. Heights of objects ashore, such as lighthouses, are calculated from mean high tide. The CG has been known to try and confuse the question by inserting the time of tide with something like ZD +5. The ZD means Zone Description, simply referring to your time zone, i.e., five time zones west of Greenwich, namely, the US east coast.

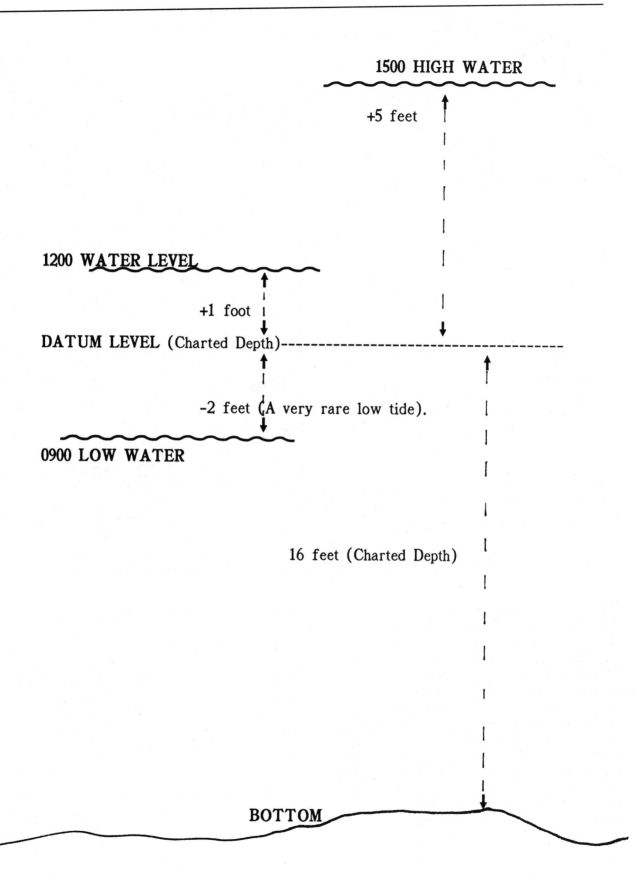

1500 HIGH WATER

+5 feet

1200 WATER LEVEL

+1 foot

DATUM LEVEL (Charted Depth)

-2 feet (A very rare low tide).

0900 LOW WATER

16 feet (Charted Depth)

BOTTOM

Study the tidal abstract on the next page. Sorry it's mounted sideways, but the enlargement makes it easier to read. Fed Gov pubs were never known for large print.

These are stations and ports in the Puget Sound, which, if anyone should ask on your Rules quiz, is considered international waters. The info here is based on Seattle. One looks first at Seattle for the time and height of tide then adds or subtracts time or height of tide from their station of interest. We don't have Seattle here, the table indicates it is located on page 98 of this particular tide book. We'll make up some Seattle times and heights then take it from there. First, let's try the last one on the list; Stellacoom.

If Seattle experienced a high tide of 6.2 feet, at 0815, Stellacoom's **high tide** could be determined by adding 22 minutes -which would make it 0837 in Stellacoom- and +1.8 feet making it 8.0' at 0837. **CAREFUL:** The CG delights in leaving off the "+" mark in their exams which confuses some people into believing they should subtract. Subtract only when the "-" sign is indicated.

Do it again. Give the time and height of Stellacoom's low tide when (let's say) Seattle's **low** tide occurs at 1430 and -1.5.

You should get 1505 and -1.5. To Seattle's time of 1430 you must add 35 minutes making the 1505. Stellacoom's low tide registers 0.0, so adding the -1.5 means -1.5 for the final answer.

Let's try another sub-station. Try the times and heights for **both** high and low tides on #925, Port Blakely, when Seattle's high (let's say) is 4.9 at 1935, and her following low of -1.2 at 0155.

Go down the **high water** column under "Time" to Port Blakely which states you should add two minutes. That would make for two more minutes added to Seattle's 1935 yielding 1937 for a high tide. Now, how high? Down the High Water under the "Height" column to Port Blakely we find 0.2'. Not much. Add that to

Seattle's 4.9 and you get 5.1' for high tide. Under low tide come down the Low Water "Time" column to Blakely which shows 0.03 meaning three minutes are to be added to Seattle's low tide. To 0155 one must add three minutes giving 0158. Under Low Water "Height" we find 0.0 again, so Seattle's -1.2 stands unchanged at Port Blakely.

We're not through yet. One more concept here.

Let's assume Seattle's low tide is -1.2 on a certain date at, say, 0500. We need the time of low tide at #943, Arletta, Hale Passage (AHP) and the height of that particular low tide. The "Time" part isn't difficult. For low water it says you should add 36 minutes meaning low tide will be at 0536. The probability of confusion starts when we hit the "Height" column. According to this entry, you are supposed to add 1.7 feet. The answer you want is 0.5 feet for low tide at AHP at 0536.

If that little bit of arithmetic confuses you and the eighth grade was too many years ago, glance at page 88 and pick an imaginary point **below** the datum level and call it -1.2 feet which, recall, was the original low tide reading in Seattle at 0500. Says here you must add 1.7 feet. Thus, if you go "up" to the Datum Level from your chosen -1.2 foot position you will have gone "up" a total of 1.2 feet. How much further must you go? Subtracting 1.2 from 1.7 yields 0.5 feet to go!

Always remember, if metal fatigue overtakes you in the exam room you can always draw diagrams. Sometimes it's safer.

⚓

TABLE 2.—TIDAL DIFFERENCES AND OTHER CONSTANTS

No.	PLACE	POSITION		DIFFERENCES				RANGES		Mean Tide Level
		Lat.	Long.	Time		Height		Mean	Diurnal	
				High water	Low water	High water	Low water			
		° '	° '	h. m.	h. m.	feet	feet	feet	feet	feet
903	Port Ludlow	47 55	122 41	-0 27	-0 18	*0.88	*0.88	6.4	9.9	5.9
905	Port Gamble	47 51	122 35	-0 17	-0 17	*0.91	*0.91	6.7	10.3	6.2
907	Bangor	47 45	122 44	-0 20	+0 04	-0.3	0.0	7.3	10.9	6.4
909	Seabeck	47 38	122 50	-0 03	+0 03	+0.3	+0.1	7.8	11.6	6.8
911	Union	47 21	123 06	-0 09	+0 04	+0.4	0.0	8.0	11.7	6.8
	Puget Sound									
913	Point No Point	47 55	122 32	-0 16	-0 16	*0.92	*0.92	6.7	10.4	6.1
915	Port Madison	47 42	122 32	-0 08	-0 08	+0.1	0.0	7.7	11.4	6.6
917	Poulsbo, Liberty Bay	47 44	122 39	+0 02	+0 08	+0.6	+0.1	8.1	11.9	6.9
919	Brownsville, Port Orchard	47 39	122 37	+0 02	+0 08	+0.4	0.0	8.0	11.7	6.8
921	SEATTLE (Madison St.), Elliott Bay	47 36	122 20	Daily predictions on SEATTLE, p.98				7.6	11.3	6.6
923	Eighth Ave. South, Duwamish River	47 32	122 19	+0 05	+0 07	-0.1	0.0	7.5	11.1	6.5
925	Port Blakely	47 36	122 30	+0 02	+0 03	+0.2	0.0	7.8	11.5	6.7
927	Pleasant Beach, Rich Passage	47 36	122 32	+0 01	+0 07	+0.2	0.0	7.8	11.5	6.7
929	Bremerton, Port Orchard	47 33	122 38	+0 07	+0 12	+0.4	0.0	8.0	11.7	6.8
931	Tracyton, Dyes Inlet	47 37	122 40	+0 30	+0 56	+1.0	0.0	8.6	12.3	7.1
933	South Colby, Yukon Harbor	47 31	122 32	+0 01	+0 07	+0.3	0.0	7.9	11.6	6.7
935	Des Moines	47 24	122 20	+0 03	+0 09	+0.4	0.0	8.0	11.7	6.8
937	Burton, Quartermaster Harbor	47 23	122 28	+0 07	+0 13	+0.6	0.0	8.2	11.9	6.9
939	Gig Harbor	47 20	122 35	+0 06	+0 14	+0.6	0.0	8.2	11.8	6.9
941	Tacoma, Commencement Bay	47 17	122 25	+0 07	+0 06	+0.5	0.0	8.1	11.8	6.8
943	Arletta, Hale Passage	47 17	122 39	+0 23	+0 36	+1.9	1.7	9.3	13.0	7.4
945	Home, Von Geldern Cove, Carr Inlet	47 16	122 45	+0 27	+0 39	+2.3	+0.2	9.7	13.6	7.8
947	Wauna, Carr Inlet	47 23	122 38	+0 20	+0 36	+1.8	0.0	9.4	13.1	7.5
949	Stellacoom	47 10	122 36	+0 22	+0 35	+1.8	0.0	9.4	13.1	7.5

On page 164 we will start your education in piloting, but actually you should give serious consideration to working it into your other studies as you go along. In other words, alternate between Rules of the Road, the Deck Modules and piloting. That way nothing gets forgotten while another subject is mastered.

To encourage you to practice what we preach, some of your plotting is shown here, but it doesn't take charts, plotter and dividers. This is because on your charting, (piloting) section maybe one or two of the ten answers can be found in either the *Light List* of the *Coast Pilot*. What are in them that you can use? We talked about the *Coast Pilot* on page 81, but be sure to go through a copy of one of these gems long before you even consider visiting the REC. Do it even if your finances demand you visit your local chandlery and simply thumb through one.

Now to the *Light List*. Assume a charting problem takes you all over the chart and finally winds up in a small obscure bay with a ring of light houses ashore. The final question asks, "How far are you from the Old North Light?" After a half-hour of charting it would be nice to know which one they mean. None of them have names on the chart. So, go to the *Light List*, that handy volume in the REC and look up the Old North Light in the index. It will refer you to a certain page where the Old North Light is described. It will also give you its latitude and longitude which means you can find the blasted light, measure the distance and get on with your test.

Two good friends: *Coast Pilot* and *Light List*.

Another excellent use of the *Light List* are the opening pages wherein are displayed all of the buoys in full color, but read our pages 93 to 97 first. Then there's the Luminous Range Diagram (also in our appendix), but it's also near the front of each *Light List*.

We won't bore you with more on the *Light List*. Go find one and get familiar.

The Coast Pilot is a trove of information, including the Weather Advisories they used to fly from the Harbor Masters flag pole.

Also note that some answers to your question are written right on the chart itself. Buy our chartlets or go find them in a chandlery and start reading up.

Now, here's a biggie for those of you who are rich. Almost all of the data bank questions are for sale at your friendly local Government Book Store. The addresses and phone numbers are listed in our appendix and they take MasterCard and VISA. They are voluminous books and memorizing all the answers would be impossible, fruitless and not all apply to the lower licenses like Six Pac and 100 ton masters. But they are there. Best to drop by and ask to see their Marine test books. There are ones on Rules of The Road, Deck Questions and Navigation Problems. They are also constantly updating, so get the latest. By phone, you might get the oldies they're trying to unload.

‡

PUBLICATIONS

1) Tide Tables   Dept. of Commerce
                   National Ocean Survey

2) Current Tables-Coast Pilot   NOS

3) Light Lists and   USCG
   Local Notice to Mariners

4) Notice To Mariners   Dept of
                         Transportation
                         (DOT)

5) Coast Pilot   NOS

6) Charts and   Defense Mapping
   Sailing Directions*   Agency
                      Hydrographic/
                      Topographic
                      Center
                      (DMAHTC)

CG tests have been known to ask who publishes what. The Government Printing Office **prints** publications. However, the above agencies are the ones who **publish** the books and pamphlets. If in doubt, you can always check the shelves in the exam room.

We call her Tadpole because of the wiggling tail piece. When she showed up in the Charter Skipper class the first night I knew I wouldn't have to worry about absenteeism. By then, she was a regular around the harbor, but not for long. She's a short girl with tight brown curls all over her head. She has an exceptionally small waist and things get neat and curvy going both ways from there. She barely avoids arrest by wearing two pieces of string around the harbor and that mahogany tan is flat out vulgar. I later learned she was educated to be a school teacher, but after a year of the heebie jeebies she landed in Santa Barbara with a few saved dollars and decided to stay. A short time later she had come a long way from starting out with paint and varnish work and putting names on boats. Now she's licensed.

Tadpole works a scalene triangle and does it with real panache. Late spring and summer finds her in Santa Barbara working the charter boats. Dive, fish or sight-seeing; she doesn't seem to care. When fall rolls around she stuffs things into a deep straw bag and pushes it under the seat of a jet heading for Hawaii. Sometimes she works the Cats off Kona, sometimes Oahu or Kauai's north shore. Before leaving she unwinds for a few weeks on Kauai by hiking over the Kalalau trail to her favorite beach. That beach is like a lot of Santa Barbara beaches; no one calls the cops if you forget the strings. In late December, after the hurricane season, she heads for Mexico or the Virgins.

She works those vacation clubs where everyone is always smiling and only one string is required even during working hours. She runs a boat and teaches water skiing to N.Y. and L.A. outpatients. I asked her once why they hire U.S. licensed skippers in those foreign places. She explained that those Clubs have to carry liability insurance and only the U.S. or G.B companies will underwrite it. One of their requirements is the use of licensed skippers. I still say it's because she makes a nice ornament for the Clubs. Tadpole works her triangle on a declared income the government would consider poverty level. She keeps her needs as slim as her waistline and saves a lot of money doing it. She likes to be paid in cash and generally is. We won't talk about her tips. Last year she paid cash for her own thirty footer to charter and live aboard while in California. When away, she bare boats it through a boat rental agency. She's a girl you could easily hate.

*Sailing Directions are Coast Pilots of foreign shores.

‡

THE LATERAL BUOYAGE SYSTEM

> ### READ THIS OR FAIL

In this case, the term "lateral" means "sides" which is where these buoys are located. They're along both sides and serve to guide vessels up or down the channel. Some buoys, while not lateral aids, are still related to coastal navigation. Some indicate anchorage areas, Special Aids, Regulatory and Information Marks. Then there are the Aids to Navigation on Western Rivers and the Intracoastal Waterway (ICW) aids. Also there's the system maintained by each state in accordance with a national standard. It's called the Uniform State Waterway system. Keep in mind if you're shooting for a coastal ticket, you need to know them all.

The entire lateral buoyage system underwent changes a few years back and not simply black buoys being painted green. There are two systems in this new International Association of Light-house Authorities (IALA) called Regions A & B. The U.S. is in Region B along with Japan, Korea, and the Philippines. Never mind about the other one, you've got enough to worry about. In the exam room we cannot over-emphasize your reference is *The Light List*. Read the shaded box in the next column.

As will be mentioned again, identification of these buoyage systems on your CG exams will frequently be by chart *symbol* rather than by a full-blown picture of the buoy itself. Thus, learning both symbols and buoys is equally important. A good example is our matching quiz on page 105.

Whip out your felt tips and do the buoys as you go. Surprising how it helps things stick in your mind.

Here's a color code. The rest are noted or obvious.

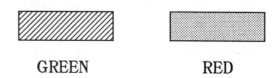

GREEN   RED

AN OPEN BOOK EXAM TIP

The Coast Guard can include just about any question regarding buoys they desire if for no other reason than this is part of an open book exam. The question is; where does one look for the answers? For buoys and lights ashore refer to their copy of the *Light List*. There's one for each area. Beautiful color plates in the front pages to remind you of what you are reading here. While at your local chandlery try thumbing through this volume to become acquainted with **all** of the information contained therein. Also pull a copy of the *Coast Pilot* and check what this book contains in the way of miscellaneous but important local marine information. There will probably be two to three questions on your charting exam that could be answered quickly by referring to this volume instead of floundering around on your chart looking for information not printed on the chart itself. The reference books and knowing them is important which is one reason we included a section on them with our video on *The Coast Guard License* showing all of them and explaining how they are used, indexes, tables of contents, subject matter location, etc.

⚓

I) Nuns, Cans and Spars

There are six things to remember about the nuns, cans and spars. 1) All are numbered progressively **from seaward** working upstream, (never lettered). 2) The nuns are conical shaped, red and numbered evenly. 3) The cans have straight tops, look like cans, and are green with odd numbers. 4) The rare spar buoys look like telephone poles bobbing about, can go on either side of the channel, be either color and hence, bear any number. The nuns are on your right entering from sea. (Red right returning). The cans are on the far left side of the channel coming in, thus they define the safe channel boundaries. 5) Another way to put it: the nuns are off your starboard coming in from sea, the cans off your starboard going out to sea. 6) They are all **unlighted aids.** See figure #1 below, study them, then close your eyes and try to recall the six attributes outlined above.

The pictures are nice, but be sure you have three things straight before you finish this buoy section. Know which ones are numbered, which ones are lettered and **know the chart symbols defining each buoy.**

On your exam sometimes you will be referred to diagrams in the back of your test booklet and asked to identify various pictures and symbols. As regards the symbols keep in mind that any letter or number in quotation marks, like say "4" or "L", means that is what is painted right on the buoy. Note also the diamond chart symbol for buoys. If a vertical line runs through the diamond the buoy is vertically striped. A horizontal line indicates the buoy is banded. Updated charts have colored diamond chart symbols. The dot beneath the buoy indicates the exact position of the buoy.

II)

The **daymarks** replace nuns and cans upstream in shallow water. Red triangles on the right, green squares on the left. Basically, these are signs mounted on pilings. If they are hooked up to a battery they become daybeacons or **"minor lights"**. Note the symbols; odd green and even red pattern for numbers still holds. Fig. #2

III)

Now for the **lighted** buoys marking channels. If a buoy is red, the light flashes red. If it is green, the light flashes green. Red on the right coming in from sea, green on the left. The red and green colors have the same meaning as their unlighted counterparts; "red right returning" and green on your right heading out. Note the symbol now has a circle around the dot to indicate a lighted aide. The dot still indicates the position of the buoy. Fig. #3

IV)

Unlighted mid-channel buoys are spherical in shape and painted with red and white vertical stripes. This buoy, or its lighted counterpart, can be passed on either side. These buoys use **letters** for identification and note the color of the buoy is indicated by the RW in the symbol. The line running vertically on the triangle indicates vertical striping on the buoy. SP is for spherical. Again, what is written in quotation marks on the symbol is what is painted on the buoy. The daymark equivalent will be **octagonal** in shape and red and white; always on exams. They are on pilings upstream like the triangles and squares replacing upstream nuns and cans. Fig. #4

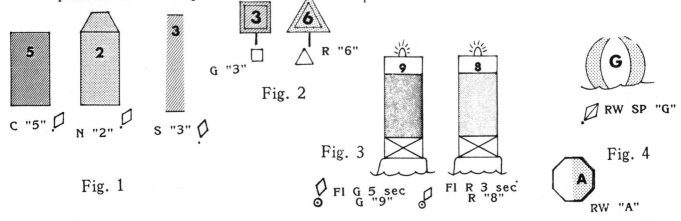

C "5"   N "2"   S "3"   Fig. 2   G "3"   R "6"

Fig. 1

Fig. 3   Fl G 5 sec G "9"   Fl R 3 sec R "8"

RW SP "G"   Fig. 4   RW "A"

V) Lighted mid-channel buoys are vertically striped red and white and lettered for identification. They blink a Morse Code "A" for their light signal (short-long flashing - a characteristic exclusive of this buoy) and the light will be white. Note again the circle around the dot to indicate a lighted aide. Fig. #5

VI) Preferred channel buoys are most important. They are not numbered but **can be** lettered. These are color banded nuns, cans and spars which can generally be passed on either side. On the nuns the top band is red meaning the **preferred channel** is accessed by leaving the buoy to starboard of your craft. If the can buoy has a green top band keep the buoy off your port side. Any spars so banded can be on either side of the channel, but are treated the same. These buoys mark two things; either channel junctions or hazards like wrecks or sandbars. They catch your attention and encourage you to refer to your chart to determine if a hazard or junction exists and if so, where. The equivalent upstream daymarks on pilings are **triangles** red-over-green on the right coming in and green-over-red **squares** on the left side. RG is the symbol for red-over-green; GR for green-over-red. Fig. #6

VII) There is also a **lighted preferred channel buoy**. Like nuns and cans it is banded red and green on the right side coming in from sea then green (top) and red on the opposite side of the channel.

The light is a group flash 2 + 1 meaning it flashes twice, pauses, then flashes once. Again, this banded buoy thing is for channel junctions and/or underwater obstructions like sand bars, subsurface wrecks, etc. Fig. #7

VIII) Cardinal Marks are horizontally striped **yellow** and **black** buoys with **white** lights and top marks. They indicate a particular "point of interest," meaning a shoal, spit or bend in channel. These buoys indicate the safe passage deep water side of the obstruction to which the buoy is stationed. An easterly coded buoy is stationed to the east of the shallow water or obstruction. The **white light** cycles, **triangle topmarks** and **colors** all have directional meaning. If there was no light, the topmark would indicate the direction. The arrangement of the yellow-black banding is also directionally significant.

See the pictures in Chart #1 which doesn't really tell it all, then read this along with it.

Let's try an easy code for the flashing lights. Quick flash (60/min) = ⇑. Short flash (30/min) = ↑. A long flash (about one second duration) = △.

North - Top is black, lower portion yellow. Topmarks vertically arrange both pointing up. Light cycle is ⇑⇑⇑⇑⇑⇑⇑⇑⇑⇑⇑⇑⇑⇑⇑⇑⇑⇑⇑⇑ ↑↑↑↑↑↑↑↑↑↑. (20 quicks, 10 shorts).

South - Top is yellow, lower portion black. Topmarks both point down. Light cycle is ⇑⇑⇑⇑⇑⇑△   ⇑⇑⇑⇑⇑⇑△ ↑↑↑↑↑↑△   ↑↑↑↑↑↑△.

East - Banded from top; black-yellow-black. Topmarks are base to base. Light cycle is ⇑⇑⇑ ⇑⇑⇑ ↑↑↑ ↑↑↑.

West - Banded from top; yellow-black-yellow. Topmarks are tip to tip. Light cycle is ⇑⇑⇑⇑⇑⇑⇑⇑⇑   ↑↑↑↑↑↑↑↑↑.

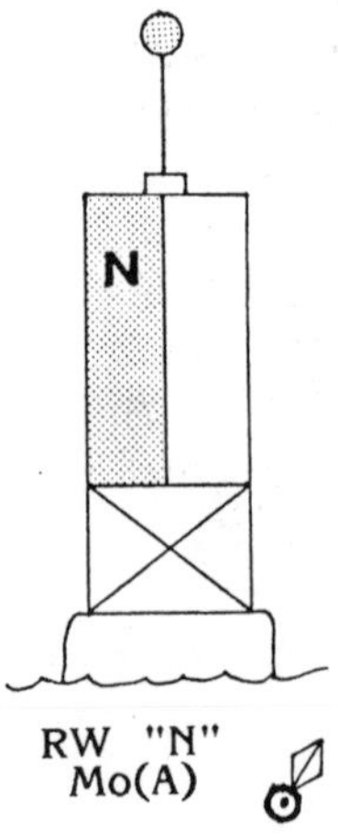

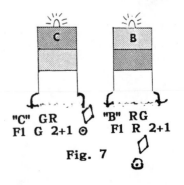

N

C "D" GR ▱   N "J" RG

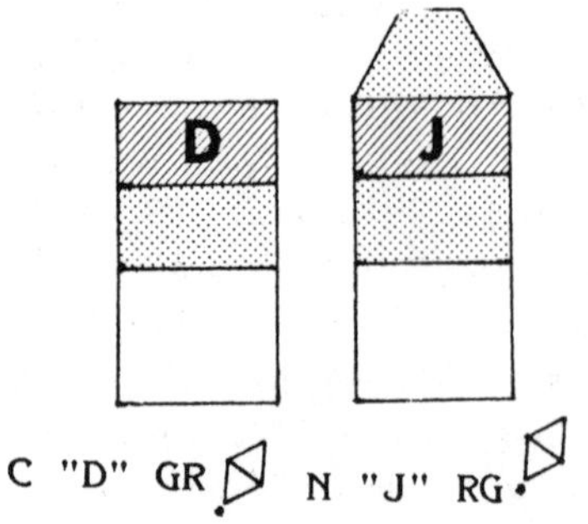

Fig. 6

RW "N"
Mo(A)

Fig. 5

□   A   □   B

□ GR "A"   RG "B" △

"C" GR
Fl G 2+1

"B" RG
Fl R 2+1

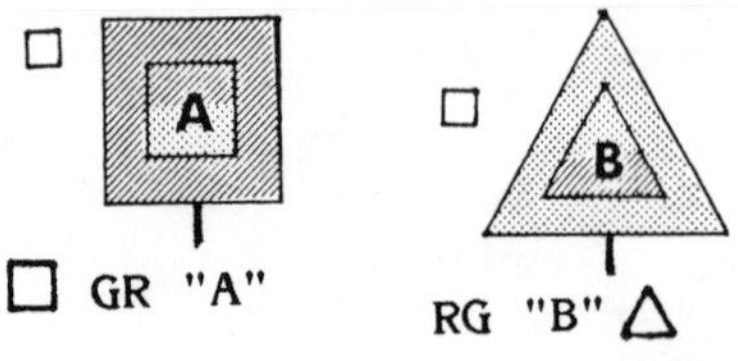

Fig. 7

The Special Aids

Block #1 to your right contains the lighted and unlighted versions, but they share one thing in common. They are all yellow and if lighted, the light is yellow. These buoys are positioned in the navigable channels and plainly labeled: No swimming, 5 knots, No Water Skiing, Nude Beach, whatever.

The Regulatory and Information Marks

Block #2: These are *privately maintained*, banded white and orange with symbols printed right on the buoy. If the symbol is a **diamond** it's a danger area, (Rocks, Sand Bar) **circle** for controlled area, (Anchorage or No Wake)) and a **cross-hatched diamond** for exclusion area, (Swimming Only). If lighted-white.

The Uniform State Buoyage System.

The states are responsible for buoys in Block #3. Same system for all. Found mostly on rivers or lakes around recreation areas. Frequency on exam will not necessarily be proportionate to the number of these buoys in your district. Know them.

1 Obstruction buoy. Painted vertically red and white. Don't go between this buoy and the shoreline.

2 White buoy with red top. Pass this buoy only on the south or west side.

3 White buoy with black top. Pass this buoy only on the north or east side.

4 Red or black. Can buoys to leave on your starboard or port side respectively.

5 White buoy with blue band. Mooring buoy. Watch for dangling lines, or submerged spreader lines.

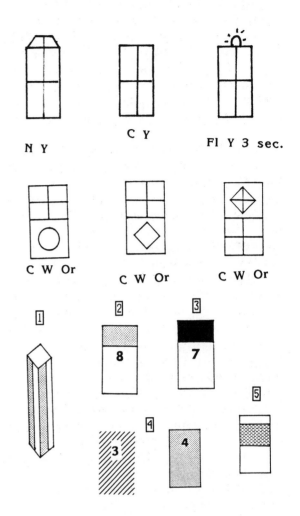

N Y   C Y   Fl Y 3 sec.

C W Or   C W Or   C W Or

The Intracoastal Waterway System. (ICW)

Recent CG exams have placed emphasis on this system, but not to worry as it resembles the lateral system in many respects. For example: Red nuns or lighted red buoys on the starboard side (when entering or traveling the system **from** north and east **proceeding** south and west) and black ones on the port. *Even and odd numbered* respectively. Daymarks are the same; red triangles to starboard and green squares to port. The big test thing seems to be the thin yellow horizontal **line** on each ICW buoy and daymark *or* the yellow **triangles and** squares seen on **some.** When do the yellow triangles replace the yellow horizontal lines and what do they mean? The yellow triangles show up when coming onto the ICW from seaward or when confusion runs rampant as two or more ICW's form a junction or "coincide". When either one of these things happens - **no matter what color or shape of buoy-** keep the triangles on your starboard hand and the squares on your port hand...when sailing south or west, for example, from New Jersey to Texas. (See why you should go buy Chart #1?)

The ICW (preferred channel) junction and obstruction nuns, cans and lighted aids are banded red over black and black over red and are lettered (no numbers) just like the lateral aids. When lighted these banded junction buoys show an interrupted-quick-flash such as four quick flashes -a pause- then four more quick flashes. On the starboard hand, red over black banded buoys, the light will be either red or white. On the port hand, black over red banded buoys, the light will be white or green.

The mid-channel buoy can be a lettered (no numbers) nun, can or lighted buoy, but all three are vertically striped black and white. The light flashes the familiar MoA and the daymark is octagonal black on the right side of the octagon and white on the left side. Sound familiar? The only difference is the color.

LIGHTS AND AIDS ASHORE

By lights ashore it is meant those which are not afloat. They are high on a hill in a lighthouse, sticking out on a peninsula or nailed to a wharf or pier. They are marked on charts with symbols, but with teardrops instead of diamonds.

As mentioned earlier, **minor lights** are small lights upstream resembling day-beacons and nailed to pilings. They are as rare as **station buoys** which are small

backup buoys situated next to big sea buoys in case the big guy gets run down or carried away. Rare, hence always on exams.

The height of lights ashore is measured from mean high water and the distance they can be seen is presumed to be when your eyes are at sea level. A numerical symbol (26M=26 miles) indicates the nominal range (the distance visible due to brilliance of the light) and the light characteristic. If no light color is indicated, assume white. If you get stuck remember this exam is open book, but **most** REC OinC's insist you use only books in the exam room. Look around for Chart #1 or the Light List (which **must** be there) for clues. Preferably Chart #1 which is a pamphlet you should own. See your local chandlery or the list of Fed Gov bookstores in the appendix.

Major lights, like many other chart symbols are colored magenta. Many war and merchant vessels have red "battle lights" on the bridge so night vision is not destroyed by a glare. Under red lights magenta turns black on a chart and is easier to see.

Concentric circles on a chart indicate a radio beacon marked by the unmistakable R Bn letters.   ⊙   R Bn 294 ▬ ▬ ▬ / ▬ ‥

The Morse Code signals and radio frequency are also listed on the chart. Find the frequency on your radio direction finder (RDF) and if you are within about ten miles of the transmitter you should pick up the signal and home in on it listening for the distinct Morse Code signal it broadcasts. Turn the RDF antenna until you receive the "null" sound -not the loudest- and make sure you aren't going in precisely the opposite direction. Most embarrassing.

⚓

COMPASS ERROR

Compass error comes in two distinct types. Variation and deviation. The object is to compensate for these disturbing factors. Courses on charts are always plotted "true" from one point to the next. Straight up on a chart is always north...or more appropriately, 000° which is the same thing as 360°. South is 180°...down. West is 270°, to the left. East is to the right, or 090°.

The problem arises when we plot a course "true" on the chart and draw lines to where we want to go. Anyone with experience around boats will tell you that it's impossible to plot the course on the chart then expect the compass to take you directly there without a few simple arithmetic adaptations. That's because a magnetic pull deep in the earth's core keeps pulling the needle off preventing it from pointing north as it should.

The adjustments are on paper. The object is to adjust the compass course to match the true course plotted on the chart.

Compasses are strange instruments ...sometimes. They need two types of adjustment. Again; for variation and deviation.

VARIATION

Some compass error can't be helped. The earth's magnetic pull forces the compass card the wrong way. The compass card has small magnets mounted beneath it. This pull from the earth is called variation. Variation differs in different parts of the world. You have to look at the chart to determine the degree of variation at your location. We'll come to that.

Along the coast of California it varies from about 14 degrees down near San Diego to 18 degrees off San Francisco.

On the west coast variation is always "east" meaning the magnetic attraction pulls the compass needle too far to the east. Too far from what? Too far from true...you know, straight up towards the north pole; the direction we call "true north". Thus, no matter which way the craft is facing, the variation is the same in that locale. The ideal situation would be for you to live in an area which had no variation whatsoever. Rare locations.

Charts are made with true north at the top. If we didn't want to do the paper work we would have to buy a new chart every time variation changed and that could get expensive. So we make all charts with north towards the top of the chart and learn to compensate with a little arithmetic. And let's not kid ourselves ...it's not math. It's arithmetic.

The local variation is printed in the centers of the compass roses which appear on every chart.

1) Plot your course "true" on the chart. Look at the **next page and follow along.** Say from Stud Island to Bunny Isle is true north or 000°. To call it 360° would be the same thing.

2) Write down the true course on a scrap of paper. Since the compass needle is pulled 14° degrees east, too far to the right, simply subtract the variation from the true course.

3) 000° (or 360°) minus 014° variation = 346°.

4) Steer 346° by **compass** to travel 000° **true** to Bunny Isle.

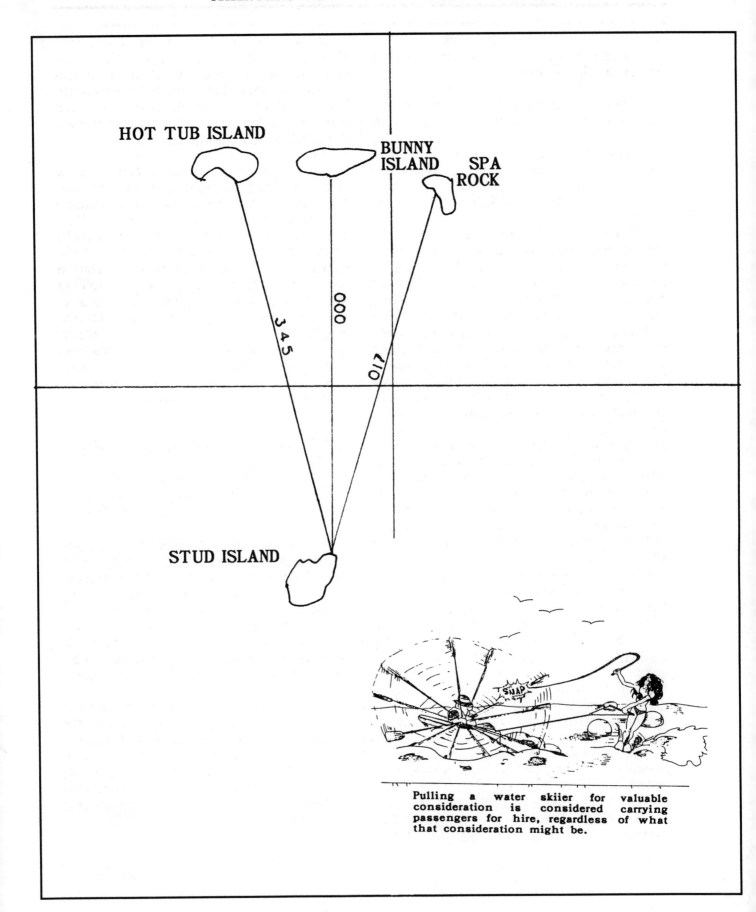

HOT TUB ISLAND

BUNNY
ISLAND   SPA
ROCK

345

000

017

STUD ISLAND

Pulling a water skiier for valuable
consideration is considered carrying
passengers for hire, regardless of what
that consideration might be.

Another one. What's the magnetic course to Spa Rock?

What's the magnetic course to Hot Tub Island?

Answers: Spa Rock = 003º, and Hot Tub = 331º.

DEVIATION

Things would be fine now if it weren't for another compass error. This other one is called deviation. Deviation is caused by various ferrous metals aboard a vessel and **generally** located less than three feet from the compass. That includes magnets from radios and speakers, keys left lying about and various tools left up on the console by the compass. On sailboats with flush mounted bulkhead compasses it is frequently something mounted behind the compass inside the cabin. On big boats, hydraulic fittings are dynamite to a compass and always seem to be situated directly beneath the compass. They make a compass do strange things so you call in an expert to correct the compass as much as possible. To do this he will swing the ship completely around and check various courses to see if they are correct. It's called "swinging Ship" to correct for the **deviation**. If you want a compass adjustor, look in the yellow pages under, ahem, "swinging deviate". There's one in every harbor, but make sure he uses sun azimuths for his bearings.

Unlike variation, deviation can change by the heading of the vessel. Different heading...different deviation.

Sometimes only limited correction is possible so the expert makes what is called a "deviation table". This table shows how far the compass is being pulled off from the magnetic reading on various courses. Most deviation tables worth

their salt are calibrated for **at least** each 15 degrees of the compass. The table also indicates in which direction the needle is being pulled. You can then compensate (add or subtract) to get the reading on your compass to take you whichever direction you wish to go.

Let's assume you plot a course on a chart and find your destination is 175º true from your departure point. Also assume the local variation is 15º east. That means 175º - 15º = magnetic course 160º. Let's also assume the deviation table indicates the deviation on magnetic course 160º is 5º west. Thus, 160º + 5º = 165º to be steered on your compass. This course of 165º, then, really is the direction originally worked out on your chart. Make sure you express ALL courses with three digits, even if you only need one or two. Variation and deviation are expressed in only one or two digits.

True.....175º
Variation 15º E. (so subtract 15º)
Mag.   160º
Dev.   5º W. (so add 5º)
Compass 165º (Compass course to steer in order to make good 175º true.

In plotting, everything begins when you plot your course TRUE on the chart. With the subsequent arithmetic you eventually arrive at the course you are to steer by compass. The secret is in when to subtract and when to add. When working for compass course from TRUE TO COMPASS, westerly error is added to the course line and any easterly is subtracted.

Another example: Assume true course to be 285º. Variation (always east on the West Coast and west on the East Coast) is 15º E. Deviation for the magnetic course is 10º W. What compass course would you steer? (Incidentally, compass course is often referred to as PSC - per steering compass).

T 285°
V 15° E (-)
M 270°
D 10° W (+)
C 280°

On this course the westerly deviation almost made up for the easterly variation. When working **down** from **true** to **compass** always add west and subtract east. Or, as the old sea memory crutch adage has it, so the proper arrangement of the letters is not forgotten:

T rue
V irgins
M ake
D ull
C ompany

So, **ADD WHISKEY.** "W-hiskey" to remember "W-est". Add west coming down. Now–if you add west it stands to reason you would have to subtract east.

Could you reverse the method? That is, could you start with a compass and work your way back up to true? Try it, and this isn't just for fun. You need this. Starting at "C" or compass and moving "up" the TVMDC lineup, things would change a bit. You would have to **subtract** the **west**erly deviations and variations then **add** the **east**erly errors.

Back to T V M D C. Let's try a few practice problems. See if you can fill in the blanks. Please note: Calling for some westerly variation wasn't a mistake. The CG will throw both kinds at you no matter where you live. Good exercise for self-teaching...which indicates that if you have gotten this far, you're a prime candidate for the license. You've got tenacity and this thing must mean a great deal to you. Hang in and plow on.

The exercises following have blanks in various spots. The answers are on the next page to check out the first few making sure you are on the right track, but after that **no fair looking** until you complete the series. In case you're not honest with yourself, well, there's two series.

Series One

T	015°	*221*	*016*	049°	137°
V	15°E	14°W	1°E	15°W	7°W
M	*000*	*235*	015°	*064*	*144*
D	*15E*	6°W	3°W	10°E	5°E
C	345°	241°	*018*	*054*	*139*

Series Two

T	000°	010°	*185*	200°	*050*	*168*
V	*15E*	*15E*	15°W	*15E*	14°E	10°W
M	345°	355°	200°	185°	036°	*178*
D	*15W*	*5W*	*8W*	*13E*	3°W	13°E
C	000°	000°	192°	172°	*039*	165°

TIME OUT

The Coast Guard has recently inserted questions into exams regarding chart symbols which denote certain depths in fathoms. They are found in Chart #1 under Section I, but here are the more common ones they are using.

Symbol	Depth In Fathoms
....	4
....	5
--- ---	6
·-·-·-·-	10
-··-··-··	20
-···-···-···	30
-····-····-····	40

Get it? Adding a dot adds 10 fathoms.

ANSWERS

SERIES ONE

T	---	221°	016°	---	---
V	---	---	---	---	---
M	000°	235°	---	064°	144°
D	15°E	---	---	---	---
C	---	---	018°	054°	139°

SERIES TWO

T	---	---	185°	---	050°	168°
V	15°E	15°E	---	15°E	---	---
M	---	---	---	---	---	178°
D	15°W	5°W	8°E	13°E	---	---
C	---	---	---	---	039°	---

⇒ SUFFER THE GYRO COMPASS ⇐

One recent addition to the CG repertoire of stymies is this business of dealing with gyro compasses. One doesn't frequently find gyros on vessels traveling less than 200 miles from shore, or even a six-pac boat in general; they're too costly, but that's probably why you'll get one.

Without going into unnecessary detail, simply regard a gyro compass as a compass run by machinery rather than being attracted to the magnetic north pole like a magnetic compass. The gyro can be set to read any heading, thus it is set to read true courses. Kind of sweet, really. You don't have to fool with variation and deviation when moving from the plotting sheet to the gyro, but most navigators do, as all courses are logged. The point is, gyro error works the same as magnetic compass error indicated in the exercises above.

If your exam says the gyro has an error of 1° east (E) and the true course is 197°, all you have to do is subtract that one degree. That produces a true course of 196° on the gyro. So, what's so difficult about that? Nothing really, but don't lose your head when they start mixing in this thing called **leeway.**

In this case it's easier to teach the concept with a charting problem. Don't get excited. No chart needed in this and many chart problems.

Problem: What gyro compass course would you steer to make good a magnetic course of 075°? Gyro error is 1° E. Deviation is 3° E. and variation is 9° W. There is a 4° leeway caused by a southerly wind.

Let's do some rough sketching. Draw the first course line as the one you need, that is, a **magnetic course** of 075°. Now draw a line *pointing* north representing the wind *coming out of* the south. This wind is trying to push your vessel more northerly, so you need to oversteer to your right, or more southerly, (or clockwise on the compass). Four degrees more southerly. Add four degrees, now making a **magnetic course** of 079°. That doesn't mean **magnetic compass course.** It means the "M" of TVMDC, not the "C". What gyro compass would you steer? That's like asking you what **true course** would you steer. Actually, all we're doing here is going from "M" up to "T" for true. Dirty trick. You don't really need the deviation, do you? If the local variation cited is 9° W, then wouldn't you subtract the 9° from the **magnetic course** of 079°? Wouldn't you then get 070° for a gyro course?

Not quite. Just enough error to make your entire answer incorrect. Did you forget the 1° E gyro error? Try 069°.

What gyro course would you have to steer to make a magnetic course of 265° under the same circumstances? You should get 251°.

⚓

Compass Adjustment Using Ranges

Not too much in this volume is practical, granted. Like, show me the sailboat with his sails up and engine running who hoists the little black dayshape of a down-pointing cone. On the other hand, once in a while along comes a real gem. This is one. And, you have to know it. Don't misunderstand. No self-respecting compass adjustment man would go near this idea on a commercial basis, but it could get you close to home in a fog if you are suspicious of your own compass. By the nature of the beast it tags along with the T V M D C theory on compass error. Here's how it works.

Before you whip your boat out of the slip, pick up a local harbor chart and start lining things up. Find two buoys or aides over 1,000 yards apart. Better yet, see if some of those tall buildings, radio antenna towers and tanks ashore are indicated on your chart. From the sea or river you might be able to line up two of them. Using your course plotter, find out their true bearing on the chart. Apply the local variation then see how close your compass comes. The difference is your deviation **on that course.** Again, deviation unlike variation, differs by the heading of the vessel. Study the sketch below.

On the first one, the boat has lined up on two buoys with an 065° bearing.
The skipper knows his local variation is 15° east. Once lined up on his markers, for which he knows the true bearing is 065°, he glances down at his compass which says 055°. He jots down the following:
T 065°
V 15°E
M 050°
D ? °
C 055°

You just finished the exercises on pages 101 & 102. What's the deviation on the course above?

Incidentally, if there's no reliable compass man in your area -one who uses "sun azimuths" to obtain his bearings- try adjusting it yourself. On the T V M D C above, the compass **should say** the same as the magnetic heading; 050°. Using a piece of brass or copper with a sharp edge like a screwdriver, you can adjust the compass by turning those little slotted screw heads near the base... assuming your compass has internal magnets. If the course you are adjusting is closer to a north-south line, like the one in our example, use the screw head which runs athwartship. If the course bearing is closer to the east-west line, use the one running fore and aft. Caution: some of those adjustment bars are held fast with a set screw inside the base of the compass which should be loosened first.

Now look **below** at the next example. The boat is now turned around and a reciprocal stern bearing is taken by adding 180° to the first bearing. Variation is the same, but there's still some deviation because the compass says 225° heading away from the buoys instead of directly at them.

T 245°
V 15°E
M 230°
D ?°
C 225°

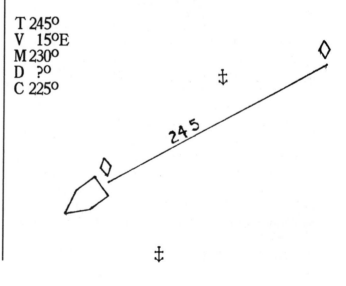

Doubling The Angle On The Bow

The object in this one is to determine how far offshore your vessel is. The only tools you are allowed is your boat compass and the ability to calculate speed, distance and time. Well, maybe a pelorus if you have one lying about.

First let's talk about relative bearings. In using relative bearings the compass plays no part and it doesn't make any difference which way your vessel is facing. Relative bearings are measured from the bow of the boat clockwise. Off to your starboard side would therefore be 90⁰. Off your stern is 180⁰ and off the port side is 270⁰. Dead ahead is either 000⁰ or 360⁰, whichever one turns you on. Imagine cruising up the coast like the first vessel on the next page. Off your starboard bow you spot a lighthouse perched high on a cliff or maybe it's a simple outcrop easy to see.

When the object ashore bears 045⁰ off your bow, look at your watch. How do you determine when it's 45⁰ off your bow? One way would be to add 45 to your compass course and try an eyeball lineup over the top of your compass. If your course was 105⁰ you could add 45⁰ and try to wait for the object to line up on 150⁰ on your compass. There is also an inexpensive plastic pelorus available for taking relative bearings. It even has a sighting vane and we'll discuss it later. Anyhow, back to the watch.

First you line up the object 45⁰ off your bow and note the time. When the same object lines up 090⁰ off your bow, (starboard side) you check the time and **always** knowing the speed of your craft, you can do a speed-time-distance problem with your information. Since you know your speed and how long underway, your calculation will yield the distance traveled. Since the second bearing was exactly twice

the first bearing (2 x 45⁰ = 90⁰) the distance travelled is the distance off the object. Before you blink, go back and read the first sentence in paragraph one.

In short, anytime you double your angle on something off the bow, the distance travelled is the distance off the object when you arrive at the second bearing.

Study diagram #1 on the next page. It's the one we just did. Fifteen minutes at twelve knots makes him three miles off.

Diagram #2: A 40⁰ angle the first time and an 80⁰ angle the second time. Time of first angle was 0330 with time of second angle 0400. Half hour underway at 12 knots. It doesn't take a mental giant to see that's six miles. Thus, you would be six miles off point "C".

Diagram #3: Assume the first bearing was taken at 1345 and the second bearing at 1405. Speed is 8.5 knots and the angle **is** doubled when going from 30⁰ to 60⁰. Calculator-wise that's S x T divided by 60. (8.5 x 20 [minutes]) divided by 60. Ans: 2.8 miles off. Time for you try your first one.

1) Diagram #4: Speed is 9.4 knots. Assume first bearing taken at 1740 and second bearing at 1805. Was the angle doubled? Okay, then how far off was he on the second bearing?

Try making your own sketches to the following. Answers in shaded box on next page.

2) A vessel approaching a lighthouse ashore bearing relative 35⁰ at 1145. Making 10.2 knots a second bearing on the same lighthouse is taken at 1210 when the lighthouse bears 070⁰. How far off is the lighthouse at the time of the second bearing?

3) At 1640 you take a 40º relative bearing on a prominent cliff overhang. Your boat speed is 14.6 knots. At 1655 the same cliff bears 080º. How far off the cliff are you at the second bearing?

4) At 0815 you take a 315º relative bearing on a building ashore as you are making 12.6 knots up the channel. At 0830 the same building bears 270º. How far off the building was your boat as you passed by?

Wrong side of the boat, right? No problem. Subtract each bearing from 360º. Is the one twice the other? If so, you have doubled the angle and the plan still holds. Compute the distance travelled and you have the answer.

5) Your first relative bearing on an object ashore is 340º at 2005 while making 14.7 knots. Taking a second bearing at 2030 it proves to be 320º. How far off the object is your vessel? ‡

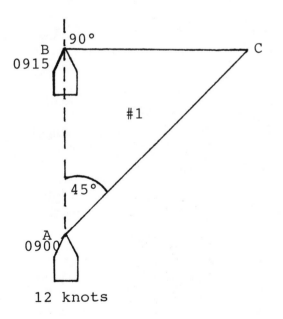

12 knots

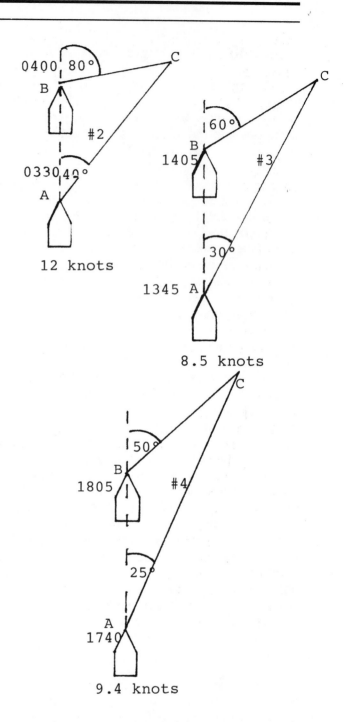

12 knots

8.5 knots

9.4 knots

ANSWERS
1) 3.9 MI, 2) 4.3 MI, 3) 3.7 MI, 4) 3.2 MI, 5) 6.1 MI.

General Knowledge - Chart Symbols

Place the letter from Column "A" to the left of the correct chart symbol listed in column "B". Some may be used several times, some not at all.

Column "A"

a) Light ashore.
b) Light ashore, not flashing.
c) Range markers.
d) Daybeacon. Pass to starboard entering from sea.
e) Offshore mooring buoy.
f) Unlighted hazard-junction buoy.
g) Green lateral buoy-lighted.
h) Sunken rock not dangerous to navigation.
i) Masts exposed at datum level-dangerous to navigation-position doubtful.
j) Oil platform.
k) Radio beacon.
l) Red lateral buoy flashing red.
m) Major light equipped with radio beacon.
n) Sunken rock dangerous to navigation.
o) 20 fathom line.
p) Daymark replacing buoy upstream.
q) Lighted mid-channel buoy.
r) Lighted junction buoy.
s) Marks hazardous curve in channel.
t) Green can buoy.
u) Green buoy w/reflector.
v) Green flashing buoy.
w) Six fathom line.
x) Red buoy w/ radar reflector.
y) Mid-channel buoy.

Column "B"

1) ____
2) ____ Fl G "5"
3) ____ Fl 2+1 "L"
4) ____ Fl R "4"
5) ____ Fl "5"
6) ____ R BN
7) ____ Fl 10sec 16M
8) ____
9) ____ RG "J"
10) ____
11) ____
12) ____ G "1"
13) ____ PD
14) ____
15) ____ C "3"
16) ____ RW SP "M"
17) ____
18) ____ GR "R" C
19) ____ N "4" Ra Ref
20) ____ Qk Fl "G"
21) ____ C "7" Ref
22) ____ RW "Z" MoA
23) ____ F
24) ____ R BN
25) ____

26) Unlighted red and green horizontally banded buoys with the topmost band red:

a) Are cylindrical shaped and called can buoys, b) Are conical shaped and called nun buoys, c) May either be cylindrical or conical since the shape has no significance, d) Are triangular shaped to indicate that it may not be possible to pass on either side of the buoy.

27) When displayed under a single-span fixed bridge, red lights indicate:

a) The channel boundaries, b) That vessel must stop, c) The bridge is about to open, d) That traffic is approaching from the other side.

28) When you are steering on a pair of range lights and find the upper light is above the lower light you should:

a) Come left, b) Come right, c) Continue on the present course, d) Wait until the lights are no longer in a vertical line.

29) A buoy having red and green horizontal bands would have a light characteristic of:

a) Interrupted quick-flashing, b) Composite group-flashing, c) Morse (A), d) Quick flashing.

30) Which buoy is lettered?

a) Green can buoy, b) Preferred channel buoy, c) Red lighted buoy, d) Green gong buoy.

31) You are approaching a swing bridge at night. You will know that the bridge is open for river traffic when:

a) The fixed, green light starts to flash, b) The amber light changes to green, c) The red light is extinguished, d) The red light changes to green.

32) When using a buoy as an aid to navigation which of the following should be considered?

a) The buoy should be considered to always be in the charted location, b) If the light is flashing the buoy should be considered to be in the charted location, c) The buoy may not be in the charted position, d) The buoy should be considered to be in the charted position if it has been freshly painted.

33) When approaching a preferred channel buoy, the best channel is NOT indicated by the:

a) Light characteristic, b) Color of the uppermost band, c) Shape of an unlighted buoy, d) Color of the light.

34) You are approaching a multiple-span bridge at night. The main navigational channel span will be indicated by:

a) A red light on the bridge pier on each side of the channel, b) A steady blue light in the center of the span, c) 3 white lights in a vertical line in the center of the span, d) A flashing green light in the center of the span.

35) A pilot navigating a vessel:

a) Can always rely on a buoy to be on station, b) Can always rely on a buoy to show proper light characteristics, c) Should assume a wreck buoy is directly over the wreck, d) Should never rely on a floating aid to maintain its exact position.

36) The color of a station buoy is:

a) Yellow with green stripes, b) White with green stripes, c) The same as the aid which it represents, d) Irrelevant.

37) When should a navigator rely on the position of floating aids to navigation?

a) During calm weather only, b) During daylight only, c) Only when inside a harbor, d) Only when fixed aids are not available.

38) In the U.S. Aids to Navigation system, red and green horizontally banded buoys mark:

a) Channels for shallow draft vessels, b) General anchorage area, c) Fishing grounds, d) Junctions or bifurcations.

39) The reference datum used in determining the heights of land features on most charts is:

a) Mean sea level, b) Mean high water, c) Mean low water, d) Half-tide level.

40) Which of the following indicates a dual purpose buoy?

a) Red buoy with a horizontal yellow band, b) Red and white vertically stripped buoy with a vertical yellow stripe, c) Red and white vertically stripped buoy with a red spherical topmark, d) Green buoy with a yellow square.

41) Red lights may appear on:

a) Horizontally banded buoys, B) Vertically striped buoys, c) Yellow buoys, d) Spherical buoys.

42) A preferred channel buoy may be:

a) Lettered, b) Spherical, c) Showing a white light, d) All of the above.

43) A buoy with a composite group-flashing light would signal a/an:

a) Bifurcation, b) Fish net area, c) Anchorage area, d) Dredging area.

44) Lights on preferred channel buoys will show:

a) A white light whose characteristic is Morse (A), b) A group-occulting white light, c) A composite group-flashing (2 + 1) white light, d) A composite group-flashing (2 + 1) red or green light.

45) A lighted preferred channel buoy may show a:

a) Fixed red light, b) Morse (A) white light, c) Composite group-flashing light, d) Yellow light.

46) Green lights may appear on:

a) Horizontally banded buoys, b) Vertically striped buoys, c) Yellow buoys, d) Spherical buoys.

47) Aids to navigation marking the intracoastal waterway can be identified by:

a) The letters ICW after the aid's number or letter, b) Yellow stripes, squares or triangles marked on them, c) White retro-reflective material, d) The light characteristic and color for lighted aids.

48) A safe water mark buoy may be:

a) Vertically striped, b) Spherical, c) Showing a white light, d) All of the above.

49) You are sailing south on the ICW, when you sight a red nun buoy with a yellow square painted on it. Which of the following is true?

a) You should leave the buoy on your port hand, b) This buoy marks the end of the ICW in that geographic area, c) The yellow is retro-reflective material used to assist in sighting the buoy at night, d) The yellow square is in error and it should be a yellow triangle.

50) A vertically striped buoy may be:

a) Striped black and green, b) Striped black and yellow, c) Lighted with a red light, d) Lighted with a white light.

51) A green buoy has a yellow triangle on it. This is:

a) An information or regulatory buoy that has lateral significance, b) A buoy that is off-station and is painted to warn mariners of its wrong position, c) A dual purpose marking used where the ICW and other waterways coincide, d) A buoy that was set in error and it will be replaced with a red nun buoy.

52) Safe water buoys are:

a) Equipped with triangular shaped topmarks, b) Numbered, c) Painted with red and white horizontal bands, d) Sometimes lettered.

53) You are entering an east coast port and sea a buoy with a yellow diamond painted on it. This indicates:

a) You are in the vicinity of the ICW, b) You must leave the buoy to starboard, c) The buoy is off station, d) The buoy designates a sharp turn in the channel.

54) Under the U.S. Aids to Navigation System, spherical buoys are found on a:

a) Sailing chart, b) General chart, c) Coast chart, d) All of the above.

55) Buoys and day beacons exhibiting a yellow triangle or square painted on them are used:

a) In minor harbors where the controlling depth is 10 feet or less, b) On isolated stretches of the ICW to mark undredged areas, c) Where the ICW and other waterways coincide, d) At particularly hazardous turns of the channel.

‡

WEATHER

1) A warm air mass is characterized by:

a) Stability, b) Instability, c) Gusty winds, d) Good visibility.

2) A strong, often violent, northerly wind occurring on the Pacific coast of Mexico, particularly during the colder months, is called:

a) Tehuantepecer, b) Papagoyo, c) Norther, d) Pamero.

3) A katabatic wind blows:

a) Up an incline due to surface heating, b) In a circular pattern, c) Down an incline due to cooling of the air, d) Horizontally between a high and a low pressure area.

4) Wind direction may be determined by observing all of the following EXCEPT:

a) Low clouds, b) Waves, c) Whitecaps, d) Swells.

5) The largest waves (heaviest chop) will usually develop where the wind blows:

a) At right angles to the flow of the current, b) Against the flow of the current, c) In the same direction as the flow of the current, d) Over slack water.

6) A veering wind will do which of the following?

a) Change direction in a clockwise manner in the Northern Hemisphere, b) Circulate about a low pressure center in a counterclockwise manner in the Northern Hemisphere, c) Vary in strength constantly and unpredictably, d) Circulate about a high pressure center in a clockwise manner in the Southern Hemisphere.

7) Wind velocity varies:

a) Directly with the temperature of the air mass, b) Directly with the pressure gradient, c) Inversely with the barometric pressure, d) Inversely with the absolute humidity.

8) An approximate idea of the distance to the storm center can be gained by noting the increasing hourly rate of fall of the barometer. If the rate of fall were 0.08 - 0.12 inches per hour, approximately how far would you be from the storm center?

a) 50 to 80 miles, b) 80 to 100 miles, c) 100 to 150 miles, d) 150 to 250 miles.

9) The process in which an air mass changes in temperature and or moisture characteristics is called:

a) Sublimation or condensation, b) Modification, c) Consolidation, d) Association.

10) The diurnal pressure variation is most noticeable in the:

a) Polar regions, b) Horse latitudes, c) Roaring forties, d) Doldrums.

11) The direction of the surface wind is:

a) Directly from high pressure toward low pressure, b) Directly from low pressure toward high pressure, c) From high pressure toward low pressure deflected by the earth's rotation, d) From low pressure toward high pressure deflected by the earth's rotation.

12) In the Northern Hemisphere, a wind that shifts in a counterclockwise manner is a:

a) Veering wind, b) Backing wind, c) Reverse wind, d) Chinook wind.

13) A U.S. Weather Bureau forecast states that the wind will commence backing. In the Northern Hemisphere, this would indicate that it:

a) Will shift in a clockwise manner, b) Will shift in a counterclockwise manner, c) Will continue blowing from the same direction, d) Velocity will decrease.

14) A U.S. Weather Bureau forecast states that the wind will possibly commence "veering" in the Northern Hemisphere. This would indicate that the:

a) Wind will shift in a clockwise manner, b) Wind will shift in a counterclockwise manner, c) Wind will continue blowing from the same direction, d) Wind velocity will increase.

15) A local wind which occurs during the daytime and is caused by the different rates of warming of land and water is a:

a) Foehn, b) Chinook, c) Land breeze, d) Sea breeze.

16) At night, which of the following winds result from a land mass cooling more quickly than an adjacent water area?

a) Coastal breeze, b) Sea breeze, c) Land breeze, d) Mistral.

17) Which Beaufort force indicates a wind speed of 65 knots?

a) Beaufort force 2-6, b) Beaufort force 7-10, c) Beaufort force 11, d) Beaufort force 12.

18) Wind velocity varies most closely with the:

a) Temperature of the air mass, b) Pressure gradient, c) Barometric pressure, d) Absolute humidity.

19) In reading a weather map, closely spaced pressure gradient lines would indicate:

a) High winds and seas in that area, b) Settled weather in that area, c) Calms in the area, d) Fog in the area.

20) Which of the following wind patterns generally influences the movement of frontal weather systems over the North American continent?

a) Subpolar easterlies, b) Northeast trades, c) Prevailing westerlies, d) Dominant southwesterly flow.

21) Steady precipitations is typical of:

a) Coming cold weather conditions, b) A warm front weather condition, c) High pressure conditions, d) Scattered cumulus clouds.

22) If your weather bulletin shows the center of a low pressure area to be 100 miles due east of your position, what winds can you expect?

a) East to northeast, b) East to southeast, c) North to northwest, d) South to southeast.

23) If an observer in the Northern Hemisphere faces the surface wind, the center of low pressure is:

a) Toward his left, slightly behind him, b) Toward his right, slightly behind him, c) Toward his left, slightly in front of him, d) Toward his right, slightly in front of him.

24) According to Buys Ballot's law, when an observer in the Northern Hemisphere experiences a northeast wind, the center of low pressure is located to the:

a) Northeast, b) west-southwest, c) Northwest, d) South-southeast.

25) To best check your barometer you would:

a) Check it with a barometer on another vessel, b) Take readings from several barometers and average them, c) Check it with the barometer at the ship chandlery, d) Check it against radio or Weather Bureau reports of the immediate vicinity.

26) Wind velocity may be measured by a/an:

a) Hydrometer, b) Barometer, c) Psychrometer, d) Anemometer.

27) On a working copy of a weather map, an occluded front is represented by what color line?

a) Red, b) Blue, c) Alternating red and blue, d) Purple.

28) A hygrometer is a device used for determining:

a) The absolute temperature, b) Atmospheric pressure, c) Wind velocity, d) Relative humidity.

29) Which publications should you check for complete information on Puget Sound weather conditions?

a) Sailing Directions, b) Light Lists, c) Coast Pilot, d) C & GS Charts.

30) A mariner would expect fog in which of these situations?

a) Warm weather at night, b) A low pressure area, c) An anticyclone, d) Lack of frontal activity.

For some time the Coast Guard called the "National Weather Service" the "U.S. Weather Bureau" which explains the use of the term in this test. By now, they should have it straight, but it makes a nice protest.

Incidentally, if number 17 threw you, the Beaufort Scale is in the back of the Coast Pilot and this is an open book test.

⚓

1) The period at high or low tide during which there is no change in the height of the water is called the:

   a) Range of the tide, b) Plane of the tide, c) Stand of the tide, d) Reversing of the tide.

2) "Stand" of the tide is that time when:

   a) The vertical rise or fall of the tide has stopped, b) Slack water occurs, c) Tidal current is at a maximum, d) The actual depth of the water equals the charted depth.

3) The term "spring tides" means tides which:

   a) Have lows lower than normal and highs higher than normal, b) Have lows higher than normal and highs lower than normal, c) Are unpredictable, d) Occur in the spring of the year.

4) What is the datum of soundings for charts on the Atlantic Coast of the United States?

   a) Mean low water, b) Mean lower low water, c) Mean low water springs, d) Mean normal low water.

5) What does the term "tide" refer to?

   a) Horizontal movement of the water, b) Vertical movement of the water, c) Mixing tendency of the water, d) Salinity content of the water.

6) On charts of the east coast of the United States, the datum used for soundings is:

   a) Mean low water springs, b) Mean lower low water, c) Mean low water, d) Half tide level.

7) The range of tide is the:

   a) Distance the tide moves out from the shore, b) Duration of time between high and low tide, c) Difference between the heights of high and low tide,

d) Maximum depth of the water at high tide.

8) The height of tide is the:

   a) Depth of water at a specific time due to tidal effect, b) Measurement between the surface of the water and the area's tidal datum, c) Measurement between the surface of the water and the high water tidal level, d) Measurement between the surface of the water at high tide and the surface of the water at low tide.

9) Charted depth is the:

   a) Vertical distance from the chart sounding datum to the ocean bottom, plus the height of tide, b) Vertical distance from the chart sounding datum to the ocean bottom, c) Average height of water over a specified period of time, d) Average height of all low waters at a place.

10) Which of the following is the correct definition of height of tide?

   a) The vertical distance from the tidal datum to the level of the water at any time, b) The vertical difference between the heights of low and high water, c) The vertical difference between a datum plane and the ocean bottom, d) The vertical distance from the surface of the water to the ocean floor.

11) The datum from which the predicted heights of tides are reckoned in the tide tables is:

   a) Mean low water, b) The same as that used for the charts of the locality, c) The highest possible level, d) Given in table three of the tide tables.

12) When there are small differences between the heights of two successive high tides or two successive low tides, the tides are called:

   a) Diurnal, b) Semi-diurnal, c) Solar, d) Mixed.

13) On the west coast of North America, charted depths are taken from:

a) High water, b) Mean tide level, c) Mean low water, d) Mean lower low water.

14) A tide is called diurnal when:

a) Only one high and one low water occur during a lunar day, b) The high tide is higher and the low tide is lower than usual, c) The high tide and low tide are exactly six hours apart, d) Two high tides occur during a lunar day.

15) When utilizing a Pacific Coast chart, the reference plane of soundings is:

a) Mean low water springs, b) Mean low water, c) Mean lower low water, d) Lowest normal low water.

16) The lunar or tidal day is:

a) About 50 minutes shorter than the solar day, b) About 50 minutes longer than the solar day, c) About 10 minutes longer than the solar day, d) The same length as the solar day.

17) The average height of the surface of the sea for all stages of the tide over a 19 year period is called:

a) Mean high water, b) Mean low water, c) Half-tide level, d) Mean sea level.

18) Mean high water is correctly defined as the average height of:

a) The higher high waters, b) The lower high waters, c) The lower of the two daily tides, d) All high waters.

19) Mean low water is correctly defined as the average height of:

a) The surface of the sea, b) High waters and low waters, c) All low waters, d) The lower of the two daily tides.

20) Priming of the tides occurs:

a) At times of new and full moon, b) When the Earth, Moon, and Sun are lying approximately on the same line, c) When the Moon is between first quarter and full and between third quarter and new, d) When the Moon is between new and first quarter and between full and third quarter.

21) Tropic tides are caused by the:

a) Moon being at its maximum declination, b) Moon crossing the equator, c) Sun and Moon both being at the equator, d) Moon being at perigee.

22) How many high waters usually occur each day?

a) one, b) Two, c) Three, d) Four.

23) What is the frequency at which diurnal tides normally occur?

a) Two high and two low waters occur each tidal day, b) A single high and a single low water occur each tidal day, c) The number of occurrences in a tidal day varies by geographic area, d) One high or one low water, but not both, occurs in each tidal day.

24) An important lunar cycle affecting the tidal cycle is called the nodal period. How long is this cycle?

a) 16 days, b) 18 days, c) 6 years, d) 19 years.

25) The class of tide that prevails in the greatest number of important harbors on the Atlantic Coast is:

a) Interval, b) Mixed, c) Diurnal, d) Semidiurnal.

⚓

1) If possible, a vessel's position should be plotted by bearings:

a) Of buoys close at hand, b) Of fixed known objects on shore, c) Of buoys at a distance, d) The choice of method makes no difference.

2) In calculating a running fix position, what is the minimum number of fixed objects needed to take your lines of position from?

a) One, b) Two, c) Three, d) None.

3) A position that is obtained by taking lines of position from one known object at different times and advancing them to a common time by applying your vessel's course and speed is known as a/an:

a) Dead reckoning position, b) Estimated position, c) Fix, d) Running Fix.

4) A single line of position when combined with a dead reckoning position results in a/an:

a) Assumed position, b) Estimated Position, c) Fix, d) Running fix.

5) Which of the following positions includes the effects of wind and current?

a) Dead reckoning position, b) Leeway position, c) Estimated position, d) Set position.

6) A position that is obtained by using two or more lines of position from known fixed objects at about the same time is known as a:

a) Dead reckoning position, b) Estimated position, c) Fix, d) Running fix.

7) Which of the following describes an accurate position that is NOT based on any prior position?

a) Dead reckoning position, b) Estimated position, c) Fix, d) Running fix.

8) A position that is obtained by applying only your vessel's course and speed to a known position is known as a:

a) Dead reckoning position, b) Fix, c) Probable position, d) Running fix.

9) The path that a vessel is expected to follow on a chart (assuming no current), is represented by a line termed a/an:

a) Advance speed curve, b) Track line, c) Relative motion plot, d) Course correction plan.

10) When possible, a DR track should always be started from which of the following?

a) Any position, b) A known position, c) An assumed position, d) None of the above.

11) If your vessel is turning R.P.M.'s for 10 knots and making good a speed of 10 knots, the current:

a) Is with you at 10 knots, b) Is against you at 10 knots, c) Is slack, d) Cannot be estimated.

12) Your vessel is making way through the water at a speed of 12 knots. Your vessel traveled 30 nautical miles in 2 hours 20 minutes. What current are you experiencing?

a) A following current of 2.0 knots, b) A head current of 2.0 knots, c) A following current of 0.9 knots, d) A head current of 0.9 knots.

13) You are steering a southerly course, and you note that the chart predicts an easterly current. Without considering wind, how may you allow for the set?

a) Head your vessel slightly to the right, b) Head your vessel slightly to the left, c) Decrease your speed, d) Increase your speed.

14) You are proceeding up a channel at night marked by a range which bears 185 degrees True. You steady up on a compass course of 180 degrees with the range dead ahead. This indicates that you:

a) Must come right to get on the range, b) Must come left to get on the range, c) Are on the range, and your compass has some easterly error, d) Are on the range, and your compass has some westerly error.

15) A line of position will be in what form?

a) An irregular line, b) A straight line, c) An arc, d) Any of the above.

16) At 0000 you fix your position and plot a new DR tracking. At 0200 you again fix your position, and it is 0.5 miles east of your DR. Which of the following statements is true?

a) The current is westerly at 0.5 knots, b) You must increase speed to compensate for the current, c) The current cannot be determined, d) The drift is 0.25 knots.

17) The wind speed and direction observed from a moving vessel is known as:

a) Coordinate wind, b) True wind, c) Apparent wind, d) Anemometer wind.

18) A line of position formed by sighting two charted objects when in line is called a/an:

a) Relative bearing, b) Rangeline, c) Tracking line, d) Estimated position.

19) How many points are there in a circle?

a) 4, b) 8, c) 24, d) 32.

20) The term "current" refers to:

a) The vertical movement of the water, b) The horizontal movement of the water, c) The density changes in the water, d) None of the above.

21) What publication contains descriptions of the coast line, buoyage systems, weather conditions, port facilities, and navigation instructions for the United States and its possessions?

a) Coast Pilots, b) Sailing Directions, c) Port Index, d) Light List.

22) Which of the following tables is NOT found in the U.S. Coast Pilots?

a) Climatological table, b) Geographic Range table, c) Meteorological table, d) Coastwise Distance table.

23) The "drift" and "set" of tidal, river, and ocean currents refer to the:

a) Position and area of the current, b) Speed and direction toward which the current flows, c) Type and characteristic of the current's flow, d) None of the above.

24) The set of the current is:

a) The speed of the current at a particular time, b) The maximum speed of the current, c) The direction from which the current flows, d) the direction in which the current flows.

⚓

1) The normal variation between actual depth of water and the indicated depth on an electronic depth sounder due to water conditions is on the side of safety. This would not be true in a case when the water:

a) Has high salinity, b) Is unusually warm, c) Is very dense, d) Is extremely cold.

2) The speed of sound through ocean water is nearly always:

a) Faster than the speed of calibration for the fathometer, b) The same speed as the speed of calibration for the fathometer, c) Slower than the speed of calibration for the fathometer, d) Faster than the speed of calibration for the fathometer, unless the water is very warm.

3) The elapsed time of a fathometer signal (from sound generation to the return of the echo) is 1 second. What is the depth of the water at the point sounded?

a) 400 feet, b) 400 fathoms, c) 800 feet, d) 800 fathoms.

4) Your vessel's fathometer transmits a signal which is returned 1.5 seconds later. Your vessel is in how much water?

a) 1,800 feet, b) 3,600 feet, c) 5,400 feet, d) 7,200 feet.

5) When operated over a muddy bottom, a fathometer may indicate:

a) A shallow depth reading, b) A zero depth reading, c) No depth reading, d) Two depth readings.

6) When using an echo sounder in deep water, it is NOT unusual to:

a) Receive a strong return at about 200 fathoms during the day, and nearer the surface at night, b) Receive a first return near the surface during the day, and a strong return at about 200 fathoms at night, c) Receive false echoes at a constant depth day and night, d) Have to recalibrate every couple of days due to inaccurate readings.

7) When using a recording depthfinder in the open ocean, which of the following phenomena is most likely to produce a continuous trace which may not be from the actual ocean bottom?

a) Echoes from a deep scattering layer, b) Echoes from schools of fish, c) Multiple returns reflected from the bottom to the surface and to the bottom again, d) Poor placement of the transducer on the hull.

8) What should you apply to a fathometer reading to determine the depth of water?

a) Subtract the draft of the vessel, b) Add the draft of the vessel, c) Subtract the sea water correction, d) Add the sea water correction.

9) Readings on a fathometer indicate:

a) Actual depth of water, b) Actual depth of water below keel, c) Average depth from waterline to hard bottom, d) Average depth of water to soft bottom.

10) An electronic depthfinder operates on the principle that:

a) Radio signals reflect from a solid surface, b) Sound waves travel at a constant speed through water, c) Radar signals travel at a constant speed through water, d) Pressure increases with depth.

11) The recording fathometer produces a graphic record of the:

a) Contour of the bottom against a time base, b) Depth underneath the keel against a time base, c) Contour of the bottom against a distance base, d) Depth of water against a distance base.

12) In modern fathometers, the sonic or ultrasonic sound waves are produced electrically by means of a/an:

a) Transmitter, b) Transducer, c) Transceiver, d) Amplifier.

13) Which of the following factors has the greatest effect on the amount of gain required to obtain a fathometer reading?

a) The salinity of water, b) The temperature of water, c) The atmospheric pressure, d) The type of bottom.

14) The needle of an aneroid barometer points to 30.05 on the dial. This indicates that the barometric pressure is:

a) 30.05 inches of mercury, b) 30.05 millimeters of mercury, c) 30.05 millibars, d) Falling.

15) The instruments most commonly used to measure dew point and relative humidity is:

a) An hydrometer, b) A psychrometer, c) A barometer, d) An anemometer.

16) Corrections which must be applied to an aneroid barometer reading include:

a) Height error, b) Gravity error, c) Temperature error, d) All of the above.

17) A hand held instrument used to measure distances between objects and the ship is a:

a) Vernier, b) Psychrometer, c) Hygrometer, d) Stadimeter.

18) What is the basic magnetic principle on which the operation of the magnetic compass is based?

a) Magnetic materials of the same polarity repel each other and those of opposite polarity attract, b) The Earth's magnetic lines of force are parallel to the surface of the Earth, c) Magnetic meridians connect points of equal magnetic variation, d) The compass needle(s) will, when properly compensated, lie parallel to the isogonic lines of the Earth.

19) When operating a Loran-C receiver, the blinking of a signal would indicate:

a) That the signal is in proper sequence, b) There will be no increase or decrease in kHz, c) There is an error in the transmission of that signal, d) That it has the proper GRI.

20) Most modern Loran-C receivers, when not tracking properly, have a/an:

a) Bell alarm to warn the user, b) Lighted alarm signal to warn the user, c) Alternate signal keying system, d) View finder for each station.

21) If transmission of Loran-C signals from a pair of stations becomes unsynchronized, the receiver operator is warned of the situation when the:

a) Signals begin to blink, b) Signals begin to shift, c) Stations discontinue transmission, d) Stations transmit grass

22) Most modern Loran-C receivers automatically detect station blink which is enough to:

a) Automatically shift to another station, b) Trigger alarm indicators to warn the operator of a malfunction, c) Automatically shift down the receiver, d) Enable the receiver to shift automatically to an alternate station.

23) A Loran-C fix taken many times at a known location will give positions normally varying:

a) Less than 40 feet, b) More than 300 feet, c) More than 500 feet, d) Less than 300 feet.

24) Loran-C may be used for safe navigation in harbor areas due to:

a) Multipulse grouping, b) Repeatability of readings, c) Synchronization control, d) Using secondary slave stations.

25) A "full service" Loran-C receiver will provide:

a) Matching pulse rates of at least 20 stations, b) An automatic on and off switch, c) A horizontal matching of all delayed hyperbolic signals, d) Automatic signal acquisition and cycle matching.

⚓

CHARTS

1) Lines on a chart which connect points of equal magnetic variation are called:

a) Magnetic latitudes, b) Magnetic declination, c) Dip, d) Isogonic lines.

2) Which of the following nautical charts is intended for coastwise navigation outside of outlying reefs and shoals?

a) Approach charts, b) General charts, c) Sailing charts, d) Coast charts.

3) A chart with a natural scale of 1:150,000 is classified as a:

a) Sailing chart, b) General chart, c) Coast chart, d) Harbor chart.

4) A chart with a scale of 1:80,000 would fall into the category of a:

a) Sailing chart, b) General chart, c) Coast chart, d) Harbor chart.

5) If you were using a chart with a scale of 1:45,000, it would be considered a:

a) Harbor chart, b) Coast chart, c) General chart, d) Sailing chart.

6) The scale on a chart is given as 1:5,000,000. This means that:

a) 1 inch is equal to 5,000 inches on the Earth's surface, b) 1 nautical mile on the chart is equal to 5,000 inches on the Earth's surface, c) 1 inch is equal to 5,000,000 inches on the Earth's surface, d) 1 nautical mile on the chart is equal to 5,000,000 inches on the Earth's surface.

7) Which symbol represents a 20-fathom curve?

a)-··-··-··-·· , b) -- -- -- -- --, c)--·--·--·--·--, d)- - - - - - - -.

8) The chart symbol indicating that the bottom is coral is:

a) C, b) Cl, c) Co, d) c.

9) Which chart symbol indicates the bottom is clay?

a) Cy, b) Cla, c) Cl, d) C.

10) Which statement is true concerning a simple conic chart projection?

a) It is an equal-area projection, b) It is conformal projection, c) Meridians appear as curved lines, d) The scale is correct along any meridian.

11) You would find the variation on a polyconic projection chart:

a) On the compass rose, b) On the mileage scale, c) Written on the chart title, d) At each line of longitude.

12) Which government agency publishes the U.S. Coast Pilot?

a) Army Corps of Engineers, b) Defense Mapping Agency, c) National Ocean Survey, d) U.S. Coast Guard.

13) What department of the U.S. Government issues charts of U.S. waters, Coast Pilots, Tide Tables, and Tidal Current Tables?

a) National Ocean Survey, b) Defense Mapping Agency, c) U.S. Coast Guard, d) U.S. Naval Observatory.

14) In addition to the Notice to Mariners, chart correction information may be disseminated through all of the following excect the:

a) Summary of Corrections, b) Local Notice to Mariners, c) Daily memorandum, d) Chart Correction Card.

15) Mariners are FIRST warned of serious defects or important changes to aids to navigation by means of:

a) Marine broadcast Notice to Mariners, b) Weekly Notices to Mariners, c) Corrected editions of charts, d) Light Lists.

16) Information about temporary, short term changes affecting the safety of navigation in U.S. waters is disseminated to navigational interests by the:

a) Daily Memorandum, b) HYDRO-LANT or HYDROPAC broadcasts, c) Local Notice to Mariners, d) Summary of Corrections.

17) Which of the following is a weekly publication which advises mariners of important matters affecting navigational safety?

a) Light List, b) Notice to Mariners, c) Coast Pilot, d) Sailing Directions.

18) Which of the following is published by the U.S. Coast Guard?

a) Light List, b) Nautical Charts, c) Tide Tables, d) U.S. Coast Pilot.

19) On an isomagnetic chart, the line of zero variation is the:

a) Zero variation line, b) Isogonic line, c) Variation line, d) Agonic line.

‡

The highest priority of the right-of-way is bestowed upon the vessel not under command, presumably adrift.

MATCHING

1) C
2) G, V
3) R
4) L
5) V, G
6) K
7) A
8) N
9) D
10) J
11) H
12) P
13) I
14) O
15) T
16) Y
17) W
18) F
19) X
20) S
21) U
22) Q
23) B
24) M
25) E

AIDS

26) B
27) A
28) C
29) B
29) B
30) D
31) C
32) A
33) C
34) D
35) C
36) D
37) D
38) B
38) D
39) A
39) A
40) A
41) D
42) C
43) A
44) B
45) D
46) A
47) D
48) C
49) D
50) A
51) B
52) C
53) A
54) B
55) C

WEATHER

1) A
2) C
3) C
4) D
5) B
6) A
7) B
8) B
9) B
10) D
11) C
12) B
13) B
14) A
15) D
16) C
17) D
18) B
19) A
20) C
21) B
22) C
23) B
24) D
25) D
26) D
27) D
28) D
29) C
30) A

TIDES

1) C
2) A
3) A
4) A
5) B
6) B
7) C
8) B
9) B
10) A

11) B
12) B
13) D
14) A
15) C
16) B
17) D
18) D
19) C
20) D
21) A
22) B
23) B
24) D
25) D

NAVIGATION

1) B
2) A
3) D
4) B
5) C
6) C
7) C
8) A
9) B

10) B
11) C
12) C
13) A
14) C
15) D
16) D
17) C
18) B
19) D
20) B
21) A
22) B
23) B
24) D
25) D

INSTRUMENTS

1) D
2) A
3) B
4) B
5) D
6) A
7) A
8) B

9) B
10) B
11) B
12) B
13) D
14) A
15) B
16) A
17) D
18) A
19) C
20) B
21) A
22) B
23) D
24) B
25) D

CHARTS

1) D
2) B
3) B
4) C
5) A
6) C

7) A
8) C
9) C
10) D
11) A
12) C
13) A
14) D
15) A
16) C
17) B
18) A
19) D

Deck General is another term for all around Seamanship and don't forget that this section on the tests is *currently* being mixed in with Deck/Safety for a total of seventy questions. Breathes there the soul of a man so dead that he would believe everything on this subject could be published within a single cover? When you get your application packet back from the Coast Guard -*you have written to them for your packet, haven't you*- there should be included a page on the reference guides available in the REC exam room. Peruse them carefully. First there's Bowditch. More formally, *The American Practical Navigator*. They provide you only with volume II with an extraordinary glossary. In desperation, that's where to turn, but know now that this is more of a book on navigation than esoteric terms aboard sea-going big guys. If the body of the multiple choice question doesn't yield a reference in the Bowditch glossary try the main nouns in the four choices. Very revealing. We suspect various REC's have various references available. For example, some have *The Merchant Seaman's Manual* and *Knight's Modern Seamanship*. If possible, visit the REC and ask to view the exam room. You might do this when turning in your application and sea time forms. If you get into the room, peruse those book shelves. Take notes, if you can.

At this writing the CG seems to throw everything into six basic categories in Deck General, but here we will use six-and-a-half for good reason. No one knows why, but lately the CG has been throwing seamanship questions into the smaller license exams that sound like they would be more at home on cargo ships, transports and merchant vessels. In an effort to meet this problem the exams have been arbitrarily separated into six sections and some of their more current questions have been added to this edition. The convenience categories are: *Marlinspike, Boat Handling, Anchoring, Towing, Safety*, and a sixth catch-all called *Vocabulary*.

1) Marlinspike Seamanship - The I.D. & use of knots.

2) Boat Handling. The CG theory on maneuvering.
3) Anchoring. How much line or chain and how to use it.
4) Towing. Great questions if you need the extra endorsement on your license. You should indicate this on your application.
5) Safety. Such as rescue. Not to be confused with the module Deck Safety.
6) Vocabulary. Exam questions based on certain words you won't find around small boats; more likely around big ports, shipyards or cargo craft plying the blue waters.
6 1/2) If they throw signal questions at you look them up on the reference shelf in a small black book called the *International Code of Signals*, H.O. 102.

No fair sticking your head in the ground on the river questions even though you plan on operating only offshore or on the Great Lakes. There is often a bevy of questions regarding **river navigation**. For an area with navigable rivers this is great, but they show up in areas which have no navigable rivers, so don't plan on logic on that test. Remember, if it's an offshore license that means you're license to operate **anywhere** in U.S. waters! Some of their river questions come directly from *Knight's Modern Seamanship*.

Bank Cushion refers to the increased water pressure building up between the bow and the bank nearest you (to starboard if you are on the right side of the river) forcing you away from the bank.

Stern Suction refers to the decreased water pressure between the stern and the nearest bank. The combination of the two can cause a vessel to be thrown off course to port. Hence, you must "oversteer" to maintain the given course. Both cause an increase in intensity when the draft of the vessel is nearly the same as the depth of the water.

Some of the far out things include, but are not limited to a vocabulary list such as you will find in our glossary. Read our glossary before taking the CG tests. It might clear up a few things for you. On the other hand, Chapman's is good for the more classical things like a serving mallet used for covering and seizing wire cable with marlin. Then there's little things like broaching meaning lying parallel to the waves in a trough and is found in most seamanship glossaries. Yawing is the uncontrolled swinging of the stern when the rudder is out of the water and you lose steering. (Get some weight aft). Pitch is the distance a prop will move in one revolution assuming no slip and in still water, (better yet, thick mud). When water comes over the stern you can assume you're in shallow water. Pintle and gudgeon are parts of the rudder mounts.

Marlinspike Seamanship

Most of the time the CG doesn't have time to stand around and watch you tie knots. They do incorporate questions into their quizzes they believe are designed to test your knowledge as to what purposes the various knots serve. And remember, *bends* hold two lines together, *knots* are in one line. Some example info:

1) A knot that doesn't slip is a bowline.
2) To join two lines of **similar size** try a square knot.
3) Joining two **dissimilar** lines requires a Becket Bend.
4) Tieing up to a bollard or to tie a **knot on a spar** use a Clove Hitch.
5) To strengthen a clove hitch...add a half hitch.
6) A sheepshank serves to shorten a line. Can also be used to temporarily circumvent a break or worn spot in the line.
7) A long splice is used when it is necessary to maintain the original diameter of the line, e.g., when the line must be passed through a small metal eye or block sheave. A short splice or knot would enlarge the line.
8) Nylon line is tough stuff, but stretches and is great for absorbing shock as in dock lines. Dacron is about 10% weaker, but doesn't stretch as much. Good for sails, halyards and other running rigging, but chafes and wears much easier and sun's untraviolet nasties eat it up. Never get dacron between your feet and the deck

on a rolling craft; you'll slip for sure.
9) Polypropylene has only half the strength of nylon, but floats. It's slippery and might shear unexpectedly from fatigue.

However, now the CG is interested in not only what diameter of line will stand up against what weight, but you should be able to indicate other things like the "snap" strength and if it comes off a spool or coil and whether line is measured in diameter or circumference and the same for wire rope. Chapman states the factor is about "4" meaning the line will snap at about twenty-five percent of its stated normal load strength. The CG suggests, that a 20,000 lb. line will snap at 4,000 lbs. That's about twenty percent!
10) When you coil line it is coiled clockwise. When removing line from a newly packaged coil the line is removed from the **center** of the coil. If it doesn't seem to be coming out smoothly-kinking-then turn the entire coil over and remove from center of the opposite side.
10) **Again,** read Chapman's on Marlinspike. Chapter 13.

Maneuvering

If you get a chance to view the exam room when you make your first trip to the REC, do so. It makes it less intimidating when your turn comes up. It's not the gas chamber. Maybe someone will be in there taking an exam and he or she has just come to the maneuvering section on the Deck General module. Watch the hands. The eyes are closed and the hands are pulling on imaginary gear handles. One handle ahead, maybe the other one back, head cocked to one side. Then a firm nod the pencil is then applied to another bubble on a multiple choice answer. Try to imagine yourself just under water staring at the twin screws of a retreating craft. When going ahead the right screw is turning clockwise and the left one counter-clockwise.

THE WILLIAMSON TURN

Upon hearing the man overboard alarm, the wheel is put hard over until the ship's heading is 60 degrees off the previous heading.

The wheel is then put hard over in the opposite direction and kept there until the ship's heading is on the exact reciprocal course of the course the vessel was on when the alarm was raised.

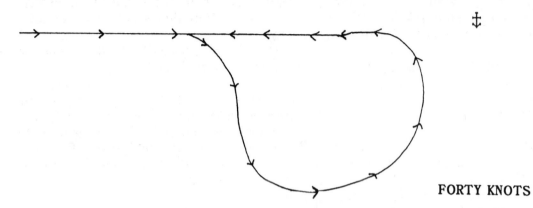

‡

FORTY KNOTS

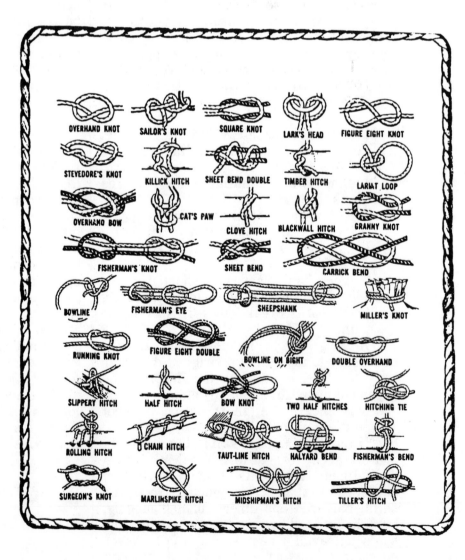

1) A fid is a:

   a) Mallet used when splicing wire rope, b) Sharp pointed crow bar used to unlay wire rope, c) Tapered steel pin used to separate wire rope, d) Tapered wooden pin used when splicing rope.

2) What is the computed breaking strength of a 4 inch manila line?

   a) 5,280 lbs., b) 7,700 lbs., c) 12,200 lbs., d) 14,400 lbs.

3) Roundline is a:

   a) Four stranded, left or right handed line, b) Three stranded, right handed line, c) Three stranded, left handed line, d) Small tarred hempline of three strands laid left handed.

4) Marlin is:

   a) Four stranded sisal line, b) Three stranded cotton line, c) Sail twine, d) Two stranded hemp cord.

5) "White Line" is made from:

   a) Cotton, b) Hemp, c) Manila, d) Sisal.

6) Line is called "small stuff" if its circumference is less than:

   a) 1/2", b) 3/4", c) 1", d) 1 3/4"

7) In the manufacture of line, plant fibers are twisted together to form:

   a) Cable, b) Line, c) Strands, d) Yarns.

8) A whipping on a fiber line:

   a) Keeps the ends from fraying, b) Strengthens it, c) Protects your hands, d) Causes the greatest depth of water to be along the outside of a bend.

9) When taking a length of new manila rope from the coil, you should:

   a) Mount the coil so it will turn like a spool and unreel from the outside, b) Roll the coil along the deck and allow the rope to fall off the coil, c) Lay the coil on end with the inside end down, then pull the inside end up through the middle of the coil, d) Lay the coil on end with the inside end up then unwind the rope from the outside of the coil.

10) Before stowing wet manila mooring lines, you should:

    a) Wash them with salt water and stow immediately, b) Dry them out without washing, c) Wash them with fresh water, dry and stow, d) Stow immediately after use so air will not cause dry rot.

11) In order to correctly open a new coil of manila line, you should:

    a) Pull the tagged end from the top of the coil, b) Pull the tagged end through the eye of the coil, c) Secure the outside end and unroll the coil, d) Unreel the coil from a spool.

12) To coil a left-hand rope, you should coil the line in:

    a) A clockwise direction only, b) A counterclockwise direction only, c) An alternating clockwise and counter-clockwise direction, d) Either a clockwise or a counterclockwise direction.

13) Using a safety factor of 6, determine the safe working load of a line with a breaking strain of 30,000 pounds:

    a) 4,000 lbs., b) 5,000 lbs., c) 20,000 lbs., d) 100,000 lbs.

14) Which mooring line has the least elasticity?

    a) Dacron, b) Nylon, c) Esterline, d) Polypropylene.

15) Which factor is most likely to impair the strength and durability of synthetic line?

a) Dry rot, b) Mildew, c) Sunlight, d) Washing with mild soap.

16) A normal safe working load for nylon rope is:

a) 20% of its breaking strain, b) 40% of its breaking strain, c) 50% of its breaking strain, d) 66% of its breaking strain.

17) Which statement is true with respect to the elasticity of nylon mooring lines?

a) Nylon can stretch over forty percent without being in danger of parting, b) Nylon can be elongated by one hundred percent before it will part, c) Nylon will part if it is stretched any more than twenty percent, d) Under load, nylon will stretch and thin out but will return to normal size when free of tension.

18) The quality that makes nylon line dangerous is that it:

a) Breaks down when wet, b) Kinks when wet, c) Is not elastic, d) Stretches.

19) What type of stopper would you use on a nylon mooring line?

a) Chain, b) Nylon, c) Manila, d) Wire.

20) Which material makes the strongest mooring line?

a) Dacron, b) Manila, c) Nylon, d) Polyethelene.

21) The critical point in nylon line elongation is considered to be:

a) 20%, b) 30%, c) 40%, 50%.

22) Which of the following lines would be least likely to kink?

a) Braided, b) Left-handed laid, c) Right-handed laid, d) Straight laid.

23) Which of the following types of line has the greatest floatability characteristics?

a) Dacron, b) Nylon, c) Old manila, d) Polypropylene.

24) What type of line is least heat resistant?

a) Wire, b) Dacron, c) Nylon, d) Polypropylene.

25) If given equal care, nylon line should last how many times longer than manila line?

a) Three, b) Four, c) Five, d) Six.

26) Nylon line is better suited than manila for:

a) Towing alongside, b) Towing astern, c) Holding knots and splices, d) Resisting damage from chemicals.

27) To find the distance the strands should be unlaid for an eye splice, multiply the diameter of the wire in inches by:

a) 12, b) 24, c) 36, d) 48.

‡

1) Sidewise pressure of the propeller tends to throw a ship's stern to the right or left, depending on rotation. The pressure is caused by:

a) Back current from the rudder, b) Greater pressure on the upper blades, c) Lower pressure on the trailing edge of the blades, d) Greater pressure on the lower blades.

2) Your single screw boat with a right-handed propeller is dead in the water, when you reverse your engine with your rudder amidship, you would expect your boat to:

a) Kick its stern to port, b) Kick its stern to starboard, c) Move astern without swinging, d) Swing its stern to starboard, then to port.

3) On a single screw vessel with a right-handed propeller, when you go full speed astern with full right rudder, the bow will swing:

a) Quickly to port, then more slowly to port, b) Slowly to port, then quickly to starboard, c) To port, d) To starboard.

4) In order to back a right-handed, single screw vessel in a straight line, you will probably:

a) Not need to use any rudder, b) Need to use some left rudder, c) Need to use some right rudder, d) Need to use full left rudder.

5) When a vessel with a single right-hand propeller backs to port, the:

a) Bow falls off to starboard, b) Vessel moves to port without changing heading, c) Bow swings to port, d) Vessel moves to starboard without changing heading.

6) Generally speaking, you are best able to keep a vessel under steering control when the vessel has:

a) Headway, b) Sternway, c) No way on with engines stopped, d) No way on with engines full ahead.

7) When backing down with sternway, the pivot point of a vessel is about:

a) At the bow, b) One-third of the vessel's length from the bow, c) One-third of the vessel's length from the stern, d) Amidship.

8) If the engine of a right handed single screw vessel with headway on is put full astern as the wheel is put hard left, what pattern will the bow follow?

a) It will swing to the left (and will swing left faster) as the ship loses way, b) It will swing to the left, straighten out and then swing to the right as the ship loses way, c) It will swing to the left without increasing or decreasing its swing, d) The bow will swing to the right.

9) A vessel is equipped with twin propellers, both turning outboard with the engines half ahead. If there is no wind or current and the rudder is amidships, which of the following will happen?

a) The bow will swing to starboard, b) The bow will swing to port, c) The vessel will steer a zig-zag course, d) The vessel will steer a fairly straight course.

10) A vessel trimmed by the stern has a:

a) List, b) Drag, c) Set, d) Sheer.

11) While moving ahead, a twin-screw ship has an advantage over a single-screw ship because:

a) Correct trim will be obtained more easily, b) Drag effect will be canceled out, c) Side forces will be eliminated, d) Speed will be increased.

12) A twin-screw vessel with single rudder is making headway with the engines full speed ahead. Both screws turn outboard. If there is no wind or current, which statement is FALSE?

a) If one screw is stopped, the ship will turn toward the side of the stopped screw, b) The principal force which turns the ship is set up by the wake against the forward side of the rudder, c) Turning response by use of the rudder only is greater than on a single-screw vessel, d) With the rudder amidships, the ship will steer a fairly steady course.

13) What is normally used to pass a mooring line to a dock?

a) Distance line. b) Gantline, c) Heaving line, d) Tag line.

14) The rudder is amidship and both screws going ahead. What will happen if the starboard screw is stopped?

a) The bow will go to port, b) The bow will go to starboard, c) The bow will remain steady, d) The stern will go to starboard.

15) A twin-screw vessel can clear the inboard propeller and maneuver off a pier best by:

a) Holding an after bow spring line and going slow ahead on the inboard engine, b) Holding a forward quarter spring line and going slow astern on the outboard engine, c) Holding an after bow spring line and going slow ahead on both engines, d) Holding an after bow spring line and going slow ahead on the outboard engine.

16) A lookout should be posted:

a) During all periods of low visibility, b) Only between the hours of sunset and sunrise, c) Only when entering and leaving port, d) At all times when the vessel is within sight of shore.

17) You are going ahead on twin engines when you want to make a quick turn to starboard. What actions will turn the boat the quickest?

a) Reverse port engine, apply right rudder, b) Reverse port engine, rudder amidship, c) Reverse starboard engine, apply right rudder, d) Reverse starboard engine, rudder amidship.

18) You are backing on twin engines with rudder amidships, when your port engine stalls. In order to continue backing on course, you should:

a) Apply left rudder, b) Apply right rudder, c) Increase engine speed, d) Keep your rudder amidship.

19) You are backing on twin engines, with rudder amidships, when your starboard engine stalls. In order to continue backing on course you should:

a) Apply left rudder, b) Apply right rudder, c) Increase your engine speed, d) Keep your rudder amidships.

20) "Right hard rudder" means:

a) Put the rudder over all the way right, b) Jam the rudder against the stops, c) Meet a swing to the right, then return amidships, d) Put the rudder over 15 degrees right.

21) Leeway is the:

a) Difference between true and compass course, b) Momentum of a vessel after her engines have been stopped, c) Lateral movement of a vessel downwind of her intended course, d) Gross displacement of a vessel.

22) The best way to steer a twin screw vessel if you lost your rudder is by using:

a) One engine and a steering oar, b) Both engines at same speed, c) One engine at a time, d) One engine running at reduced speed and controlling the boat with the other.

23) In twin-screw engine installations while going ahead, maneuvering qualities are most effective when the tops of the propeller blades both turn:

a) To starboard, b) Outboard from the center, c) To port, d) Inboard from the center.

24) The effect known as "bank cushion" acts in which of the following ways on a single screw vessel proceeding along a narrow channel?

a) It forces the bow away from the bank, b) It forces the stern away from the bank, c) It forces the entire vessel away from the bank, d) It heels the vessel toward the bank.

25) The effect known as " bank suction" acts in which of the following ways on a single screw vessel proceeding along a narrow channel?

a) It pulls the bow toward the bank, b) It pulls the stern toward the bank, c)It pulls the entire vessel toward the bank, d) It heels the vessel toward the bank.

26) Which of the following is NOT an advantage of the Williamson turn?

a) In a large vessel (VLCC) much of the headway will be lost thereby requiring little astern maneuvering, b) When the turn is completed, the vessel will be on a reciprocal course and nearly on the original trackline,

c) The initial actions are taken at well defined points and reduce the need for individual judgment, d) The turn will return the vessel to the man's location in the shortest possible time.

27) You suspect that a seaman has fallen overboard during the night and immediately execute a Williamson turn. What is the primary advantage of this maneuver under these circumstances?

a) You will be on a reciprocal course and nearly on trackline steamed during the night, b) The turn provides the maximum coverage of the area to be searched, c) The turn enables you to reverse course in the shortest possible time, d) You have extra time to maneuver in attempting to close the man for rescue.

28) A common occurrence when a vessel is running into shallow water is that:

a) The wake is less pronounced, b) The vessel is more responsive to the rudder, c) "Suck down" will cause a decrease in bottom clearance and an increase in draft, d) All of the above.

29) In a Williamson turn, the rudder is put over full until the:

a) Vessel has turned 90 degrees from its original course, b) Vessel has turned 60 degrees from its original course, c) Vessel is on a reciprocal course, d) Emergency turn signal sounds.

‡

1) On an anchor windless, the wheel over which the anchor chain passes is called:

a) Brake compressor wheel, b) Devil's claw, c) Wildcat, d) Winchhead.

2) What best describes an anchor buoy?

a) A black ball that is hoisted when the ship anchors, b) A buoy attached to the anchor, c) A buoy attached to the scope of an anchor chain, d) A mark of the number of fathoms in an anchor chain.

3) The part of an anchor which takes hold on the bottom is the:

a) Arm, b) Base, c) Fluke, d) Stock

4) If the winch should fail while you are hauling in the anchor, what prevents the anchor cable from running out?

a) Chain stopper, b) Devil's claw, c) Hawse rachet, d) Riding pawl.

5) Generally speaking, the most favorable bottom anchoring is:

a) Very soft mud, b) Rocky, c) A mixture of mud and clay, d) Loose sand.

6) How many fathoms are in a shot of anchor cable?

a)6, b) 15, c) 20, d) 30.

7) What is meant by veering the anchor chain?

a) Bringing the anchor to short stay, b) Heaving in all the chain, c) Locking the windlass to prevent more chain from running out, d) Paying out more chain.

8) How many feet are there in 2 shots of anchor chain?

a) 50, b) 60, c) 180, d) 360.

9) On a small boat, which of the following knots is best suited for attaching a line to the ring of an anchor?

a) Clove hitch, b) figure eight knot, c) Fisherman's knot, d) Overhand knot.

10) Which of the following in NOT a part of an anchor?

a) Bill, b) Devils claw, c) Palm, d) Crown.

11) When anchoring, it is a common rule of thumb is to use a length of chain:

a) Five to seven times the depth of water, b) Seven to ten times the depth of water, c) Twice the depth of water, d) Twice the depth of water plus range of tide.

12) Which of the following would be the best guide for determining the proper scope of anchor chain to use for anchoring in normal conditions?

a) One shot of chain for every ten feet of water, b) one shot of chain for every fifteen feet of water, c) One shot of chain for every thirty feet of water, d) One shot of chain for every ninety feet of water.

13) When anchoring, good practice requires 5 to 7 fathoms of chain for each fathom of depth. In deep water you should:

a) Use the same ratio, b) Use more chain for each fathom of depth, c) Use less chain for each fathom of depth, d) use two anchors with the same ratio of chain.

14) In a strong wind and current, what should be the length of chain with a single anchor?

a) 5 times the depth of water, b) 7 times the depth of water, c) 10 times the depth of water, d) 14 times the depth of water.

15) If you pay out more anchor line, you:

a) Decrease the holding power of your anchor, b) Decrease the swing of your boat while at anchor, c) Increase the holding power of your anchor, d) Increases the possibility that your boat will drag anchor.

16) Using a scope of five, determine how many feet of chain you should put out to anchor in 12 fathoms of water?

a) 60 feet, b) 72 feet, c) 360 feet, d) 450 feet.

17) To safely anchor a vessel, there must be sufficient "scope" in the anchor cable. Scope is the ratio of:

a) Weight of cable to weight of vessel, b) Weight of cable to weight of anchor, c) Length of anchor to depth of water, d) Length of cable to depth of water.

18) Using a scope of 6, determine how much cable would have to be used in order to anchor in 24 feet of water?

a) 4 feet, b) 18 feet, c) 30 feet, d) 144 feet.

19) In moderate wind and current what should be the length of chain with a single anchor?

a) 5 times the depth of water in good holding ground, b) 10 times the depth of water in good holding ground, c) 2 times the depth of water in good holding ground, d) 8 times the depth of water in good holding ground.

20) Using a scope of 6, determine how many feet of anchor cable you should put out to anchor in 12 feet of water?

a) 2 feet, b) 18 feet, c) 48 feet, d) 72 feet.

21) To "ease" a line means to:

a) Cast off, b) Double up so that one line does not take all the strain, c) Pay out more line to remove most of the tension, d) Slack it off quickly.

22) Which part of the patent anchor performs the same function of an old fashioned anchor; that is, forces the fluke to dig in?

a) Bill or pea, b) Arm, c) Shank, d) Tripping palm.

23) While anchoring your vessel, the best time to let go of the anchor is when your vessel is:

a) Dead in the water, b) Moving slowly astern over the ground, c) Moving fast ahead over the ground, d) Moving fast astern over the ground.

24) When preparing to hoist the anchor, the first step should be to:

a) Engage the wildcat, b) Put the brake in the off position, c) Take off the chain stopper, d) Take the riding pawl off the chain.

⚓

1) The catenary in a towline is:

a) A short bridle, b) The downward curvature of the hawser, c) Another name for a pelican hook, d) Used to hold it amidship.

2) Which of the following will NOT reduce yawing of a tow?
a) Increasing the length of the towing hawser, b) Trimming the tow by the stern, c) Stowing deck loads so the sail area is aft, d) Drogues put over the stern.

3) In towing, "in step" refers to:

a) The towed vessel following exactly in the wake of the towing vessel, b) Absence of catenary in the towing hawser, c) When turning, both the tow and towing vessel turn on track, d) Both the towed and towing vessels reach a wave crest or trough at the same time.

4) The biggest problem you generally encounter while towing a single tow astern is:

a) Hawser size, b) The bridle, c) Speed, d) Yaw.

5) While towing, sudden shock-loading caused during heavy weather can be reduced by:

a) Using a short tow hawser, b) Using a non-elastic type hawser, c) Using a heavier hawser, d) Decreasing the catenary in the hawser.

6) You are being towed by one tug. As you lengthen the bridle legs, you:

a) Increase your chances of breaking the towing hawser, b) Reduce the yawing of your vessel, c) Reduce the spring effect of the tow connection, d) Increase your chances of breaking the bridle legs.

7) Which of the following could be used as fairleads on a towed vessel?

a) Chocks, b) Double bits, c) Roller chocks, d) All of the above.

8) When making up a tow connection, you should use:

a) Safety hooks, b) Plain eye hooks, c) Round pin shackles, d) Screw pin shackles.

9) If the situation arose where it became necessary to tow a disabled vessel, which statement is true concerning the towing line?

a) The towing line between the two vessels should be clear of the water, b) The towing line should be taut at all times between the vessels, c) There should be a catenary so the line dips into the water, d) None of the above.

10) You are towing a large barge on a hawser. Your main engine suddenly fails. What is the greatest danger?

a) Tug and tow will go around, b) Tow will endanger other traffic, c) Tow will over run tug, d) Tow will block the channel.

11) Compare a twin screw tug to a single screw tug. Which of the following concerning the twin screw tug is FALSE?

a) The failure of one engine does not mean loss of control of the tow, b) It is more maneuverable, c) It develops more bollard pull, d) It is generally subject to more propeller damage from debris in the water.

12) While towing, what is the principal danger in attempting to swing a barge on a hawser in order to slow the barge's speed?

a) The barge may pass under the hawser and capsize the tug, b) The barge may swing too quickly and run over the tug, c) Free surface effect of liquid inside the barge may rupture the barge bulkheads when turning too quickly, d) Dangerous wakes may result from the swinging barge and capsize the tug.

13) A "loose" tow may cause all of the following EXCEPT:

a) Loss of maneuverability, b) Lines to part, c) Damage to the tug and tow, d) A saving in the transit time.

14) If a tow sinks in shallow water, you should:

a) Release it immediately, b) Attempt to beach it before it goes under, c) Pay out cable until it's on the bottom and buoy the upper end, d) Shorten cable to keep it off the bottom.

15) You are attempting to take a dead ship in tow. All lines have been passed and secured. How should you get underway?

a) Order minimum turns until the towing hawser is just clear of the water, then reduce speed to that necessary to keep the line clear of the water, b) If the towline is properly adjusted and weighted you can order slow or dead slow and the towline will act as a spring to absorb the initial shock, c) Order minimum turns until the towing hawser is taut and then continue at that speed until towing speed is attained, d) Order minimum turns until the catenary almost breaks the water, then stop. Order more turns as the hawser slackens but keep the catenary in the water.

16) When being towed by one tug, the towing bridle should be connected to:

a) Towing bits with figure eights, b) Towing padeyes, with a pelican hook, c) Towing padeyes with a safety hook, d) All of the above.

17) When being towed, a fairlead is a:

a) Fabricated shape used to change the direction of a flexible member of the tow hook-up, b) Fabricated shape used to secure the tow hook-up to the towed vessel, c) Line connecting the fish-plate to the bridle legs, d) Line connecting the tow bridle to the towed vessel.

18) The bridle for ocean tows consists of how many legs?

a) One, b) Two, c) Three, d) Four.

19) Back-up wires on a towed vessel provide:

a) A factor of safety, b) Additional strength, c) A distribution of the towing load, d) All of the above.

20) You have a large, broken-down vessel in tow with a wire rope and anchor cable towline. Both vessels have made provision for slipping the tow in an emergency; however unless there are special circumstances:

a) The towing vessel should slip first, b) The vessel towed should slip first, c) They should slip simultaneously, d) Either vessel may slip first.

⚓

1) While underway, if one of your crew members falls overboard from the starboard side, you should IMMEDIATELY:

a) Apply left rudder, b) Throw the man a life preserver, c) Begin backing your engines, d) Position your vessel to windward and begin recovery.

2) A crew member has just fallen overboard off your port beam. Which of the following actions should you take?

a) Immediately put the rudder over hard right, b) Immediately put the rudder over hard left, c) Immediately put the engines astern, d) Wait until the stern is well clear of the man and then put the rudder over hard right.

3) Fire fighting equipment requirements for a particular vessel may be found on the:

a) Certificate of Inspection, b) Certificate of Seaworthiness, c) Classification Certificate, d) Certificate of Registry.

4) You must evacuate a seaman by helicopter lift. Which of the following statements is true?

a) The ship should be stopped with the wind off the beam while the helicopter is hovering overhead, b) The basket or stretcher must not be allowed to touch the deck, c) The tending line of the litter basket should be secured to the ship beyond the radius of the helicopter blades, d) The hoist line should be slack before the basket or stretcher is hooked on.

5) By regulation, a user of marijuana may be subject to:

a) Loss of pay during the period of such use, b) Reprimand by the Coast Guard, c) Revocation of license or certificate, d) Termination of employment.

6) The penalty for failing to give aid without reasonable cause in the case of collision is:

a) $500 or 1 year imprisonment, b) $1000 or 2 years imprisonment, c) $1500 or 2 years imprisonment, d) $2000 or 2 years imprisonment

7) You shall notify the nearest U.S. Coast Guard Marine Inspection Office as soon as possible when one of your crew members remains incapacitated from an injury for over:

a) 24 hours, b) 48 hours, c) 60 hours, d) 72 hours.

8) Which of the following would require you to furnish notice of marine casualty to the Coast Guard?

a) You collide with a buoy and drag it off station with no apparent damage to the vessel or the buoy, b) A seaman slips on ice on deck and is bed ridden for two days before returning to duty, c) Your vessel is at anchor and grounds at low tide with no apparent damage, d) Storm damage to the cargo winch motors requiring repairs costing $19,000.

9) Grade D combustible liquids have a maximum flashpoint of:

a) 109 degrees Fahrenheit, b) 100 degrees Fahrenheit, c) 149 degrees Fahrenheit, d) 80 degrees Fahrenheit.

10) A combustible liquid with a flashpoint of 90 degrees Fahrenheit would be grade:

a) B, b) C, c) D, d) E.

11) As chief officer of a vessel underway, it comes to your attention that the vessel is, in some manner, unseaworthy. Under such circumstances the Master is required to take action upon receiving:

a) Information of such condition from yourself, b) Notification of such condition from yourself and the second officer, c) Notification of such condition from yourself and any other member of the crew, d) Notification of such condition from yourself or the second officer.

12) Grade E combustible liquids have a flashpoint of :

a) 80 degrees Fahrenheit to 150 degrees Fahrenheit, b) 150 degrees Fahrenheit or above, c) 60 degrees Fahrenheit to 100 degrees Fahrenheit, d) 90 degrees Fahrenheit to 120 degrees Fahrenheit.

13) When evacuating a seaman by helicopter lift, what course should the ship take?

a) Downwind so that the apparent wind is close to nil, b) A course that will keep a free flow of air, clear of smoke, over the hoist area, c) A course that will have the hoist area in the lee of superstructure, d) With the wind dead ahead because the helicopter is more maneuverable when going into the wind.

14) When evacuating a seaman by helicopter lift, which of the following statements is true?

a) When lifting from an area forward of the bridge, the apparent wind should be about 30° on the port bow, b) The vessel should be slowed to bare steerageway, c) If the hoist is at the stern, booms extending aft at the lifts hove taut, d) The litter should not be touched until it has been grounded.

15) You are proceeding to a distress site and expect large numbers of people in the water. Which of the following is true?

a) You should stop to windward of the survivors in the water and only use the ship's boats to recover the survivors, b) If the survivors are in inflatable rafts you should approach from windward to create a lee for the survivors, c) An inflatable life raft secured alongside can be an effective boarding station for transfer of survivors from the boats, d) Survivors in the water should never be permitted alongside due to the possibility of injury from the vessel.

16) The single turn method of returning to a man overboard should be used only if:

a) The man is reported missing rather then immediately seen as he falls overboard, b) The vessel is very maneuverable, c) The conning officer is inexperienced, d) A boat will be used to recover the man.

17) Which of the following statements is false?

a) In small, shallow-draft vessels, the man overboard should be picked up on the weather bow, b) The ship pickup is difficult with very large vessels due to lack of maneuverability, c) You should always place your vessel upwind of a survivor in the water to create a lee, d) The ship pickup is faster than using a small boat.

18) A man was sighted as he fell overboard. After completing a Williamson turn, the man is not sighted. What type of search should be conducted?

a) Expanding circle, b) Sector search, c) Parallel track pattern, d) Datum-drift search.

19) Safety equipment on board vessels must be approved by the:

a) Coast Guard, b) Safety Standards Bureau, c) Occupational Health and Safety Agency (OSHA), d) National Safety Council.

20) While underway in thick fog you are on watch and hear the cry "Man Overboard." What type of maneuver should you make?

a) Be sure the man is clear, back down until stopped, then send a boat, b) Round turn, c) Race track turn, d) Williamson turn.

‡

Fishing vessels shall not fish in traffic patterns and relinquish their rights-of-way when they do so.

1) What is the difference between net tonnage and gross tonnage?

a) Net tonnage is the gross tonnage less certain deductions, b) Net tonnage is tonnage of cargo compared to tonnage of the whole ship, c) Net tonnage is gross tonnage minus engine and bunker space, d) Net tonnage is the net weight of the ship.

2) The term "lee side" refers to the:

a) Side of the vessel exposed to the wind, b) Side of the vessels sheltered from the wind, c) Port side, d) Starboard side.

3) The "iron mike" is a/an:

a) Pilot, b) Speaker, c) Standby wheel, d) Automatic pilot.

4) The extension of the after part of the keel in a single screw vessel upon which the stern post rests is called the:

a) Boss, b) Knuckle, c) Skeg, d) Strut

5) A "dog" is a:

a) Crow bar, b) Device to force a water tight door against the frame, c) Heavy steel beam, d) Wedge.

6) Water may boil up around the stern of a vessel in a channel due to:

a) Slack water when upbound, b) Shallow water, c) A cross current, d) A head current.

7) The pitch of a propeller is a measure of the:

a) Angle that the propeller makes with a free stream of water, b) Angle that the propeller makes with the surface of the water, c) Number of feet per revolution the propeller is designed to move in still water without slip, c) Positive pressure resulting from the difference of the forces of both sides of the moving propeller in still water without slip.

8) The terms "cant frame" and "counter" are associated with the vessel's:

a) Cargo hatch, b) Forecastle, c) Steering angle, d) Stern.

9) The term "pintle" and "gudgeon" are associated with the:

a) Anchor windlass, b) Jumbo boom, c) Ruddering engine, d) Steering engine.

10) A condition where two currents meet at the downstream end of a middle bar can be determined by a:

a) Small whirlpool, b) Smooth patch of water, c) V-shaped ripple with the point of the V pointing downstream, d) V-shaped ripple with the point of the V pointing upstream.

11) The upward slope of a ship's bottom from the keel to the bilge is know as:

a) Camber, b) Slope, c) Dead rise, d) Keel height.

12) When a vessel is swinging from side to side off course due to quartering seas, the vessel is:

a) Broaching, b) Pitching, c) Rolling, d) Yawing.

13) When a boat turns broadside to heave seas and winds, thus exposing the boat to the danger of capsizing, the boat has:

a) Broached, b) Pitchpoled, c) Trimmed, d) Yawed.

14) When the period of beam seas equals the natural rolling period of a vessel which of the following will most likely occur?

a) Excessive pitching, b) Excessive yawing, c) Excessive rolling, d) No change would be evident.

15) Freeboard is measured from the upper edge of the:

a) Bulwark, b) Deck line, c) Gunwale bar, d) Sheer strake.

16) With a following sea, a vessel will tend to:

a) Heave to, b) Pound, c) Reduce speed, d) Yaw.

17) When using the term "limber system" one is referring to a:

a) Cleaning system, b) Drainage system, c) Strengthening system, d) Weight reduction system.

18) One function of a bulwark is to:

a) Help keep the deck dry, b) Prevent stress concentrations on the stringer plate, c) Protect against twisting forces exerted on the frame of the vessel, d) Reinforce the side stringers/

19) The "carrick bend" is used to:

a) Add strength to a weak spot in a line, b) Join two hawsers, c) Be a stopper to transfer a line under strain, d) Join lines of different sizes.

20) The garboard strake is the:

a) Raised flange at the main deck edge, b) Riveted crack arrester strap on all-welded ships, c) Riveting pattern most commonly used in ship construction, d) Row of plating nearest the keel.

Sailboats less than 7 meters in length and rowboats need not use sidelights if impractical. A torch is sufficient.

⚓

MARLINSPIKE

1) D
2) D
3) B
4) D
5) A
6) D
7) D
8) A
9) C
10) C
11) B
12) B
13) B
14) A
15) C
16) A
17) D
18) D
19) B
20) C
21) C
22) A
23) D
24) D
25) C
26) B
27) C

BOATS

1) D
2) A
3) C
4) C
5) A
6) A
7) C
8) B
9) D
10) B
11) C
12) C
13) C
14) B
15) D
16) A
17) C
18) B
19) A
20) A
21) C
22) D
23) B
24) A
25) B
26) D
27) A
28) B
29) B

ANCHORING

1) C
2) B
3) C
4) D
5) C
6) B
7) D
8) C
9) C
10) B
11) A
12) B
13) C
14) C
15) C
16) C
17) D
18) D
19) A
20) D
21) C
22) D
23) B
24) A

TOWING

1) B
2) C
3) D
4) D
5) C
6) B
7) D
8) D
9) D
10) C
11) C
12) A
13) D
14) C
15) D
16) A
17) A
18) B
19) D
20) A

SAFETY

1) B
2) B
3) A
4) D
5) C
6) B
7) D
8) C
9) C
10) C
11) B
12) B
13) B
14) D
15) C
16) B
17) C
18) B
19) A
20) D

VOCAB.

1) A
2) B
3) D
4) C
5) B
6) B
7) C
8) D
9) C
10) C
11) C
12) D
13) A
14) C
15) B
16) D
17) B
18) A
19) B
20) D

The last of the four modules is Deck/Safety with six categories. The categories, like the others, are arbitrary to enable the distribution of the types of questions for easier mastery. Remember, this is an open book exam, but in only a few cases is the research alternative practical in a test that must be finished within a given time frame. For example, look at number two in the pollution test. If you're stuck, you know (see page 22) you can refer to the appropriate CFR's for your answer. In the case of pollution see 33 CFR-Parts 130-137 under subchapter M, or subchapter O, parts 151-159.

As for fire, some of which is based on the National Fire Prevention Association's (NFPA) small, but packed manual, or directly from CFR 46 and applicable parts. In short, read again page 22 and make sure you know how the CFR system works, index, table of contents and all.

As a candidate perusing the following test questions you will undoubtedly notice that many of the questions, like those in the Deck/General module, appear to be more applicable to the *Queen Mary* than the relatively small boats you plan to operate. Good examples of this are the Signaling and Distress sections. The CG claims most of it comes from *The American Merchant Seaman's Manual*, which doesn't leave much room for choices. Go buy it, hope for the best or find some more questions just like these. A lot depends on whether you pass the first time out or have to keep going back for various modules. No way can Charters West squeeze all the questions into this manual without more than tripling the size and the price. Besides, the total module package wasn't ready when this volume went to press. Actually, if you have a problem it would be cheaper to purchase the extra question manual on the order form.

Text exposure here aims primarily at the two big ones under Deck/Safety: Fire and First Aid. Remember, the divisions are selected for easy study, but the quiz questions on your CG test module will be well mixed. Recall also this module will have about forty questions which averages out to about seven questions on each subject. Here you are working on more than three times that many on each subject. This should be a pretty fair exposure.

1) Fire - meaning fire fighting, extinguishers, causative factors and the types of fires.

2) Pollution: Mostly from CFR 33.

3) Regulations: Substantially from CFR 46, subchapter C found in parts 24-26; for Master 100 tons found in subchapter T parts 175-187.

4) Distress: This can cover a myriad of subjects, but you will get the feel for it in the following questions.

5) First Aid: A great deal taken by the CG from a book entitled: *The Ship's Medicine Chest*, readily available in most chandleries, but you should get the hang of it from the extensive list of questions which follow. Note, that even though you must have your CPR rating, there will be some of these questions on your exam.

6) Signaling: Admittedly, a small sampling compared to the others, but the topic itself is rather limited when applied to Six Pac and Master 100 tons.

Let's go for a run-down on First Aid first.

FIRST AID.

1) Heat exhaustion: Body temp normal or sub-normal. Perspiration profuse. Get patient out of sun. Cool him off before he loses all body moisture. Bathe with cool cloths. Rest. Immobilize.

2) Heat stroke: Body temp high and skin dry and hot to the touch. Get him out of sun and/or heat. Call doctor immediately.

3) Burns:

a) 1st degree; reddening of skin. 2/3 of body is serious.

b) 2nd degree; blistering. 1/3 of body is seriously burned.

c) 3rd degree; loss of skin in burned area. 1/10 of body is serious.

Burn treatment: Cold water quickly. No grease or butter. Wrap in sterile gauze to prevent infection. Do not bind tightly.

4) Blood loss: Body has five qts. Loss of one pint not serious. Two pints can cause shock. Capillary blood is brick red and oozes slowly. Venous blood is dark and escapes in steady even flow. Arterial blood is bright red and if near surface, spurts. If deep, blood comes in a steady stream. For heavy bleeding, apply direct pressure to wound. Tourniquets only as a last resort to stop uncontrollable bleeding. (Had your dinner yet?)

5) Broken bones: With "simple fracture" bone does not penetrate skin. Compound fracture ruptures skin. Bleeding occurs. Never attempt to set. Immobilize-prevent movement. Call doctor.

6) Do not attempt to treat or administer first aid to unknown injury.

7) Never try to give liquids to unconscious person.

8) When choking, do not slap on back, especially between shoulder blades. Might force object into lungs. Heimlich is the way to go with quick sharp upward thrust when you have him, **or her,** clasped with your arms folded just beneath the rib cage. (First aid can be fun).

9) Heart failure: Symptoms-pain on left side below breastbone, numbing of left arm or fingers. Pain down left arm. Cold sweat and pale. Lips blue, pulse weak. Treatment: Immobilize patient. Keep him from any exertion. If heart stops, go to CPR. (First aid could be more fun if it wasn't only *men* always having the heart attacks.)

10) Drowning: CPR. Clear mouth and make sure air passage open prior to commencing CPR. Review your course material particularly on timing, both on adults and babies. (Have you lined up your CPR course yet? Get on it.)

11) Shock: Symptoms-Shallow breath, low blood pressure, ashen face. Immobilize, raise feet, lower head and make comfortable.

12) Compound fracture shows bleeding from area of fracture; could be puncturing skin. Immobilize patient and immobilize fracture if possible, in any fracture case.

FIRE

I) To create a decent respectable fire you must have three elements. Remove any of these elements and the fire dies. They are:

FUEL - OXYGEN - HEAT

Better known as the "Fire Triangle."

II) There are three **types** of fire. Each has a capital letter to identify it. You're supposed to know these.

Type A: Wood, paper, and trash in general.

Type B: Petroleum-Such as gas, alcohol, diesel, paint, thinner, kerosene

Type C: Electrical.

Type D: Combustible metals. Prime examples used are magnesium and sodium.

III) There are four basic types of fire extinguishers:

a) **Water.** This stuff isn't good on just **any** kind of fire. Only on Type "A" fire. In the form of nozzle spray it is known for taking the heat out of a fire faster than CO_2. Water can be used on alcohol fire, but not petroleum. Just spreads it around.

However, water can be used on alcohol fires.

b) **Carbon Dioxide.** Better known as CO_2. Great stuff on petroleum fires, (Type "B") and even on Type "A". Not to be used on electrical. It evaporates quickly and the theory is the fire will restart. Never use CO_2 on an **energized** electrical fire. This leads to a cute catch. The first thing to do with an electrical fire is to cut off the source of power; de-energize it. Thus, if some of the questions use CO_2 as an alternate choice to fighting electrical fires then accept it as a plausible answer. Why? Because, one would **guess** they assume, you have already de-energized the burning line. If you are suspicious consider filing a protest **before they grade your exam.**
This is difficult, but better you know now and here rather than later. CO_2 on a hot electrical fire evaporates too quickly and re-ignition occurs. CO_2 also eats up oxygen in a small compartment. However, CO_2 is recognized as one **extinguisher** capable of taking heat out of a fire very quickly. CO_2 extinguishers are measured by weight. A 15 lb. CO_2 extinguisher contains 15 lbs of carbon dioxide. When they get even close to 90% capacity, they should be recharged.

c) **Dry Chemical.** This is a capacity extinguisher measured by weight as in a can of coffee. Good on any fire. Particularly on petroleum fires. Sometimes mistaken for the old "soda-acid" extinguisher which had to be turned upside down to activate. Most dry chemical extinguishers have gauges on them indicating current reliability status. Dry chemical uses CO_2 as a trigger and emits CO_2 when set off.

d) **Foam.** Foam smothers. Not generally found on small boats. Takes a special "mixing" nozzle and two separate chemicals. This is the stuff they "foam" down airport runways with when a crippled plane is coming in. Great on petroleum fires, but should be bounced off a bulkhead so it will spread out over the fire.

All of the above provides us with a jungle of possibilities regarding which extinguisher should be used on what fire. Here's some statements the CG utilizes to construct their fire quiz.

1) Type "A" fires are fought with water.

2) Type "B" need CO_2 or foam. Dry chemical will do it, but the former two are preferred.

3) Do not use CO_2 on still-energized electrical fires. Evaporation problem.

Next-Take a few minutes out to familiarize yourself with these classifications. This is one of those "short-term" memory things you cram down at the last minute before you visit the REC. Same for those CFR references on page 22.

U.S. Coast Guard Extinguisher Classifications

Extinguisher Type	Size	Water Gallons	Foam Gallons	CO_2 Pounds	Dry Chemical Pounds
A	II	2½	2½	--	--
B	I	--	1¼	4	2
B	II	--	2½	15	10
B	III	--	12	35	20
B	IV	--	20	50	30
B	V	--	40	100	50
C	I	--	--	4	2
C	II	--	--	15	10

‡

WL=waterline   K=keel

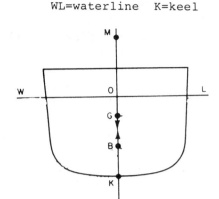

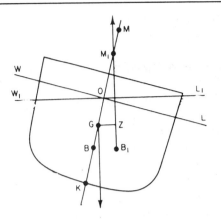

ANTI-CAPSIZING FORCES

One way of viewing anti-capsizing is by considering the center of gravity of a ship. We mean forces that are "pushing down" on the hull. Look at this pressure as that which prevents the ship from heeling too far. That "point" which is "pushing down" is referred to as the center of gravity and represented by the letter "G" in stability references and equations. More appropriately, it is the point at which the weight of the ship is centered.

It's what happens if you add or subtract weights above or below "G" that counts. In other words, what if you use fuel underway and empty some tanks without pumping in sea water to make up the difference? Or, what if you add weight on deck? Some would call it getting top heavy. First, let's get a mental picture of "G". Feature a ship's outline and you're looking at it from either side. See above. Think of "G" situated on a line which runs fore and aft. Anyplace along that line is fine as long as it's the real center of weight. That's called the *longitudinal*. Now also look at it from the stern and "G" should be situated midships with the line running from one side to the other. That's the *transversal*. Now you have a line running through "G" both ways: fore and aft and then amidships. Again, point "G" is considered to be the point at which all of the weight of the ship is centered. If you could pick it up and balance it on your finger tip, "G" is where you would put your finger. "G" has a *downward* thrust.

BUOYANCY

If "G" has a *downward* thrust, "B" (buoyancy) has an *upward* thrust. They work against each other. If "G" is the center of weight, "B" is the *geometric* center of the **underwater part** of the ship which means (rather simplified) that there is equal **space** all around that point of buoyancy. It's pushing **up** from that point. When the ship is upright, "G" and "B" are located on the same line, more specifically the *vertical centerline* of the ship. The distance from "B" to "G" in feet is called the *metacentric height* and is labeled "GM."

Now watch that vertical centerline as the ship heels. Point "G" remains on that centerline but "B" moves off to the heeled side. Drawing a line from "B" straight up to the centerline reveals the so-called *metacenter* "M". "M" is always the metacenter. Drawing another straight line, this time from "G" downwards makes these two lines parallel. Draw another line horizontally between these two lines and you have what is termed the *righting arm*, GZ.

If the ship continues to heal the righting arm shrinks until we reach "0" with the righting arm and the craft could go either way. When "M" works down below "G" over she goes with what they call a "negative righting arm."

That's a terribly brief summary as various hull forms and hull lengths produce different stability factors. Knowing what little you do from the above try the questions at the end of the following quiz which came directly from a recent CG data bank.

1) An inflatable liferaft is in the water, still in its container and attached to the ship by the painter line. You see that the ship is sinking rapidly. What action should you take with respects to the liferaft container?

a) Cut the painter line so it will not pull the liferaft container down, b) Swim away from the container so you will not be in danger as it goes down, c) Take no action because the painter will cause the liferaft to inflate and open the container, d) Manually open the container and inflate the liferaft with the handpump.

2) Liferafts are less maneuverable than lifeboats due to their:

a) Weight, b) Shallow draft, c) Large sail area, d) All of the above.

3) If an inflatable liferaft is overturned, it may be righted by:

a) Filling the stabilizers on one side with the water, b) Releasing the CO2 cylinder, c) Pushing up from under one end, d) Standing on the inflatable cylinder and pulling on the straps on the underside of the raft.

4) The lifesaving signal indicated by a horizontal motion of a white light or white flare means:

a) Landing here highly dangerous, b) Negative, c) Avast hauling, d) All of the above.

5) If a vessel rolls slowly and sluggishly in a seaway, this condition indicates that the vessel:

a) Has off-center weights, b) Is taking on water, c) Has a greater draft forward than aft, d) Has poor stability.

6) Life preservers must be marked with the:

a) Stowage space assigned, b) Vessel's name, c) Vessel's homeport, d) Maximum weight allowed.

7) If you are forced to abandon ship in a lifeboat, you should:

a) Remain in the immediate vicinity, b) Head for the nearest land, c) Head for the closest sea-lanes, d) Vote on what to do, so all hands will have a part in the decision.

8) Which item is NOT required to be marked with the vessel's name?

a) Hand-portable fire extinguisher, b) Life preserver, c) Firehose, d) Lifeboat oar.

9) If a fire breaks out in the forward part of your vessel while underway, the first thing you should do is:

a) Call for assistance, b) Abandon ship to windward, c) Put the vessel's stern into the wind, d) Keep going at half speed.

10) How should an "EPIRB" be mounted?

a) Under lock and key, b) Where it can float free, c) In the engine room, d) By a 10 foot lanyard.

11) Which statement concerning storm oil is correct?

a) It has a moderate effect in surf, b) It is most effective in shallow water, c) It reduces friction between wind and water, d) Mineral oil is the most effective type.

12) In order to get the most benefit from the use of storm oil in heavy seas, the storm oil should be spread:

a) Around the rudder and screws, b) Completely around the vessel, c) To leeward of the vessel, d) To windward of the vessel.

13) A person has fallen overboard and is being picked up with a lifeboat. If the person appears in danger of drowning, the lifeboat should be maneuvered to make:

a) An approach from leeward, b) An approach from windward, c) The most direct approach, d) An approach from across the wind.

14) Which type of oil is suitable for use as storm oil?

a) Fish oil, b) Crude oil, c) Lube oil, d) Mineral oil.

15) The purpose of storm oil in a sea anchor is to:

a) Weigh down the anchor, b) Lubricate the anchor, c) Repel dangerous fish, d) Smooth the sea.

16) Spreading oil on the open sea has the effect of:

a) Diminishing the height of the seas, b) Lengthening the distance between successive crests, c) Preventing hypothermia to anyone overboard, d) Preventing the wave crest from breaking.

17) Which of the following is true concerning personal flotation devices (life preservers) which are severely damaged?

a) They must be replaced, b) They must be tested for buoyancy before continued use, c) They can be repaired by a reliable seamstress, d) They can be used for children.

18) Kapok life preservers require proper care, and should NOT be:

a) Stowed near open flame or where smoking is permitted, b) Used as seats, pillows, or foot rests, c) Left on open decks, d) Any of the above.

19) Which of the following statements is NOT true concerning life preservers?

a) They come in two sizes, child and adult, b) They are required to be of a highly visible color, c) The "bib" life preserver will not support an unconscious wearer in an upright position, d) They must be able to support the wearer in an upright position.

20) The national distress, safety and calling frequency is channel:

a) 13, b) 16, c) 18, d) 22.

21) Which statement is true concerning life preservers?

a) Buoyant vests may be substituted for life preservers, b) An adult size life preserver may be used for children, c) Life preservers must always be worn with the same side facing outwards, d) Life preservers are not designed to turn a person's face clear of the water when unconscious.

22) An emergency sea anchor may be constructed by using:

a) A boat bucket, b) An air tank filled with water, c) An oar and canvas weighted down, d) Any of the above.

‡

1) If your liferaft is to leeward of a fire on the water, you should first:

a) Cut the line to the sea anchor, b) Paddle away from the fire, c) Splash water over the liferaft to cool it, d) Get out of the raft and swim to safety.

2) What is the most important characteristic of the extinguishing agent in fighting a class "C" fire?

a) Weight of the extinguishing agent, b) Temperature of the extinguishing agent, c) Electrical conductivity of the extinguishing agent, d) Cost of the extinguishing agent.

3) A B-III foam extinguisher will contain:

a) 2 1/2 gallons of foam, b) 8 gallons of foam, c) 10 gallons of foam, d) 12 gallons of foam.

4) A B-II fire extinguisher has a minimum capacity of:

a) Three gallons of foam, b) Twenty pounds of CO_2, c) Ten pounds of dry chemical, d) Any of the above.

5) Which of the following hand portable or semiportable fire extinguishers is classified as a B-II extinguisher?

a) A 2 1/2 gallon soda acid and water, b) A 1 1/4 gallon foam, c) A 2 1/2 gallon foam, d) A 15 pound dry chemical.

6) Combustible gas indicators operate by drawing an air sample into the instrument:

a) Over an electrically heated platinum filament, b) Where it is mixed with nitrogen, c) Where it is ignited by a sparking device, d) Where its specific gravity is measured.

7) Which of the following portable fire extinguishers is classified as a type B-II extinguisher?

a) 12 gallon soda acid, b) 20 gallon foam, c) 30 pound carbon dioxide, d) 20 pound dry chemical.

8) Annually, all carbon dioxide fire extinguishers aboard a vessel are:

a) Weighed, b) Discharged and recharged, c) Checked for pressure, d) Sent ashore to an approved service facility.

9) Which fire detection system is actuated by sensing a heat rise in a compartment?

a) Manual fire detection system, b) Automatic fire detection, c) Smoke detection system, d) Watchman's supervisory system.

10) Fire alarm system thermostats are actuated by:

a) Smoke sensors, b) The difference in thermal expansion of two dissimilar metals, c) Pressure loss due to air being heated, d) An electric eye which actuates when smoke interferes with the beam.

11) In weighing CO_2 cylinders, they must be recharged if weight loss exceeds:

a) 10% of weight of full bottle, b) 15% of weight of full bottle, c) 20% of weight of charge, d) 10% of weight of charge.

12) The space containing the CO_2 cylinders for the carbon dioxide fire extinguishing system shall be designed to preclude an anticipated ambient temperature in excess of:

a) 80 degrees F, b) 95 degrees F, c) 130 degrees F, d) 150 degrees F.

13) A definite advantage of using water as a fire extinguishing agent is its characteristic:

a) Alternate expansion and contraction as water in liquid state becomes vapor, b) Absorption of smoke and gases as water is converted from liquid to vapor, c) Rapid contraction as water is converted from a liquid to a vapor, d) Rapid expansion as water absorbs heat.

14) CO_2 cylinders, which protect the space in which they are stored must:

a) NOT consist of more than 200 pounds of CO_2, b) Be automatically operated by a heat actuator, c) Have an audible alarm, d) All of the above.

15) A spanner is:

a) A cross connection line between two main fire lines, b) A special wrench for tightening couplings in a fire hose line, c) A tackle rigged to support a fire hose, d) None of the above.

16) Fire hose should be washed with:

a) Salt water and a wire brush, b) Caustic soap, c) Mild soap and fresh water, d) A holystone.

17) When fighting fires in spaces containing bottles of LPG (liquified petroleum gas), you should:

a) Attempt to isolate the fire from the LPG, b) Cool the bottles or remove them from the fire area, c) See that valves on all LPG bottles are closed, d) Place insulating material over the bottles.

18) A fire must be ventilated:

a) When using an indirect attack on the fire such as flooding with water, b) To prevent the gases of combustion from surrounding the firefighters, c) To minimize heat buildup in adjacent compartments, d) If compressed gas cylinders are stowed in the compartment on fire.

19) Where possible, a fire of escaping liquified flammable gas should be extinguished by:

a) Cooling the gas below the ignition point, b) Cutting off the supply of oxygen, c) Stopping the flow of gas, d) Interrupting the chain reaction.

20) Which of the following is not part of a foam type fire extinguisher?

a) Relief valve, b) Lead stopper, c) Locking pin, d) Strainer.

21) In a foam fire extinguisher, the solutions commonly called the A and B solutions:

a) Denote the class of fire they are to be used on, b) Pertain to the NFPA rating, c) Are the two solutions that are kept separated until used, d) Describe the expansion properties of the foam.

22) Portable foam type fire extinguishers are safe and effective on:

a) Mattresses fires, b) Oil fires, c) Wood fires, d) All of the above.

⚓

1) You are alone and administering CPR to a victim. How many chest compressions and how many inflations should you administer in each sequence?

a) 5 compressions then 1 inflation, b) 15 compressions then 2 inflations, c) 20 compressions then 3 inflations, d) 30 compressions then 4 inflations.

2) When administering mouth to mouth resuscitation you should breathe at the rate of how many breaths per minute?

a) 4, b) 8, c) 12, d) 20.

3) The rescuer can best provide an airtight seal during mouth-to-mouth ventilation by pinching the victim's nostrils and:

a) Cupping a hand around the patient's mouth, b) Keeping the head elevated, c) Applying his mouth tightly over the victim's mouth, d) Holding the jaw down firmly.

4) When applying chest compression during CPR, the sternum should be depressed about:

a) 1/2 inch or less, b) 1/2 to 1 inch, c) 1 to 1 1/2 inches, d) 1 1/2 to 2 inches.

5) When administering chest compression during CPR, at what part of the victim's body should the pressure be applied?

a) Lower half of the sternum, b) Tip of the sternum, c) Top half of the sternum, d) Left chest over the heart.

6) Changing rescuers while carrying out artificial respiration should be done:

a) Without losing the rhythm of respiration, b) Only with the help of two other people, c) By not stopping the respiration for more than 5 minutes, d) At ten minute intervals.

7) The most essential element in the administration of CPR is:

a) To have the proper equipment for the process, b) The speed of treatment, c) The administration of oxygen, d) The treatment for traumatic shock.

8) Before CPR is started, you should:

a) Establish an open airway, b) Treat any bleeding wounds, c) Insure the victim is conscious, d) Make the victim comfortable.

9) You are attempting to administer CPR to a victim. When you blow into his mouth it is apparent that no air is getting to the lungs. What should you do?

a) Blow harder to force the air past the tongue, b) Raise the victim's head higher than his feet, c) Press on the victim's lungs so that air pressure will blow out any obstruction, d) Re-tip the head and try again.

10) When two people are administering CPR to a victim, how many times per minute should the chest be compressed?

a) 30, b) 45, c) 60, d) 80.

11) Antiseptics are used principally to:

a) Promote healing, b) Prevent infection, c) Reduce inflammation, d) Increase blood circulation.

12) A tourniquet should be used to control bleeding only:

a) With puncture wounds, b) When all other means have failed, c) When the victim is unconscious, d) To prevent bleeding from minor wounds.

13) A person reports to you with a fish hook in his thumb. The procedure used to remove it would be to:

a) Pull it out with pliers, b) Cut the skin from around the hook, c) Push the barb through, cut it off, then remove hook, d) Have a surgeon remove it.

14) First aid treatment for small cuts and open wounds would be to:

a) Have the patient lie down and cover the wound when the bleeding stops, b) Stop the bleeding, clean, medicate, and cover the wound, c) Apply an ice pack to the wound and cover it when the bleeding stops, d) Apply a hot towel to purge the wound, then medicate and cover it.

15) A person has suffered a laceration of the arm. The bleeding has been stopped by using direct pressure. What is the next action to be taken?

a) Apply a tourniquet to prevent the bleeding from re-starting, b) Apply a pressure bandage over the dressing, c) Remove any small foreign matter and apply antiseptic, d) Administer fluids to assist the body in replacing the lost blood.

16) In all but the most severe cases, bleeding from a wound should be controlled by:

a) Applying direct pressure to the wound, b) Submerging the wound in lukewarm water, c) Cooling the wound with ice, d) Applying a tourniquet.

17) What is the primary purpose of a splint applied in first aid?

a) Control bleeding, b) Reduce pain, c) Immobilize the fracture, d) Reset the bone.

18) A compound fracture is a fracture:

a) In which more than one bone is broken, b) In which the same bone is broken in more than one place, c) Which is accompanied by internal bleeding, d) Which causes external bleeding at the site of the fracture.

19) Unless there is danger of further injury, a person with a broken bone should not be moved until bleeding is controlled and:

a) The bone has been set, b) The fracture is immobilized, c) Radio advice has been obtained, d) The wound has been washed.

20) In any major injury to a person, the first aid includes the treatment for the injury and what other treatment?

a) Application of CPR, b) Removal of any foreign object, c) Administration of oxygen, d) Treatment for traumatic shock.

21) Which of the following is NOT a treatment for traumatic shock?

a) Keep the patient warm but not hot, b) Have the injured lie down, c) Massage the arms and legs to restore circulation, d) Relieve the pain of the injury.

22) Which of the following is a treatment for traumatic shock?

a) Administer CPR, b) Administer fluids, c) Open clothing to allow cooling of the body, d) Keep the victim in a sitting position.

‡

1) Pollution of the waterways may result from the discharge of:

a) Sewage, b) The galley trash can, c) An oily mixture of one parts oil per million, d) all of the above.

2) Which statement is true of a gasoline spill?

a) It is visible for a shorter time than a fuel oil spill, b) It is not covered by the pollution laws, c) It does little harm to marine life, d) It will sink more rapidly than crude oil.

3) Which statement is true concerning small oil spills?

a) They usually disappear quickly, b) They usually stay in a small area, c) They may cause serious pollution as the effect tends to be cumulative, d) A small spill is not dangerous to sea life in the area.

4) Under the Oil Pollution Act of 1961, prohibited zones are generally areas within how many miles of shore?

a) 2, b) 12, c) 50, d) 100.

5) The minimum distance for dumping oily mixtures offshore is 50 miles in most cases. Which of the following acts set forth this policy?

a) River and Harbor Act, b) Federal Water Pollution Control Act, c) Oil Pollution Act, d) Safety at Sea Overboard Discharge Act.

6) Prohibited zones for the discharge of oil or oily mixture are:

a) Generally areas within 50 miles offshore but may be extended to 100 miles, b) Generally 25 miles offshore but may be extended to 50 miles, c) Generally 10 to 15 miles offshore but may be extended to 25 miles, d) Generally 20 miles off the coastline.

7) A vessel violates the provisions of the Oil Pollution Act of 1961 when it discharges:

a) An oily mixture by accident within 50 miles of the coast, b) Residue from purification of fuel oil in a prohibited zone, c) Bunker C to calm the seas to launch a lifeboat, d) Solid sediment from the cargo tanks of a tanker.

8) The requirements for reporting oil spills may vary geographically; however, all oil spills must be reported to the:

a) U. S. Corps of Engineers, b) U. S. Coast Guard, c) Local police, d) Local fire department.

9) Which of the following statements concerning an accidental oil spill in the navigable waters of the U. S. is false?

a) The person in charge must report the spill to the Coast Guard, b) Failure to report the spill may result in a fine, c) The company can be fined for the spill, d) The Corps of Engineers is responsible for the clean up of the spill.

10) The pollution prevention regulations contained in the Federal Water Pollution Control Act are applicable on which of the following waters?

a) Inland waters of the U. S. only, b) Great Lakes waters of the U. S. only, c) Western Rivers of the U. S. only, d) Navigable waters, adjoining shorelines and contiguous zone of the U. S.

11) Which substance is not considered "Oil" as defined for the pollution prevention regulations?

a) Petroleum and fuel oil, b) Sludge, c) Oil mixed with dredge spoil, d) Oil refuse and oil mixed with wastes.

12) When a vessel violates the Oil Pollution Act, who may be held responsible?

a) Master only, b) Owners only, c) Licensed officers only, d) Any individual connected with the vessel involved in the operation.

13) What is the maximum fine for discharging oil in U. S. waters?

a) $500, b) $1,000, c) $5,000, d) $10,000.

14) The Federal Water Pollution Control Act requires the person in charge of a vessel to immediately notify the Coast Guard as soon as he knows of any oil discharge. Failure to notify the Coast Guard can lead to a fine of:

a) $500 or 30 days in jail, or both, b) $1,000 or 60 days in jail, or both, c) $10,000 or 1 year in jail, or both, d) $50,00 or 5 years in jail, or both.

15) The term "oily mixture" as used in the Oil Pollution Act of 1961 means a mixture with an oil content of:

a) 50 parts per thousand, b) 100 parts per thousand, c) 50 parts per million, d) 100 parts per million.

16) The term "discharge", as it applies to the pollution regulations, means:

a) Spilling, b) Leaking, c) Dumping, d) All of the above.

17) A method NOT usually allowed in cleaning up oil spills in the United States is:

a) Skimmers, b) Straw, c) Dispersants, d) Sawdust.

18) Part of the Pollution Prevention Regulations concerns:

a) Transfer operations and procedures, b) Vessel design, c) Large oil transfer facilities, d) Equipment.

19) The maximum allowable working pressure for each oil transfer hose assembly must be at least:

a) 100 psi, b) 150 psi, c) 200 psi, d) 250 psi.

20) No vessel may use or carry an oil transfer hose larger than 3 inches unless it meets certain requirements. Which of the following is NOT among those requirements?

a) Metallic reinforcement, b) A bursting pressure greater than 600 psi, c) A working pressure greater than 150 psi, c) Identification markings.

21) Which of the following vessels is NOT required to have a Pollution Placard posted on board?

a) A 15 foot passenger vessel, b) A 75 foot towing vessel, c) 50 foot cabin cruiser used for pleasure only, d) A 150 foot unmanned tank barge.

⚓

1) Records of tests and inspections of all fire extinguishing systems on board a vessel shall be kept on the vessel:

a) For 1 year, b) For 2 years, c) Until the next Coast Guard inspection, d) For the period of validity of the vessel's current Certificate of Inspection.

2) According to the communication you are required to retain a record of use of your radiotelephone for a period of not less than:

a) One month, b) Four months, c) Six months, d) One year.

3) Which of the following would be used to call all stations in your vicinity by radiotelephone?

a) Calling all stations, b) Charlie Quebec, c) Alpha Alpha, d) Kilo.

4) Radio station logs involving communications incident to a disaster shall be retained by the station licensee for a period of:

a) 4 years from date of entry, b) 3 years from date of entry, c) 2 years from date of entry, d) 1 year from date of entry.

5) You are underway in the Gulf of Mexico, when you hear a distress message over the VHF radio. The position of the sender is about 20 miles south of Galveston, TX, and you are about 80 miles ESE of Galveston. What action should you take?

a) Immediately acknowledge receipt of the distress message, b) Defer acknowledgement for a short interval so that a coast station may acknowledge receipt, c) Do not acknowledge receipt until other ships nearer to the distress have acknowledged, d) Do not acknowledge receipt because you are too far away to take action.

6) According to the Vessel Bridge to Bridge Radiotelephone Act, which is NOT required in the radiotelephone log?

a) Distress and alarm signals transmitted or intercepted, b) Times of beginning, ending, and interrupting watch, c) Routine navigational traffic, d) Details of installations, service, or repair work.

7) According to the Vessel Bridge-to-Bridge Radiotelephone Act, your record of use of the radiotelephone is required to contain:

a) A record of all routine calls, b) A record of your transmissions only, c) The home address of the vessel's master or owner, d) The substance of all distress calls and messages.

8) Which of the following documents would list all the lifesaving equipment required for a vessel?

a) Certificate of Inspection, b) American Bureau of Shipping Classification Certificate, c) International Convention for the Safety of Life at Sea Certificate, d) Certificate of Registry.

9) Which of the following is the required location of the main operation position of the radiotelephone station?

a) On the bridge or wheelhouse, b) In a separate radio compartment, c) Adjacent the main power source, d) As high as possible on the vessel.

10) Which of the following is considered primary lifesaving equipment?

a) Life preservers, b) Lifeboats, c) Ring life buoys, d) Personal flotation devices.

11) CG approved buoyant work vests are considered to be items of safety equipment and may be worn by members of the crew:

a) In lieu of life preservers during fire drills, b) In lieu of life preservers during boat drills, c) In lieu of life preservers during an actual emergency, d) When working near or over the water under favorable working conditions.

12) The lifesaving equipment on all vessels shall be:

a) Inspected weekly, b) Worn at all times, c) Readily accessible, d) Tested yearly.

13) A life line must be connected to the liferaft:

a) At the bow, b) At the stern, c) In the middle, d) All around.

14) You are required to maintain a continuous listening watch on channel:

a) 6 (156.3 MHz), b) 12 (156.6 MHz), c) 14 (156.7 MHz), d) 16 (156.8 MHz).

15) Which statement is true concerning the placard entitled "Discharge of Oil Prohibited?"

a) It is required on all vessels, b) It may be located in a conspicuous place on the bridge, c) It may be located at the bilge and ballast pump control station, d) All of the above.

16) The oil transfer procedures aboard a tanker transferring oil are NOT required to contain:

a) The name of the person designated as the person in charge of transfer, b) A line diagram of the vessel's oil transfer piping, c) Special procedures for topping off tanks, d) A description of the deck discharge containment system.

17) The transfer procedures for oil products are required to be posted:

a) In the pilothouse, b) In the officer's lounge, c) In the upper pumproom flat, d) Where they can be easily seen or readily available.

18) All towing vessels of 26 feet or over in length are required to carry which of the following items?

a) At least two lifeboats, b) A radiotelephone, c) A loran receiver, d) None of the above.

19) Which vessel would NOT be required to have a radiotelephone?

a) A 43-foot vessel engaged in towing, b) A dredge operating in a channel, c) A vessel of 150 gross tons carrying 50 passengers for hire, d) A 200 gross ton private yacht.

20) The "Vessel Bridge-to-Bridge Radiotelephone Act" applies to:

a) Every towing vessel of 16 feet or over in length while navigating, b) Every vessel of 50 gross tons and upward carrying one or more persons for hire, c) All aircraft operating on the water, d) Every power-driven vessel of 300 gross tons and upward while navigating.

⚓

1) A green signal flashing in the air from a parachute, about 300 feet above the water, would indicate that a submarine:

a) Has fired a torpedo during a drill, b) Will be coming to the surface, c) Is on the bottom in distress, d) Is in distress and will try to surface.

2) Which letter signal, when made by sound, may only be made in compliance with the International Rules of the Road?

a) D, b) F, c) Q, d) U.

3) Which single-letter sound signal may only be made in compliance with the Rules of the Road?

a) D, b) E, c) S, d) All of the above.

4) What VHF channel does the Coast Guard use to broadcast routine weather reports?

a) 13 or 14, b) 16 or 17, c) 21 or 22, d) 44 or 45.

5) If you wish to transmit a message by voice concerning the safety of navigation, you would preface it by the word:

a) Mayday, b) Pan, c) Securite, d) Safety.

6) The radiotelephone safety message urgently concerned with safety of a person would be prefixed by the word:

a) Mayday, b) Pan, c) Safety, d) Interco.

7) The VHF radiotelephone frequency designated to be used only to transmit or receive information pertaining to the safe navigation of vessels is:

a) 156.8 MHz (channel 16), b) 156.7 MHz (channel 14), c) 156.65 MHz (channel 13), d) 156.6 MHz (channel 12).

8) Your vessel has been damaged and is taking on water, but you do not require immediate assistance. Which of the following radiotelephone signals would you use to preface a message advising other vessels of your situation?

a) Mayday-Mayday-Mayday, b) Pan-Pan-Pan, c) Securite-Securite-Securite, d) SOS-SOS-SOS.

9) What frequency has the FCC designated for the use of bridge-to-bridge radiotelephone stations?

a) 156.275 MHz channel 65, b) 156.65 MHz channel 13, c) 157.00 MHz channel 28, d) 157.00 MHz channel 20.

10) Channel 13 (156.65 MHz), the designated bridge-to-bridge channel, may NOT be used for which of the following?

a) To exchange navigational information between vessels, b) To exchange navigational information between vessel and a shore station, c) To conduct necessary tests, d) To exchange operating schedules with company dispatcher.

11) The "Vessel Bridge-to-Bridge Radiotelephone Act" establishes the frequency for bridge-to-bridge communications as 156.65 MHZ or channel:

a) 12, b) 13, c) 14, d) 16.

12) You see two red lights in a vertical line at a storm warning display station. This indicates forecasted winds as high as:

a) 25 knots, b) 33 knots, c) 47 knots, d) 63 knots.

13) Which of the following Weather Bureau day storm signals indicates a hurricane warning?

a) Two square flags, red with black center, one above the other, b) One red pennant, c) One square flag, red with black center, d) Two red pennants, one above the other.

14) As specified by the Bridge-to-Bridge Radiotelephone Act, after January 1, 1974, the maximum power of all transmitters used shall be not more than:

a) 25 watts, b) 50 watts, c) 75 watts, d) 100 watts.

15) When using VHF channel 16 (156.8MHz) or 2182 KHz, and you need help, but are not in danger, you should use the urgent signal:

a) "ASSISTANCE NEEDED", b) "PAN", c) "MAYDAY", d) "SE-CURITE".

16) Which of the following Weather Bureau storm signals indicates a gale warning?

a) Two square flags, red with black centers, one above the other, b) One red pennant, c) Two red pennants, one above the other, d) None of the above.

17) Two red pennants being shown at a storm warning display station would indicate a:

a) Small craft warning, b) Gale warning, c) Storm warning, d) Hurricane warning.

18) If you are on the beach and are signalling to a small boat in distress that your present location is dangerous and they should land to the left, you would:

a) Fire a green star to the left, b) Send the letter K by light and point to the left, c) Place an orange signal to your left as you signal with a white light, d) Send the code signal S followed by L.

19) A small craft advisory signal to be shown at night at a storm warning display station of the U. S. is:

a) One red light, b) Two red lights, c) A red light over a white light, d) A white light over a red light.

20) Which should be the storm warning signal which indicates a gale warning when displayed at night?

a) A white light over a red light, b) Two white lights in a vertical line, c) A red light over a white light, d) Three red lights in a vertical line.

21) If you see a red light over a white light at a storm warning display station, the meaning is:

a) Hurricane warning, b) Gale warning, c) Small craft warning, d) Storm warning.

22) The signal employed in connection with the use of shore lifesaving apparatus to signify in general, "affirmative" is:

a) Vertical motion of the arms, b) Code signal "C" sent by light or sound signaling apparatus, c) Firing of a red star signal, d) None of the above.

⚓

1) A vessel having continuous closely spaced transverse strength members is _____

a) longitudinally framed, b) transersely framed, c) cellular framed, d) web framed

2) A vessel aground may have negative GM since the_____.

a) decrease in KM is equal to the loss of draft, b) virtual rise of G is directly proportional to the remaining draft, c) lost buoyancy method is used to calculate KM and KB is reduced, c) displacement lost acts at the point where the ship is aground.

3) When considering a vessel's stability, which spaces in a general cargo vessel are the BEST locations for the carriage of bulk grain?

a) Deep tanks, b) Lower holds, c) Lower holds at the ends of the vessel, d) Tween-decks.

4) Lighter longitudinal stiffening frames on the vessel's side plating are called_____.

a) stringers, b) side frames, c) side stiffeners, d) intercostals

5) The trim and stability booklet must be approved by the _____.

a) International Maritime Organization, b) National Cargo Bureau, c) Society of Naval Architects and Marine Engineers, d) United States Coast Guard

6) When the period of beam seas equals the natural rolling period of a vessel, which of the following will MOST likely occur?

a) Excessive pitching, b) Excessive yawing, c) Excessive rolling, d) No change should be evident

7) Reinforcing frames attached to a bulkhead on a vessel are called _____.

a) side longitudinals, b) intercostals, c) stiffeners, d) brackets

8) Beams are cambered to _____.

a) increase their strength, b) provide drainage from the decks, c) relieve deck stress, d) All of the above

9) The deck beam brackets of a transversely framed vessel resist _____.

a) hogging stresses, b) sagging stresses, c) racking stresses, d) shearing stresses

10) Which of the following statements about a vessel's stability while drydocking is TRUE?

a) Every ton of weight bearing on the blocks acts as if a ton of weight was removed at keel level, b) When the ship touches the blocks, the beam for stability purposes, increases to the beam of the drydock, c) The stability of the vessel increases as a dock is pumped out due to the support of the keel blocks, d) As the dock begins to support the weight of the vessel, stability calculations are based on the ship and dock as a single unit.

11) A continual worsening of the list or trim indicates _____.

a) negative GM, b) progressive flooding, c) structural failure, d) an immediate need to ballast

12) Concentrated heavy loads are involved in loading a LASH vessel. Which of the following does not require close attention due to such loads while working cargo?

a) GM - available and required, b) Longitudinal stress numerals. c) Tons per inch immersion numeral, d) Draft

13) Horizontal transverse motion of a vessel is known as _____.

a) pitch, b) surge, c) sway, d) heave

14) The horizontal port or starboard movement of a vessel is called _____.

a) yaw, b) sway, c) surge, d) heave

15) The period of roll is the time difference between _____.

a) zero inclination to full inclination on one side, b) full inclination on one side to full inclination on the other side, c) full inclination on one side to the next full inclination on the same side, d) zero inclination to the next zero inclination.

16) When the wave period and the apparent rolling period are the same _____.

a) synchronous rolling occurs, b) roll period decreases, c) roll period increases, d) roll amplitude is dampened.

17) Rolling is angular motion of the vessel about what axis?

a) Longitudinal, b) Transverse, c) Vertical, d) Centerline.

18) The vertical motion of a floating vessel is known as _____.

a) surge, b) sway, c) heave, d) pitch.

19) Pitching is angular motion of the vessel about what axis?

a) Longitudinal, b) Transverse, c) Vertical, d) Centerline.

20) Angular motion about the longitudinal axis of a vessel is known as _____.

a) pitch, b) surge, c) sway, d) roll.

⚓

DISTRESS

1) C
2) D
3) D
4) D
5) D
6) B
7) A
8) A
9) C
10) B
11) C
12) D
13) C
14) A
15) D
16) D
17) A
18) D
19) C
20) B
21) B
22) D

FIRE

1) A
2) C
3) D
4) C
5) C
6) A
7) D
8) A
9) C
10) B
11) D
12) C
13) D
14) B
15) B
16) C
17) B
18) B
19) C
20) C
21) C
22) D

FIRST AID

1) B
2) C
3) C
4) D
5) A
6) A
7) B
8) A
9) D
10) C
11) B
12) B
13) C
14) B
15) C
16) A
17) C
18) D
19) B
20) D
21) C
22) B

POLLUTION

1) D
2) A
3) C
4) C
5) C
6) A
7) A
8) B
9) D
10) D
11) C
12) D
13) C
14) C
15) D
16) D
17) C
18) A
19) B
20) A
21) A

RULES & REGS

1) D
2) D
3) B
4) B
5) B
6) D
7) D
8) A
9) A
10) B
11) D
12) C
13) D
14) D
15) C
16) A
17) D
18) B
19) D
20) D

SIGNALING

1) D
2) A
3) D
4) C
5) C
6) B
7) C
8) B
9) B
10) D
11) B
12) D
13) A
14) A
15) B
16) C
17) B
18) D
19) B
20) A
21) C
22) A

STABILITY

1) B
2) D
3) A
4) A
5) D
6) C
7) C
8) B
9) C
10) A
11) B
12) C
13) C
14) B
15) C
16) A
17) A
18) C
19) D
20) D

The sail endorsement is required for Masters carrying passengers for hire on sailing craft. This includes auxiliary sail boats. You will need to document one year (360 days) experience on sailing craft of one type or another. Most offices do not require the endorsement with Six Pacs. Check.

If you have any sailing experience at all here are some of their sail endorsement questions to insult your intelligence and give you a feel for the CG test questions.

1) A jibe:

a) Should be avoided, b) Moves the vessel's bow through the wind's eye, c) Moves the vessels stern through the wind's eye, d) Any of the above.

2) One reason to purposefully place your vessel in irons is to:

a) Prepare to come about, b) To reef, c) To rest, d) To set your wind vane.

3) Two very basic maneuvers in sailing are:

a) Reefing and furling underway, b) Reaching and close hauled, c) Running and yawing, d) jibing and tacking.

4) When the main boom is over the port side, your vessel is on a:

a) Starboard tack, b) Port tack, c) Run, d) Reach.

5) When sailing to windward the three components of the wind pressure are:

a) Windward, heeling and leeway, b) Leeway, windward and astern, c) Quartering, astern and reaching, d) Heeling, sideways and forward.

6) When reaching, the apparent wind is coming from:

a) One side, b) The stern, c) The bow, d) The quarter

7) The two types of sailboat hulls are:

a) Finning and displacement, b) Displacement and planing, c) Planing and furrowing, d) Furrowing and displacement.

8) To avoid placing your vessel in irons you should:

a) Sail well off the wind, b) Sail close hauled, c) Sail fast before coming about, d) Jibe before coming about.

9) The purpose of the keel is to:

a) Allow the craft to jibe without adverse affects, b) To allow the vessel to sail close hauled, c) To keep leeway to a minimum, d) To keep the affect of the apparent wind to a minimum.

10) A tiller:

a) Operates exactly the same as a helm, b) Operates opposite of a helm, c) Stabilizes the keel bolts in rough weather, d) Can substitute for a boom crutch underway in an emergency.

11) Spars are used to:

a) Extend the sails, b) Hold the lifelines suspended over the dinghy davits, c) Secure the pitchpoles, d) Stabilize the boom crutch.

12) Running rigging is used to:

a) Hold the masts in position, b) To adjust the chainplates, c) To secure the anchor to the chain when anchoring, d) Raise and lower sails.

13) Standing rigging:

a) Is secured to the chainplates, b) Is secured to the mast, c) Stabilizes the mast, d) All of the above.

14) Which two below are running rigging?

a) Backstays and headstays, b) Halyards and sheets, c) Winches and cleats, d) Lines and sheaves.

15) Which of the following is not a type of sailboat?

a) Sloop, b) Ketch, c) Gaff, d) Schooner.

16) Almost all sails today are made of:

a) Cotton, b) Polypropylene, c) Dacron, d) Nylon.

17) The three basic points in sailing are:

a) Reaching, beating and jibing, b) Wing and wing, running, down-winding, c) Pointing, close hauled and reaching, d) Beating, running and reaching.

18) A large jib could contribute:

a) As much lift as the staysail, b) As much lift as the mainsail, b) Less lift than the mainsail, d) As much lift as any mizzen.

19) Running could be:

a) Sailing down wind, b) Sailing wing and wing, c) Sailing before the wind, d) Any of the above.

20) The jib provides its own lift to windward and:

a) Helps funnel wind across the leeward side of the mainsail, b) Helps funnel wind across the windward surface of the mainsail, c) Helps to prevent funneling of the wind across the leeward side of the mainsail, d) Helps dampen the wind across the bow when jibing.

ANSWERS

1) C, 2) B, 3) D, 4) A, 5) D, 6) A, 7) B, 8) C, 9) C, 10) B, 11) A, 12) D, 13) D, 14) B, 15) C, 16) C, 17) D, 18) B, 19) D, 20) A.

When overtaking, the overtaking vessel is always the give-way craft.

Your license must be renewed every five years if only to prove you're still warm. Here's the bad news. It's going to start costing for renewals **and** for originals. How do you renew? Same old application only now you must either document a year's sea time (360 days-they can't count) **OR** take an open book test which they will mail out to you, but start early; maybe three months before expiration. You must score 90% on the renewal and if you miss any they send it back, indicating your errors and you pick a new answer for the ones missed. Then you send it back. Maybe three weeks later you get another answer saying you still missed numbers 9, 16 and 34. Would you please pick new answers for those. And so on. It's a time eater, so once again, start early. Relax, so far there's no limit on how many times you miss something. And once you get this license, never let it lapse. If you do, you must start all over. I don't care if you do become a university professor teaching Underwater Basket Weaving...some day you'll want that ticket again. Renewing is too easy.

The Rules section in this book is an excellent study guide for the renewal exam, or even the extras you can order from the back of the book. The way things change you might need a new edition, but call and we'll straighten you out with the lastest poop. Easy number to remember. 1-800-SEA TEST.

If you have been working in a closely allied field, such as shipyard, drydock or instructing in seamanship and related skills, the CG will evaluate that time and allow portions of it as creditable sea experience.

If it's convenient, write the Coast Guard when your license is about three months from expiration. Like all correspondence to the CG, keep it short. Ask in a max of three short sentences if it wouldn't be possible to mail you the exam because you're so busy working your plantation.

For renewal **and** original licenses you will have to show a valid CPR certificate granted within a year of your application and a new dope test. They will also require a new physical exam, but it is generally limited to a colorblind check. See your local optometrist. No need to spend the big bucks on an ophthalmologist unless it's time you went in to have the old glaucoma test anyway. I know, I know, colorblindness is hereditary and not acquired. Once you test okay it stays that way, but just try to tell the CG that.

You can document your own time on your own vessel for anything less than 200 gross tons. Going for anything over 100 tons means added requirements and tests. Radar plotting certification, approved fire fighting school, AB card, and Z card and the list is growing by the day. Every bureaucrat in the country is cashing in on the license.

There is one nice note. It is now much less complicated to move up the command ladder. With careful planning, a near-hobby of running a Six Pac operation can be turned into a mate's position on a 500 ton ocean's route in a very short time. With more time and sea service **plus appropriate exams** it is amazing how fast one can move up the career ladder to mates' and masters' tickets. To make head-honcho on an ocean's craft of 1600 tons isn't that difficult. The term "Oceans" infers *any* oceans, i.e. unlimited as to area of operation.

⇩ ⬇ ⇩ ⬇ ⇩ ⬇ ⬇ ⇩

⸕FREE OFFER⸕
The book you are reading is a technical teaching volume and like all such volumes, subject to change without notice and probably will. There are license, quiz updates and changes constantly in motion. Even some errata. Like, who doesn't make mistakes? Drop a self-addressed stamped envelope in the mail to Charters West and we will send you an updated errata sheet. This is a list of quiz answer changes (yes, they do change) errors, typos and other oddities brought to our attention since this issue was published. But, it's a postage stamp gamble. Maybe you will receive nothing as they aren't available yet. Thus, stand advised your envelope might not get back to you for a month, or even longer...or maybe next week. Cheap gamble.

⚓

THE COURSE PLOTTER

The following pages of diagrams and instructions are devoted to teaching you to use the course plotter. If you have completed a basic boating class with the U.S. Power Squadron or the Coast Guard Auxiliary you already know how to use it. If you hold a rank of AP in the Power Squadron, you're wasting your time on this entire section of plotting; if you remember it all.

And forget about parallel rules. This will work faster and better and more accurate. Trust me.

The top of a chart represents north; true north. The bottom is south, to the right is east and to the left is west. These terms are seldom used when plotting. North is 000° or 360°. East is 090° and west is 270°. Everything in between also has a **three digit** number.

Look at the circles on the next page. They're numbered -in the center- #1 through #6. Examine the direction of the arrows. The direction of the first arrow falls between 000° and 090°. If you were moving across a chart, your direction would be indicated by a more exact number. Maybe something like 040° or 045°.

Exactness at this point isn't necessary. We're merely looking for rough estimates. Glancing at #2, estimate the direction. 185° or even 190°? Write down your estimates for 3 through 6 before going on.

Number 3 would be someone on a course of around 280°. Number 4 would be close to 140°. Number 5 is a course line of about 080° and #6 about 240°. Don't go any further until you've established why the above answers are within rough approximations. If you missed, go do it again. Page 162 has nine more of like kind except the circles and numbers are missing. Pretend this page is a chart - north at the top- and see how close you can come by **estimating** these course lines. Looking at the first one it appears to be on a heading of less than north or 360°. Maybe 350° or 340°? Close enough for now.

Can you see that #2 is to the right of straight up or 000°? Maybe 010°? And doesn't #3 appear to be slightly greater than 090°? Perhaps 100° or 110°? Try to **estimate** the remaining six within 25° of the answers below. The object is to be within the correct quadrant.

ANSWERS

4) 245°, 5) 190°, 6) 155°, 7) 050°, 8) 290°, 9) 080°.

PSSSST! HEY BUDDY

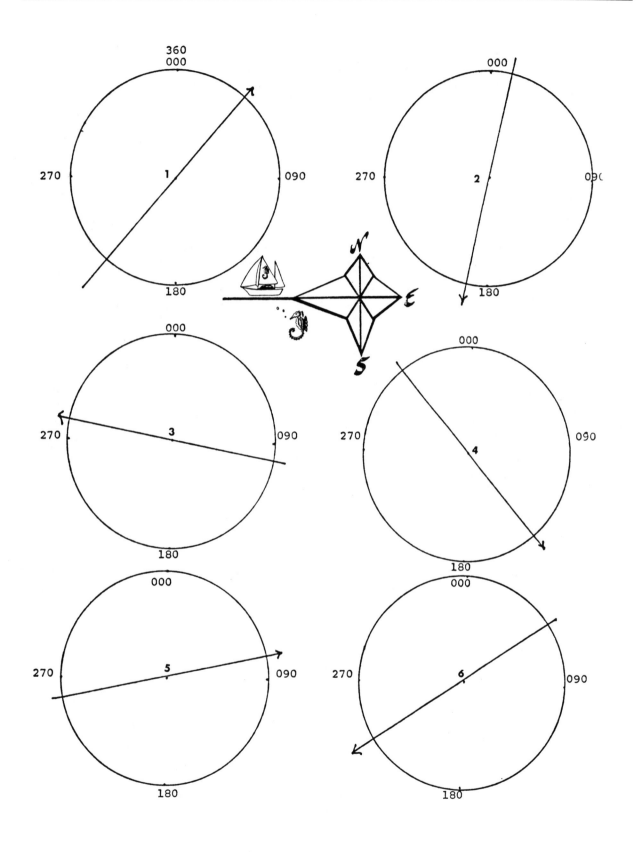

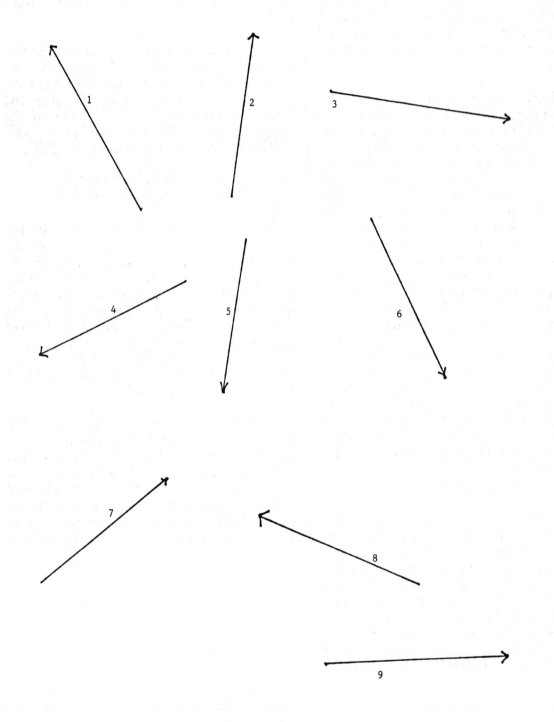

Now for the fun part. You'll need our big book chart. Flatten out a copy and grab your course plotter. **Don't put the course plotter on the chart** yet. You need to make an estimate. Estimate the course if you were travelling from the West Point Light to the Bunny Isle Light. Someplace between 000° and 090°, right? **Remember that estimate.** If you don't understand the estimate, go back until you **do** get it.

Now look at page 165 which has part of the course plotter smeared all over it. 1) Notice that the first **line** of the plotter leads from West Point Light to Bunny Isle Light. 2) Find that little circle near the bottom center of the course plotter. Line it up on any longitude line that's handy. Careful. Keep the top line of the plotter lined up on the two lights. 3) Since the plotter is plastic, you can see through it. Notice the longitude line over which you have centered the little circle (target). Follow that longitude line "up" to the top of the **outer** scale. The plotter is transparent so look right through it at the longitude line. The longitude line intersects two numbers on the outer scale. Okay, what's the course? You have two choices. 252° or 072°. **Wait!** What was that **estimate** you made a minute ago? Someplace between 000° and 090°. H-m-m-m. Must be 072° from the West Point Light to Bunny Isle Light. Sends a ripple right though the stomach, doesn't it? Let's try the next one on page 166.

This time we're heading from Bunny Isle Light to the Santa Barbara Light. Take the top line of your course plotter and arrange it so it cuts through Bunny Isle Light and the Santa Barbara Light. Now jiggle your plotter around until the target intersects that longitude line running down the middle of the page. With the bottom line intersecting the two lights and the target over the...**OH GOD!** We forgot to estimate the course first. Without an estimate, we might read the wrong number on the outer scale of the course plotter winding up with a reciprocal course and fail the charting exam. Estimate, estimate, quick. Ah, greater than 270° and less than 360°. Now, where were we?

Let's see. Top line of course plotter intersecting both lights. Target over the handiest longitude line. Look through the course plotter at the longitude line and follow it **straight up** to the top of the course plotter. What'll you have? 305° or 125°? Ah! A true course of 305°.

WAIT - DON'T TOUCH THE COURSE PLOTTER

What if you wanted to travel in the opposite direction? You know, from the Santa Barbara Light to Bunny Isle Light -if for no other reason than to find out if what they say about that island is really true. Make your estimate. Between 090° and 180°? Good. Now look again at the two choices on the outer scale. The top one is 305°, but the bottom one is 125°. Guess what the course back to Bunny Isle Light is? Another ripple, huh?

One more item before moving on. We used the top line of the course plotter on that last one. What would happen if you made a mistake and used the bottom one of some line in the middle of the plotter? Nothing. You would get the same answer. The numerous lines are so you can choose one that fits over a nearby longitude line.

Time to try the third smeared up page; page 167.

Using the bottom line of the plotter we line up Bunny Isle Light and Cavern Point Light. On this one we *could use* a longitude line to read the true course like we have with the last two. However, sometimes on true courses that come close to north or south it's difficult to find a handy longitude line. This will happen to you eventually, so listen up.

This time put the plotter target over the latitude line then follow that latitude line to your left towards the two numbers on the **lower scale**. If you were going from Bunny Isle Light to Cavern Point Light the course would seem to be closer to 218° than anything else. If you were making a wiser choice and heading back for Bunny Isle from Cavern Point, then the course would be 038°. Thus, the inner scale is for reading from latitude lines and the outer scale for reading from longitude lines. **LONG**itude lines from the **LONG**er outer scale.

The Coast Guard will want you to plot your courses to within the nearest degree so accuracy is a must. With this in mind, let's have a good lesson here. What's wrong with that last course line? Is it because the latitude line didn't *exactly* hit the 218° and 038° marks? Well, yeah, but there's something else more important here than is way out of kilter. Maybe you already spotted it.

Uh-huh, the bottom line of the course plotter on page 167 doesn't *really* line up on the light at Cavern Point. See? It's a little bit off the dot. Screws up the whole problem. The point is; the Coast Guard problems can take anything from five to fifteen minutes to solve. If your first step had a one or two degree error all the rest of your work would be in vain. Sob! Take your time, double check and look at

everything carefully.

Try these for practice. Remember to estimate your course lines first, then go for the plotter.

1) Indicate the course from Bunny Isle Light to Cavern Point Light.

2) Find the course from Cavern Point Light to West Point Light.

3) What's the course from Brockway Point Light to the Santa Barbara Fl G Bell Buoy?

4) Try going from Spa Rock Light to West Point Light.

5) How about Bunny Isle Light to the Santa Barbara Bell Buoy?

6) How about a true course from Spa Rock Light to Cavern Point Light?

ANSWERS

1) 218°, 2) 275°, 3) 046°, 4) 147°, 5) 310°, 6) 123°

⚓

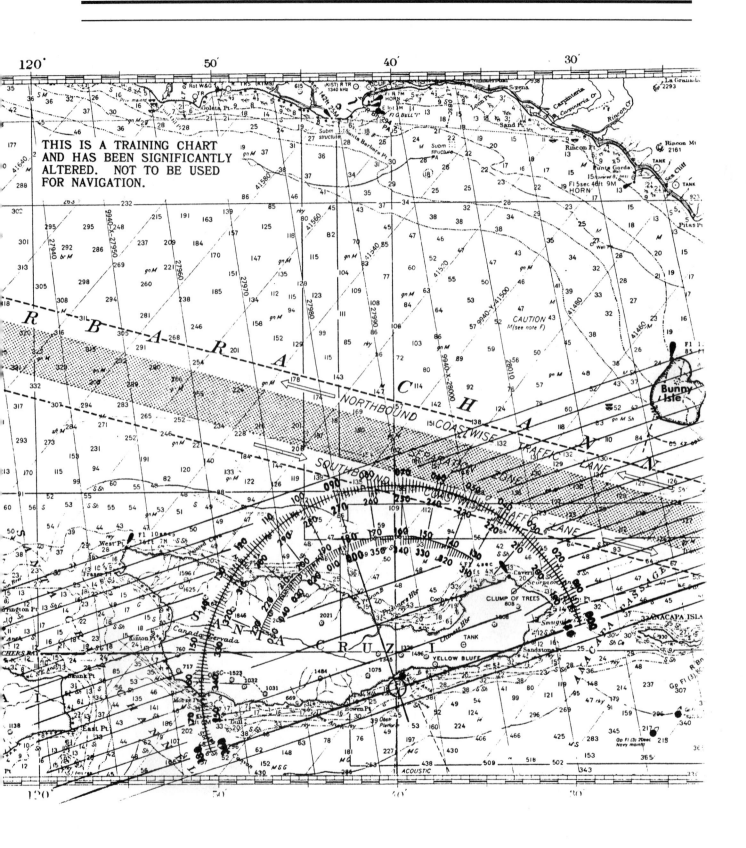

THIS IS A TRAINING CHART
AND HAS BEEN SIGNIFICANTLY
ALTERED.   NOT TO BE USED
FOR NAVIGATION.

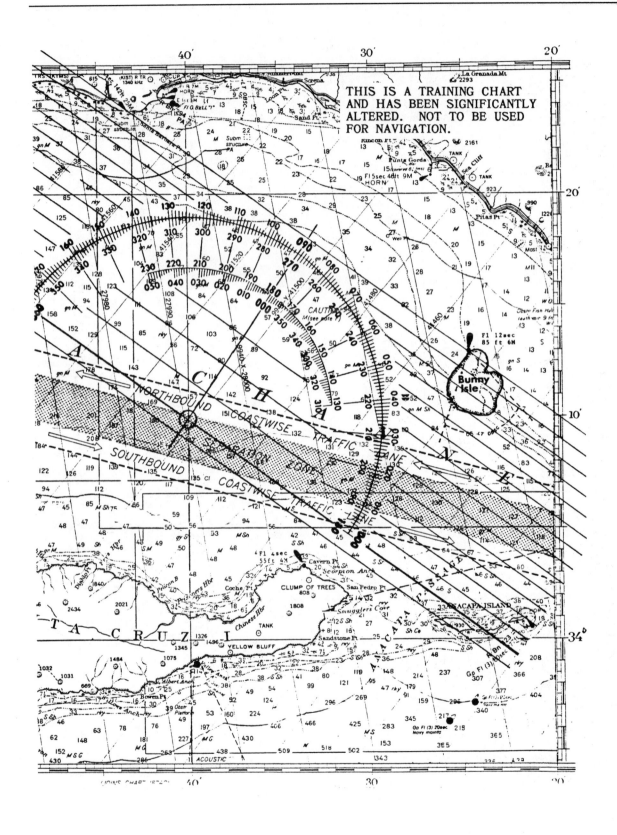

THIS IS A TRAINING CHART
AND HAS BEEN SIGNIFICANTLY
ALTERED.   NOT TO BE USED
FOR NAVIGATION.

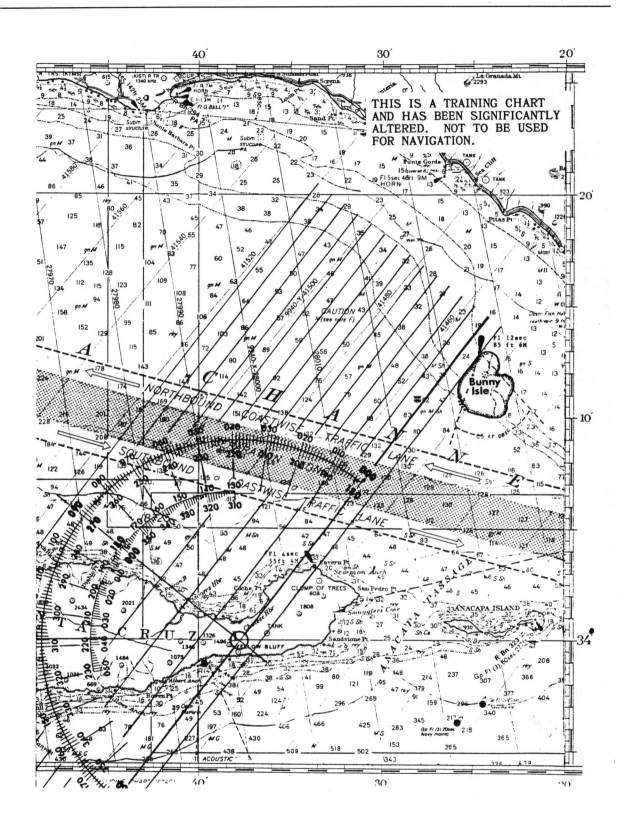

THIS IS A TRAINING CHART
AND HAS BEEN SIGNIFICANTLY
ALTERED.   NOT TO BE USED
FOR NAVIGATION.

LATITUDE AND LONGITUDE

Now for the simple stuff. This is not to say that "positioning" is unimportant. If you have been bobbing around out there for the minimum required year then you've been exposed to charts and should be aware we are located in latitude north and longitude west. Use the abbreviated Mercator world map on page 169 to confirm this and other facts as we breeze through this thing. In doing so, take note that "lat is flat". Those are the lines running horizontally across the page. The longitude lines are the ones running up and down which actually converge on the north and south poles. But, you knew that.

Latitude is always listed first in calling out a position. Latitude numbering starts from the equator and goes "up" and "down" numerically; thus you are counting along what is called "the latitude scale".

In other words, it you go north from the equator for one degree, you are in latitude 1° north. If you go south of the equator for one degree, then you're 1° south. Santa Barbara, California is about 34° north. Ka Lae (South Point) on the big island of Hawaii, is a slight bit less than 19° north latitude ranking as the southern most point in the U.S. Point Barrow, Alaska is a shade less than 72° north, making it the northern most point in the U.S. If it helps, Sydney is about 34° **south** of the equator.

I'll never know how they worked it out, but even the Russians agree that longitude counting starts at Greenwich, England. (The "w" is silent). From Greenwich, which is 0° longitude, the counting on the longitude **scale** -up at the top and along the bottom of a chart- goes east and west, but recall the **lines** are running north and south.

Starting from Greenwich working west, the numbers increase and are called "longitude west". Eventually, you get across the Atlantic and hit New York. New York is about 74° west longitude. Coming across the U.S., you hit Santa Barbara which is about 120° west longitude. Catch a plane heading across the Pacific to Hawaii and you land in Honolulu which is about 158° west longitude.

West longitude stops at 180° which is neither east nor west. The 180° line is the half-way point. Cross that line and you are in **east** longitude. From this point, you have to count backwards, (179° east, 178° east, 177° east, etc.) until you reach Greenwich again. On the way, you will hit an island in the Alaskan Aleutian Island chain called Attu. Attu is about 176° east longitude which means Alaska is the easterly most state in the U.S! Well, that's more easterly than Maine. Technically, Alaska is the northern most, western most and eastern most state in the U.S. Hawaii is the southern most.

Yards are broken down in feet. Feet break into inches. Degrees of latitude and longitude break down into "minutes". Not minutes in time, but minutes of arc. An arc is part of a circle. A closer fix on Santa Barbara Harbor would read latitude 34° 24.2' north, longitude 119° 41.6' west. That reads: Thirty-four degrees twenty-four and two-tenths minutes north and one hundred nineteen degrees forty-one and six-tenths minutes west.

The Coast Guard will want latitude and longitude to the nearest **tenth** of a minute of arc. There are sixty minutes to a degree, whether it's latitude or longitude. After looking over the world map on page 170 try writing down the positions labeled "A" through "H", then the positions labeled 1 through 10 on the same page and check you answers against those at the end of page 171.

✠

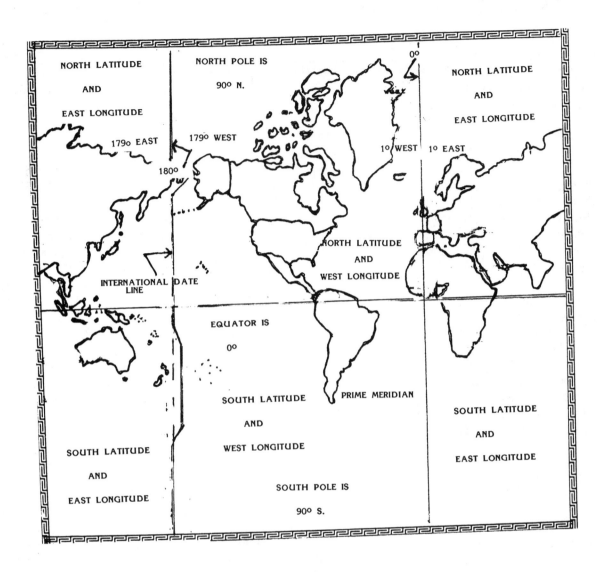

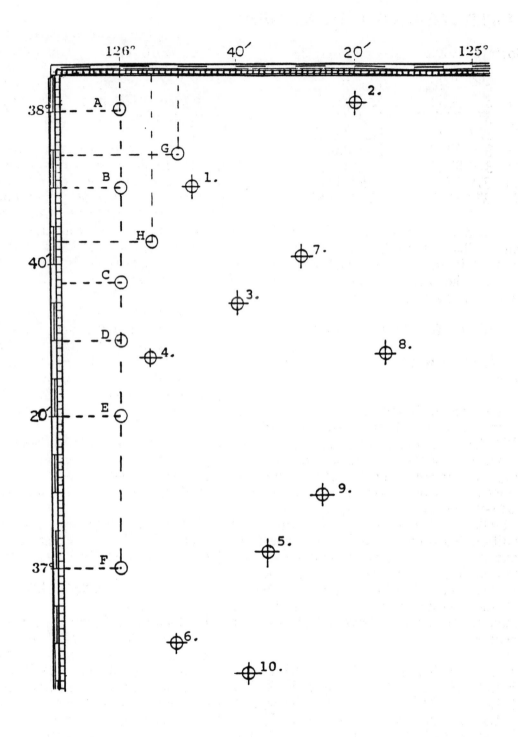

LATITUDE-LONGITUDE ANSWERS

North Latitude   West Longitude

A)	38° 00.0'	126° 00.0'
B)	37° 50.0'	126° 00.0'
C)	37° 37.5'	126° 00.0'
D)	37° 30.0'	126° 00.0'
E)	37° 20.0'	126° 00.0'
F)	37° 00.0'	126° 00.0'
G)	37° 54.2'	125° 50.0'
H)	37° 43.0'	125° 54.8'

Wondering why all the zeros? Use 'em. That's how the CG officer learned to do it in the academy and when he sees you do it he will just naturally assume you know what's you're doing.

Now go for the numbers 1-10.

Notice how the answers below are recorded.

Latitude is listed first. The "N" for north always follows latitude and the "W" for west after the longitude; at least in our hemispheres. Format can become very important when you're trying to impress someone. Develop the habit now. And don't become discouraged if you're off a tenth or two at first. To answer a position question THAT close with the spaces so small is an almost impossible task at first. However, you will get lots of practice if you follow the lesson schemes from start to finish in this volume. Surprising how adept you can become.

1)	Lat 37° 50.0'N	Long 125° 47.9'W
2)	Lat 38° 01.0'N	Long 125° 20.0'W
3)	Lat 37° 34.7'N	Long 125° 40.0'W
4)	Lat 37° 27.6'N	Long 125° 55.0'W
5)	Lat 37° 01.9'N	Long 125° 35.0'W
6)	Lat 36° 50.0'N	Long 125° 51.0'W
7)	Lat 37° 40.8'N	Long 125° 29.2'W
8)	Lat 37° 27.8'N	Long 125° 15.2'W
9)	Lat 37° 09.1'N	Long 125° 26.0'W
10)	Lat 36° 45.8'N	Long 125° 38.5'W

Page 172 is a sampling of cutouts from the book chart. The page demonstrates the conventional use of a pair of dividers to find latitude and longitude on a chart. We;re looking for the position of Spa Rock Light.

Latitude first as per page 172. Spread the dividers so one tip touches the dot representing the light's exact location while the other stretches out to meet the nearest latitude line. Next, very carefully and without moving the redius of the dividers, move it over to the left latitude scale and read it. What do you get? Should be 34° 21.5' N.

Now let's go for longitude. Open the dividers from the Spa Rock Light to the nearest longitude line. In this case, it's the 120° one. Then carefully move the dividers up to the top longitude scale and read your answer. Would you buy 120° 07.7'? Hope so, 'cause that's what I get.

Try a few. Use the textbook chart and try measuring for latitude and longitude of the following places. No fair peeking until you have finished all five.

1) The Bunny Isle Light. 2) Anacapa Island Light. 3) Cavern Point Light. 4) West Point Light. 5) Brockway Point Light.

ANSWERS

1) Bunny Isle Light: Latitude 34° 12.9' N. Longitude 119° 24.7' W.
2) Anacapa Island Light: Latitude 34° 01.0' N. Longitude 119° 21.6' W.
3) Cavern Point Light: Latitude 34° 03.4'N. Longitude 119° 33.6'W.
4) West Point Light: Latitude 34° 04.8 N. Longitude: 119° 54.9' W.
5) Brockway Point Light: Latitude 34° 01.7' N. Longitude 120° 08.7' W.

‡

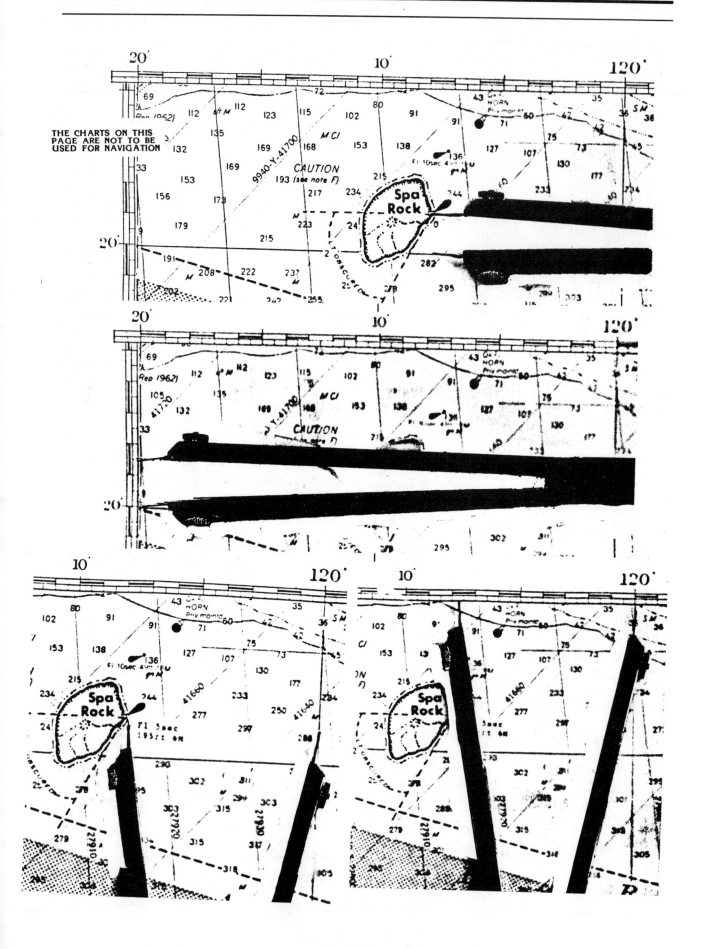

THE CHARTS ON THIS
PAGE ARE NOT TO BE
USED FOR NAVIGATION

PLOTTING

The next ten problems were measured for an easy start to charting. Your real efforts should be aimed at getting to be a fast expert with the course plotter. An excellent second aim would be to get in the habit of keeping concise and methodical notes as you work. If you attain the habit of keeping them organized, looking back to check for errors will become much easier. Don't become discouraged at first with the amount of time spent solving any given problem. It's like typing. Practice will automatically produce speed and accuracy. The solutions are on the next page following #10.

Time to turn some of the chart copies into rags. You **DID** get copies? On all problems, assume 15° east variation.

1) How long would it take to sail from the Santa Barbara Fl G Bell buoy to the West Point Light assuming you were making 15.8 knots? What will be your compass course if your deviation is 4° east on this course?

2) If you left the Santa Barbara Fl G Bell buoy at 0800 making 12.3 knots, what would be your ETA (estimated time of arrival) at the Cavern Point Light? What will be your compass course if the deviation is 3° west?

3) Friends are waiting on Bunny Isle. They're leaving at noon and taking the dancing girls with them. Thus, what is the latest time you can leave the West Point Light making 14.6 knots and drop anchor by Bunny Isle Light by 1200? What will be your compass course with deviation at 1° east?

4) Sail from Spa Rock Light at 1415 to Bunny Isle Light making 6.2 knots with deviation on this course at 3° west. What is the compass course to Bunny Isle Light and what time will you arrive?

5) From Spa Rock Light to Brockway Point Light your deviation is 7° east making 16.8 knots. On the trip back to Spa Rock Light, the deviation will be 7° west. If the speed of your craft is the same in both directions, how long will the round trip take? What are the compass courses each way?

6) Departing Bunny Isle Light at 1015 on a true course of 280° making 13.5 knots, what will be your position at 1235? (Latitude and longitude to the nearest tenth of a minute). Can you see the Spa Rock Light?

7) Departing Brockway Point Light at 1345 on a true course of 052° you take a loran reading at 1713 fixing your position at latitude 34° 20.0' N. and longitude 119° 40.0' W. Are you on course? What was your speed made good?

8) A gusty southeaster is blowing as you depart Cavern Point Light at 2230 en route to Santa Barbara's Fl G Bell Buoy. You are making what you assume to be 11.6 knots. At 2342 your loran indicates a position of latitude 34° 20.0' N and longitude 119° 50.0' W. What was your true course made good and speed made good to 2342 hours? If the wind dies off, what time will you reach the buoy? What will be your compass course if the deviation is 3° west?

9) Departing Cavern Point Light at 1335 for some channel fishing you are on a compass course of 287° with deviation of 4° west making 11.3 knots. At 1440 you stop and fish for 30 minutes before deciding to head for the harbor by Spa Rock Light. What was your true course to the fishing grounds? What was the position you stopped to fish? What were you doing wrong? If the deviation was the same as the former course, what is the compass course to Spa Rock Light? What's your ETA at Spa Rock Light?

10) You are enroute from the Bunny Isle Light to Spa Rock Light departing at 0855 making 13.4 knots. Assume deviation 3° west. One hour and forty-five minutes later you encounter a disabled craft desiring a tow to Santa Barbara. Since you are a licensed skipper you can charge them for this service and spend twenty minutes negotiating and taking their vessel in tow **after** collecting in advance.

Your speed is now reduced to 9.9 knots. At the Santa Barbara Bell Buoy, the harbor master takes your tow which takes another fifteen minutes off your schedule. From there you proceed at your former speed for Spa Rock.

a) What was your compass course from Bunny Isle to Spa Rock?

b) At what time **and** position did you encounter the disabled craft?

c) What was the true course from the disabled craft's position to the Santa Barbara Bell Buoy?

d) How long did it take to tow the craft to Santa Barbara?

e) What was your new ETA at the Spa Rock Light after leaving the tow with the harbor master and resuming your former speed?

ANSWERS

1a) 1hr 26m, b) 193°.   2a) ETA 0945, b) 152°.   3a) Depart at 1011, b) 056°.   4a) 091°, 4b) 2012.   5) 2h 22m, 160°, 354°.   6a) Latitude 34° 18.3'N-Longitude 120° 02.1'W, b) Light is visible as you are only 5.6 miles off the light which has a nominal range of 6 miles.   7a) Yes-right on course, b) Speed=8.7 knots.   8a) Course made good 321°, b) Speed made good 17.9 knots, c) ETA 0026, d) 051°.   9a) 298°, b) Latitude 34° 09.0'N-Longitude 119° 46.3'W., which is the middle of a shipping lane-fishing illegally. Shame!   9c) 294° psc, d) ETA 1705.   10a) 271°, b) 1040-Latitude 34°18.3'N., Longitude 119° 52.3'W, c) 059° d) 1h 07m, e) ETA=1403.

In restricted visibility a lookout must be posted at all times. The man on the helm cannot be considered the lookout.

PLOTTING II - BEARINGS AND FIXES

First, consider the following. Assume you are sitting offshore gazing at a lighthouse. The lighthouse bears, from your boat, 270°; in other words, west. If someone were sitting up in the lighthouse looking at your boat, what would your boat bear **from** the lighthouse?

The opposite direction, right? More appropriately, 090°. Now change the directions. If the lighthouse was bearing 225° what is the bearing from the light house to your vessel? Again, the opposite direction. Subtract 180° from 225° and you get 045°.

The next question is: How did you figure out the true direction? You only have a compass and chart on board. Simple -you aim the boat at the lighthouse and look at the compass. Assume the compass reads 320°. Now we have a T-V-M-D-C problem in which you **start** with the compass direction.

```
T 311
V  13° W from your chart rose.
M 324
D   4° E from your deviation card.
C 320
```

Now you know the true direction is 311°. Therefore, anyone in the lighthouse would look at your boat and say, "He's bearing 131° **from** the lighthouse." You could even pick up your course plotter and draw a bearing line **from** the lighthouse and know you were on that line someplace. Well, maybe you don't know how **far** you are from the lighthouse, but you have what is called a "line of position", (LOP).

If you had two (or even three) LOP's you would have a fix. So look around and find something else you can see which also shows up on your chart.

In fact, that's what the guy on the next page is doing.

First he found a buoy. Aiming his boat at it got took a bearing per steering compass (psc) of 037°. He worked that up to a true bearing of 050° and plotted it on his chart. He then turned the boat (second panel on the same page) towards a light house for a psc of 302°. That worked up to 319° true. The third panel shows the same boat taking a bearing on a rock using the same technique.

He probably could have got away with only two bearings, but just to make sure, he shot three. If one of the bearings had been off a little bit the three LOP's would not have intersected perfectly at the boat's position. Instead, he would have a small triangle. If this happens, pick the middle of the triangle.

The Coast Guard will **generally** only give you two bearings for a fix. They will either tell you the deviation on each bearing or provide you with a deviation table to use on all courses plotted throughout your test.

A fix is always better than a DR. A DR is still only an educated guess based on speed, distance and time. A fix is a more reliable thing. Notice also that the DR's are indicated by a half circle. The fixes are shown by a full circle.

There is also a certain way to label bearing lines. The time of the bearing is written on top of the line. The true bearing is recorded beneath the line.

‡

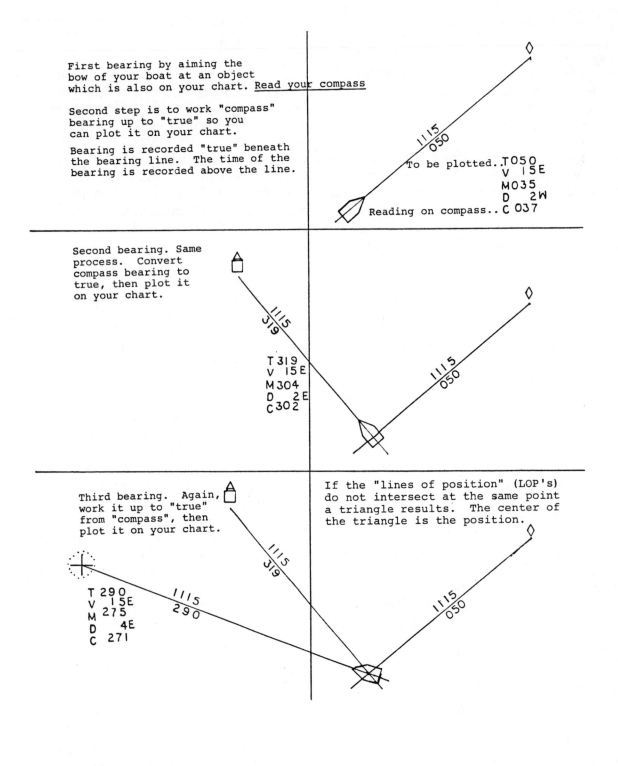

First bearing by aiming the
bow of your boat at an object
which is also on your chart. <u>Read your compass</u>

Second step is to work "compass"
bearing up to "true" so you
can plot it on your chart.

Bearing is recorded "true" beneath
the bearing line. The time of the
bearing is recorded above the line.

To be plotted.. T050
                V 15E
                M035
                D   2W
Reading on compass.. C 037

1115
050

Second bearing. Same
process. Convert
compass bearing to
true, then plot it
on your chart.

1115
319

T 319
V 15E
M 304
D   2E
C 302

1115
050

Third bearing. Again,
work it up to "true"
from "compass", then
plot it on your chart.

T 290
V   15E
M 275
D   4E
C 271

1115
319

1115
290

If the "lines of position" (LOP's)
do not intersect at the same point
a triangle results. The center of
the triangle is the position.

1115
050

This next bit is a variation on the last technique of taking bearings to establish a fix. The CG uses both types in their exams. In this case the boat isn't turned to face the buoy, lighthouse or prominent land mark. Instead, the boat maintains a steady course while the bearings are taken.

Large compasses, as found on military and merchant vessels, come equipped with an object called an azimuth circle. Azimuth means direction. This brass ring fits around the outside of the compass

sightings to true bearings, **the deviation of the ship's heading must be used each time** when working the sighting "up" the T-V-M-D-C ladder to true so it can be plotted. Since deviation is relative to the direction the vessel is travelling, the mere fact someone takes a bearing on a passing object could hardly affect the magnetic characteristics of the ship.

With this in mind, examine the first two problems on the next page. The third problem is for you to work out. **After**

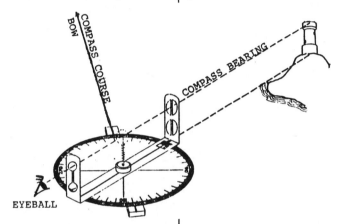

mount and can be revolved back and forth. Two sighting vanes mounted on the detachable ring permit viewing a distant object and checking the bearing simultaneously by glancing down at the compass. On smaller craft, a pelorus is used as indicated in the diagram. The revolving base is set to match the compass course and lined up on the lubber line, that is, the ship's bow. The vane is then pivoted to line up on the any object from which you seek a bearing. The bearing number can be read from the base of the pelorus. An inexpensive plastic version is made by Davis Instruments and can be found in all big chandleries. Handy to have and more fun than a basket of snakes on your ex-wife's front porch.

All of this means that while underway you can take bearings on objects without turning the vessel to face them. The one thing to remember while converting such

you have digested the sketches and worked out the third problem, come back to this page.

In #1, the vessel is on a course of 095° true. At 1055 she takes three bearings. One is almost astern, on an outcrop, another on a buoy and finally a third on a lighted buoy. Each compass bearing is worked up to true then plotted. Note: each bearing is written below the line and the time above the line.

The second panel is the same type with the vessel on a true course of 232° while shooting three objects which are also depicted on the chart. In both of these panels, practice using the course plotter before you try the third panel yourself. And how do you know you're right on the third one? All bearing lines should intersect at the same point.

⚓

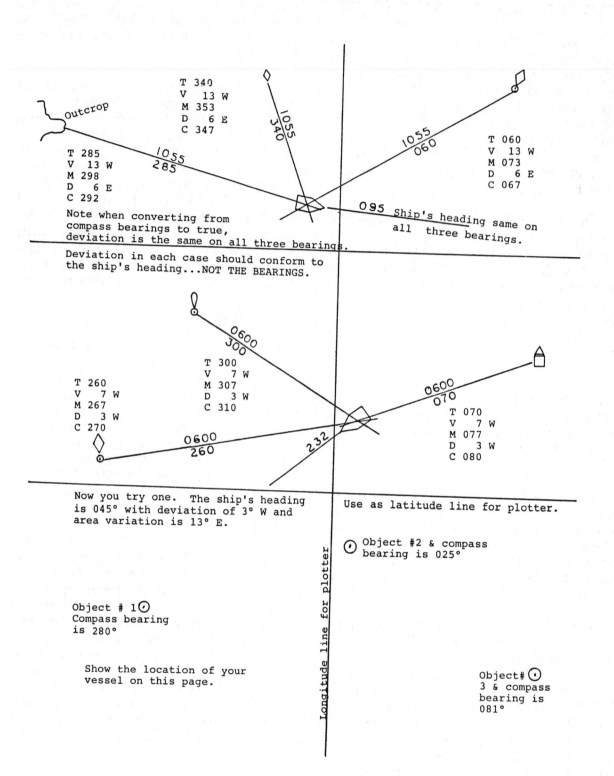

T 340
V 13 W
M 353
D   6 E
C 347

Outcrop

1055
340

1055
060

T 060
V 13 W
M 073
D   6 E
C 067

T 285
V 13 W
M 298
D   6 E
C 292

1055
285

095 Ship's heading same on
        all three bearings.

Note when converting from
compass bearings to true,
deviation is the same on all three bearings.

Deviation in each case should conform to
the ship's heading...NOT THE BEARINGS.

0600
300

T 300
V   7 W
M 307
D   3 W
C 310

T 260
V   7 W
M 267
D   3 W
C 270

0600
070

T 070
V   7 W
M 077
D   3 W
C 080

0600
260

232

Now you try one. The ship's heading
is 045° with deviation of 3° W and
area variation is 13° E.

Use as latitude line for plotter.

Object #2 & compass
bearing is 025°

Longitude line for plotter

Object # 1
Compass bearing
is 280°

Show the location of your
vessel on this page.

Object#
3 & compass
bearing is
081°

PLOTTING III - THE RUNNING FIX

If you romped through the previous exercises with any degree of accuracy the time has come for the Running Fix. A running fix infers there is only one object from which to take a bearing. On an accuracy scale of one to ten the running fix falls someplace around six or seven. Actually, the running fix is better than a DR and not nearly as good as a two or three body fix.

The next page depicts three **separate** running fixes. In #1 the vessel is on a course of 260° true. At 0205 the light ashore yields a bearing of 330° **true**. At 0225, twenty minutes later, the same light shows up as 020°. Basically is a speed-distance-time problem. The distance travelled between the two bearings is 4 miles.

Here's the hard part to understand when working with running fixes. It **doesn't matter how far the course line is plotted from the object you are shooting.** You can take the bearing from any distance off shore.

Notice where the first bearing line intercepts the course line? From that point measure 4 miles along the course line which is the distance you have travelled since the first bearing. Place a small mark on the course line to mark that twenty minute DR.

The next part is tricky. Remember that first bearing line of 330°? You need to "advance" it four miles so it crosses through the 0225 DR. So, take that mark you made on the course line indicating the 0225 DR and draw a 330° line right through that DR mark. Now both of the 330° bearing lines are parallel. That is, the first one at 0205 and the second one we just put though the 0225 DR, are parallel.

Take a close look and see how that "advanced" bearing line intersects the second bearing line of 020°. That's the running fix...or chartwise, it's called the 0225 R Fix.

The second problem is another one of like kind. This time the vessel is on a course of 080°. He takes his first bearing at 2120 and gets 040° true. Thirty minutes later (making 16.2 knots) he takes a second bearing on the same buoy and gets 330°. He marks his 2150 DR which is 8.1 miles (thirty minutes at 16.2 knots) along the course line. Then the 2120 bearing is advanced 8.1 miles **along the course line.** In other words, another 040° line is drawn through the 2150 DR. Where does that advanced bearing intersect the second bearing on the buoy? That's the 2150 R Fix.

The third problem is a repeat exercise. The vessel is on a true course of 060° making 10.6 knots. The first bearing is 110° at 1145. Then, 7.1 miles later the DR is indicated. The second bearing yielded 070° at 1225 and is plotted (true) on the chart. Next, the 1145 bearing of 110° is advanced 7.1 miles which means it will pass right through the 1225 DR. Where this advanced bearing line intersects the second bearing line one finds the 1225 R Fix.

How come all the bearings were given to you true? Well, most likely the CG will give them to you psc requiring you to work them up the T-V-M-D-C ladder to true before they are plotted. Think you can remember that? It's kind of important. If you forget, you will be plotting your bearings by compass producing a triangle the size of the side of an Egyptian pyramid. This will become rather apparent to you in some later exercises we have planned.

⚓

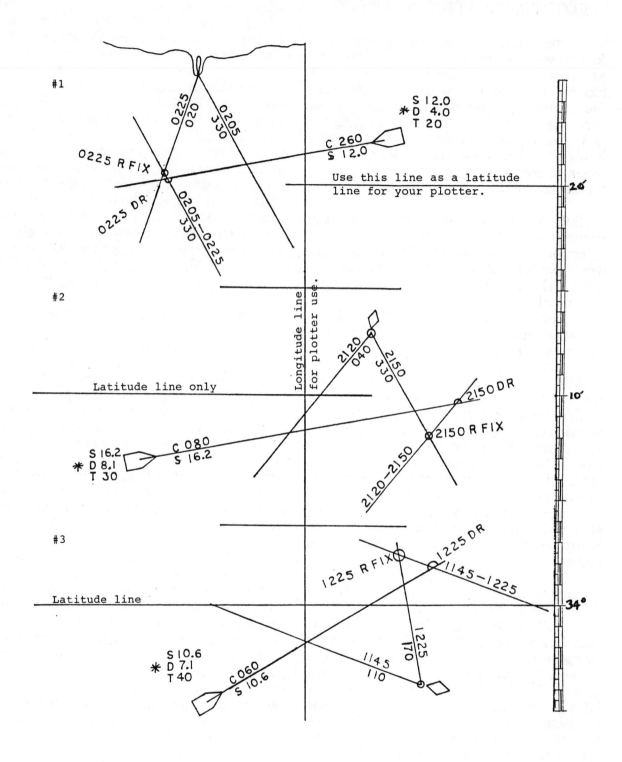

#1

0225
020
0205
330

S 12.0
✳ D 4.0
T 20

C 260
S 12.0

0225 RFIX

Use this line as a latitude
line for your plotter.

20'

0225 DR

0205—0225
330

Longitude line
for plotter use.

#2

2120
040
2150
330

2150 DR

Latitude line only

2150 RFIX

S 16.2
✳ D 8.1
T 30

C 080
S 16.2

2120—2150

10'

#3

1225 RFIX

1225 DR

1145—1225

Latitude line

34°

1225
170

1145
110

S 10.6
✳ D 7.1
T 40

C 060
S 10.6

PLOTTING IV - SET AND DRIFT

Anyone with any sea time knows it doesn't work like that. If there's any wind or the sea is rough, the boat bobs around like a soap dish. Any resemblance to course steered and course made good is pure luck. Formal plotting recognizes this and has a method for compensating. It's called Set and Drift. However, in order to compensate, you must first know the set and drift.

Set is the word used to indicate the **direction** of the current. That is, the direction the current is moving...not the direction from which it is coming, like the wind. Drift is the term used to indicate the **speed** the current is moving. Current can best be described as "all slop". Anything contributing to throwing your boat off course is current. That means wind, waves, tides, or frolicking teenage whales pushing your boat around.

We start by working a simple problem on the next page to get the basics down. We'll proceed as though the page was a chart. Notice the latitude scale on the right side for measuring distance; an important factor in set and drift problems. The two perpendicular lines running across the page are to be used as latitude-longitude lines; obviously for your course plotter.

Departure time is from point "A" at 0800. We're making 12 knots on a course of 315° true. The course line has numbers written across the top and bottom. The one on top is the true course, the one on bottom represents the speed of your boat. That is, the speed you **think** your boat is making. The speed you know you ordinarily make at a given rpm in a bath tub sea. These two facts were left out on your original plotting problems, but you had your hands full without having to worry about labeling. Get used to labeling your problems. Should you come **close** to the

answer the Coast Guard wants and one small error on the chart is making the difference, labeling could be important. The OinC, on a slow day, may ask to see your chart and you can just stand there and smile instead of showing him something that looks like it came out of the city dump. This could be the difference between receiving your license then and there, or returning on another day to start all over again. Think about that.

At 1000 you have presumably arrived at the DR (dead reckoning) point "B" so you check it out with a loran fix or bearings and oops, you're not at point "B" but point "C". Egad! Whales pushing the boat around again. Draw a line **from** "B" to "C". Using the course plotter, check the direction **from "B" to "C"**. You should find it's 270°. That's your **set**.

Since **drift** means "speed" of the water's movement, we now have a speed-distance-time problem and you will be solving for speed. This means you need the time and the distance to solve it. The distance is the length of the line from "B" to "C". From the DR to the Fix. The time is the length of time your vessel has been underway. Well, isn't that the length of time the current has been affecting your boat ever since you left home at 0800?

By measuring, you should find the BC line is four miles. You've been underway for 2h, or 120m. Thus, drift is 2.0 knots. Yep! Just like computing the speed of your boat; take the answer to the nearest tenth.

Set = 270°. Drift = 2.0 knots. Notice how they're written on the set-drift line. Set on top of the line, drift beneath it.

‡

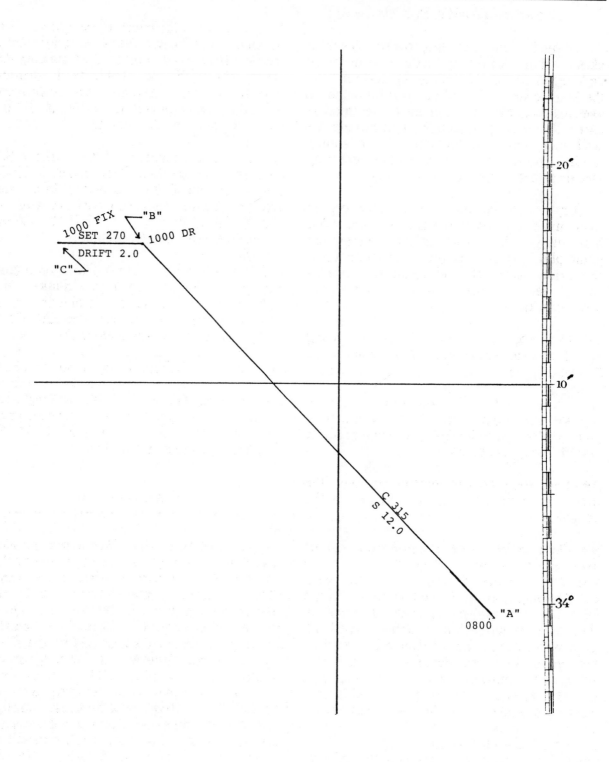

Set and Drift Practice.

Time for the real thing on our favorite chart. The following page is a slightly reduced version of the **western half** of the book chart. All of the problems below are worked out on that chart. After you learn to **work** set and drift problems we will take some time to find out how to use the information to accomplish our next step and dazzle the Coast Guard OinC.

Try these on one of your own copies then make a comparison. If you need help, turn back to page 185 and review the principle again. Briefly summarized, there are some outstanding points to watch for when methodically attacking the problems below.

①→ Plot your DR first. Find out, using speed-distance-time formulas, where you "thought" you were.

②→ Then plot the Fix which is supplied in latitude and longitude. (Most of the time you will be asked to find your own lat-long fix by using bearings.)

③→ Use your course plotter to plot the direction of the current (set) **from** the DR **to** the fix.

④→ Then do the speed-distance-time bit all over again to find the drift. The **time** will be the same as when you plotted your DR, namely, the time underway. This is because your vessel was affected by that current during your entire length of time underway. The distance is found by measuring between the DR and the fix. With your time and distance in hand...go for the **speed** because that's the **drift**. Okay, here we go. Slow and easy now.

1) Depart Brockway Point Light at 1230, speed 12.5 knots on a true course of 020. At 1400 your position is found to be latitude 34° 16.9' N & longitude 120° 05.0' W. What is your set and drift?

2) You depart Cardwell Point (lower left on chart just above 34°) at 0504 on a course to the West Point Light making 8.9 knots. At 0715 you check your location wherein a loran fix places you at latitude 34° 10.0' N & longitude 120° 00.0' W. What is your set and drift?

3) On a true course of 195° making 9.3 knots you depart Spa Rock Light at 2245. One hour and fifteen minutes later you take a fix to find yourself located at latitude 34° 11.0' N & 120° 11.9' W. What is your set and drift?

4) Leaving Spa Rock Light behind on a true course of 153° at 1324 you make 10.6 knots until 1559 when a fix places you at latitude 34° 00.0' N and longitude 120° 00.0' W. What is your set and drift?

5) Departing Goleta Point (top of chart near the 119° 50.0' mark) you set a course for Cardwell Point at 1836 making 11.6 knots. At 2040 you take a fix placing your craft at 34° 09.5' N and 120° 17.1' W. What is your set and drift?

⚓

P-s-s-s-s-t

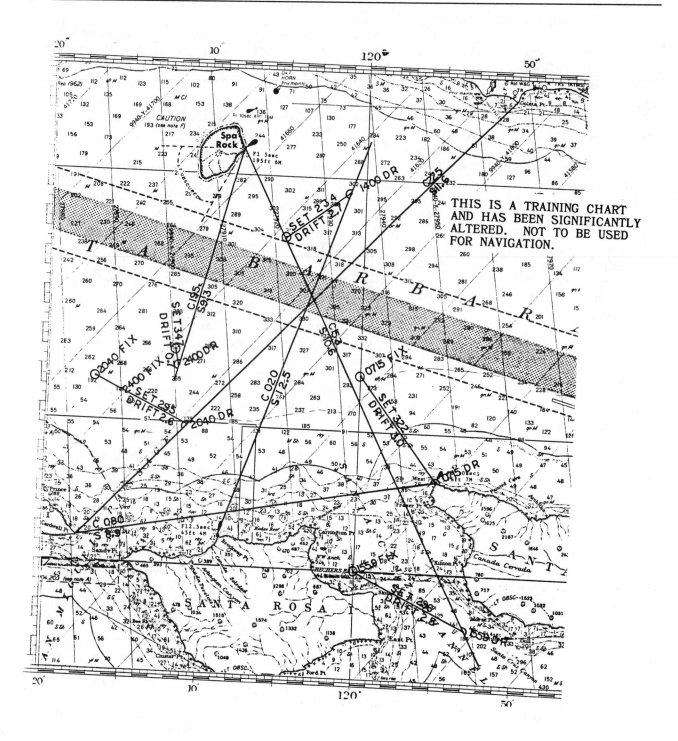

THIS IS A TRAINING CHART
AND HAS BEEN SIGNIFICANTLY
ALTERED.   NOT TO BE USED
FOR NAVIGATION.

PLOTTING V - SET AND DRIFT
TYPE #3

So you can do set and drift problems. Great! Now, what good are they? Used properly, you can sail to another location with accuracy assuming the set and drift don't change during the voyage. In short, you can pick another destination and using the information from your previously calculated set and drift, hit the new destination right on the buoy. The numbered directions below correspond to the large black numbers on the next page. It's a step-by-step procedure. Those of you who remember studying vectors in analytical geometry will be right at home, but for the sake of simplicity, we won't go into theory here. Merely step-by-step solutions. Watch the next page and follow along.

Our departure point is at the bottom of the page showing 0800. We depart on a course of 030° making 13 knots. At 1000 hours we plot our DR then take a fix.

1→ The fix (big black "1") is acquired by taking a two body fix from Ooga Island and Booga Rock. At the point of the fix we label it "O". From the DR to the fix we plot the set and drift. Note the drift is 2.0. That means the current is moving two knots. How long is the set-drift line? Go on, measure it. Four miles, right? Divided by two hours, that's a two knot current. That's what made the drift 2.0.

2→ Next, we extend the set-drift line for one hour of current movement. One hour would be two knots because that's how fast the current is moving. Thus, from point "O" we measure along a continuation of the 290° set line for two miles. That gives us point "W". In other words, whatever the drift is -written beneath the "set-drift" line- **is how far we extend the line.** If the drift worked out to be 4.2 miles, that's how far you would extend

the line. If it said 3.9 miles, extend it 3.9 miles from "O" to "W", but only after you work it out on a speed-distance-time framework like you did on page 185.

3→ Now that you know your set and drift...where would you like to go? To bed? No, no, not yet. Just a bit further. Heavy weather is coming up. Captain says head for home. So, he draws a line from where he is -the fix- to where he wants to go...home. That's the big black "3". If you saw his girl friend you'd know why he wants to go home.

4→ How do you get point "P" at big black"4"? Careful here. Spread your dividers apart to equal the rpm speed of your boat. Thirteen knots. Measure out thirteen miles on the side of the page. Steady now. Put one end of the dividers on point "W" letting the other end fall on the course line leading home. Point "P" is thirteen miles from point "W". Draw a line from "W" to "P". Never mind why, just do it.

5→ Now we have two lines. One is called line "OP". If you measure it with your dividers on the side of the page you will find the new speed you will **make good** heading for home (big black 3). Measuring the OP line carefully, you should get 12.7. Remember, line OP gives you your **new speed**. This means if you turn up the same rpm you usually do to get 13 knots, (your speed coming out from home) you will only make good 12.7 knots due to the current offset. At least now you will know what speed you will be making due to the errant whales.

6→ Whip out your course plotter and measure the other line..."WP". Did you get 192°? Good! That's the course to steer to hit home base (big black 3) right on the buoy. If you steer 192° you will offset the current working against you.

⚓

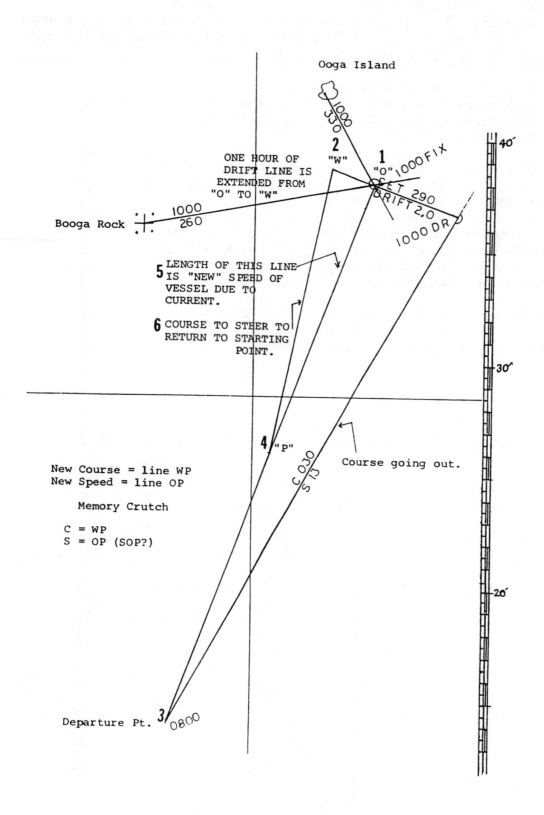

Ooga Island

1000
330

ONE HOUR OF
DRIFT LINE IS
EXTENDED FROM
"O" TO "W"

2
"W"

1
"O" 1000 FIX
SET 290
DRIFT 2.0

1000 DR

Booga Rock   1000
260

5 LENGTH OF THIS LINE
IS "NEW" SPEED OF
VESSEL DUE TO
CURRENT.

6 COURSE TO STEER TO
RETURN TO STARTING
POINT.

40'

30'

4 "P"

Course going out.

New Course = line WP
New Speed = line OP

    Memory Crutch

C = WP
S = OP (SOP?)

C 030
S 13

20'

Departure Pt. 3 0800

This is a set and drift practice problem. You have to use your course plotter, dividers and knowledge to find the answers. Taking your time is important. You will learn more in the long run and retain it longer.

    1   Start at the end of the line **after** the "X".
    2   What time should be inserted in the DR position?
    3   What time should be inserted in the fix position?
    4   What is the set and drift?

    The end of the line at "Y" marks the new destination. Extend the set-drift line for one hour of drift. Where does the letter "O" belong? Where does the letter "W" belong?

    Open your dividers to the speed of your craft. Use the distance scale over on the right side of the page for this. From "W" let the other end of the dividers intersect the course line to the new destination. Mark the intersection point "P".

    What will be your new speed over the ground? (OP)
    What will be the new course? (WP)
    Check the next page against your answers on this page.

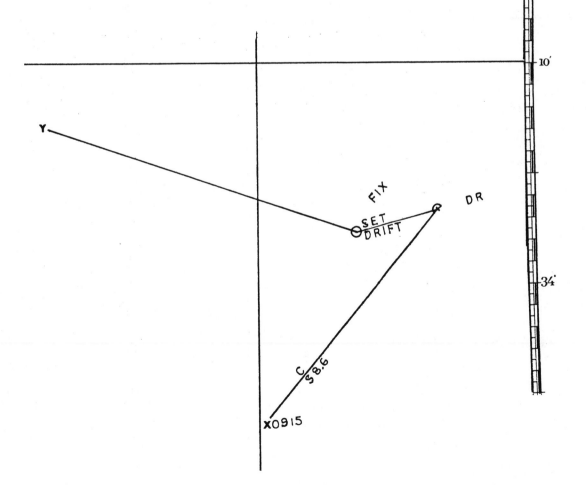

Step by step. No fair going to the next step until you understand the last one.

1) You need the distance from the 0915 departure to the DR. That's 12.3 miles and while you're at it, the course to fill in is 040º. If the speed is 8.6 & the distance is 12.3, the time must be 86m or 1h 26m. This gets added to 0915 for a 1041 DR & a 1041 fix.

2) From the DR to the fix is a distance of 4.0 miles. That current has been affecting your craft for the 86 minutes you have been underway. If D=4 & T=86 then the speed (drift) must be 2.8. The set is 255º.

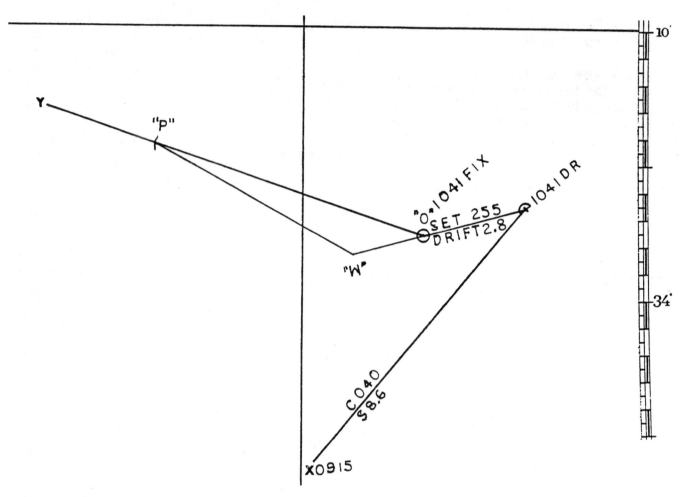

3) Extending the set-drift line for the drift of 2.8 means drawing a line 2.8 miles long. At the end of this line is "W".

4) Spread your dividers 8.6 miles. From "W" mark a point on the new course line. This is point "P". This gives you two lines: OP and WP.

5) The length of line OP gives you your new speed: 10.8 knots. (The current is working with you this time.) Line WP is your new course, 299º to reach point "Y" (new destination) despite the current. ‡

On many problems the CG will give you minimum information, but just enough to solve the problem. Take some time with this one. What you learn and discover on this page could be very helpful and rewarding on your big day. Please, a little panache and verve here. And I don't care what you say, this **is** enough information to solve the problem.

☐➔ See if you can determine your course and speed to the DR.

☐➔ Now find your fix by taking bearings on the two buoys. Your **compass** bearing on the lighted buoy is 271⁰ with deviation at 3⁰ E. and variation for the area is 12⁰ W.

The lighted buoy bears psc 057⁰, deviation 3⁰ W. From this, find your fix.

☐➔ Determine your set and drift.

☐➔ What will be the course to steer and the speed made good to your final destination?

☐➔ Assuming no time lost in computations, what will be your ETA at the final destination?

‡

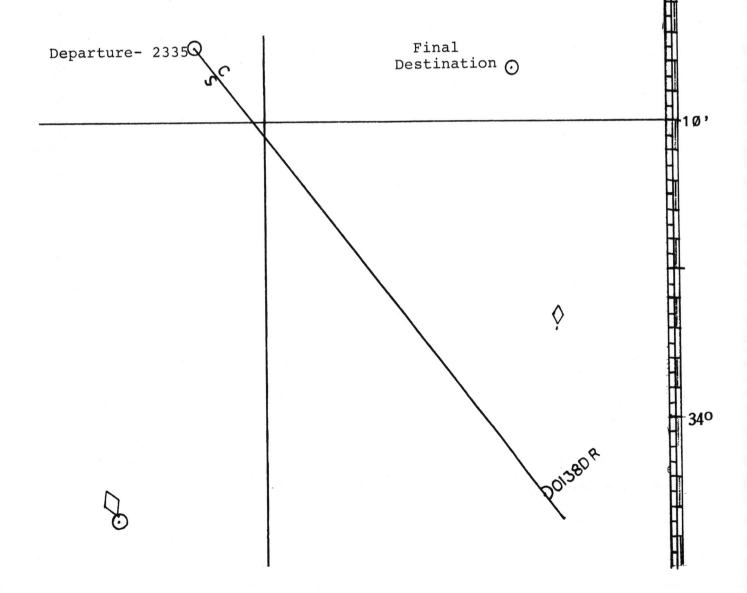

ANSWERS TO PAGE 189

The course is 141°. Departing at 2335 & arriving at 0138 makes for 2h 03m or 123 minutes. Working a S-D-T problem, that yields 9.4 knots. The lighted buoy bears 262°, the unlighted buoy 042°.

The set drift line is 4.1 miles long. D=4, T=123m, so S (drift)= 2.0. Now extend the set-drift line for 2 miles giving you point"W". Draw your track line from point "O" -also known as the fix- to your new destination. From "W" swing an arc on the new track line 9.4 miles (speed of your boat) up the line.

Line OP measures 9.1 miles which is your **new** speed assuming your craft is still turning up rpm for your original speed of 9.4 knots. Against this current it will only make 9.1 knots. Line WP is your new course which, if you use, will offset the action of the current. This is 024° true.

The ETA: The distance from your 0138 fix and the new destination is 14 miles. The new speed will be 9.1 knots. A S-D-T problem will indicate 92 minutes to make the voyage. Ninety-two minutes is 1h 32m which should be added to the 0138 departure time from the fix. 0138 plus 0132 = 0310 for an ETA.

⚓

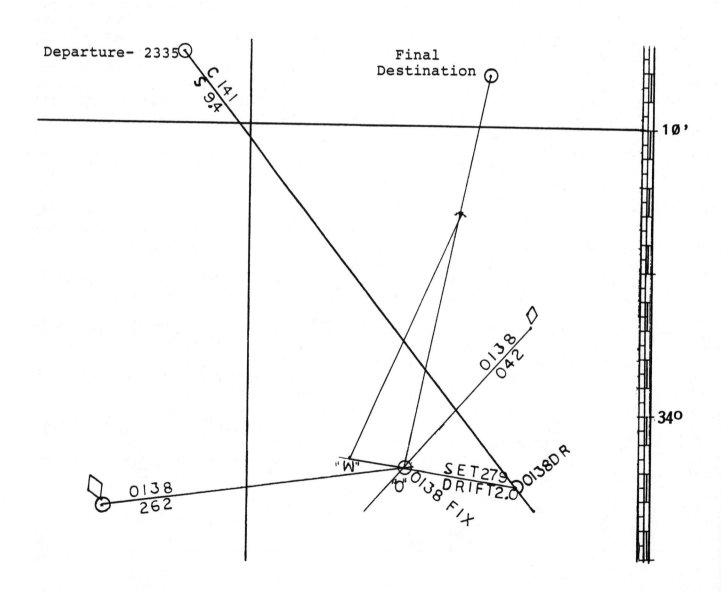

The following six problems are answered at the bottom of this page and summarized on a reduced chart on the following page. Again, assume all variation at 15° E. Recall, discouragement is forbidden.

1) Departing Sandy Point (far west end of Santa Rosa) at 1835 steering psc 340° with 5° deviation west and making 14.2 knots, you pause at 1943 for a loran fix. This results in a position of 34° 15.0' N & 120° 13.1' W. Find your set and drift. In view of your set & drift, indicate the new course and speed to Brockway Point and your ETA.

2) In your new sailboat you depart Santa Barbara's flashing green bell buoy at 1640 on compass (psc) course of 243°, speed 6.6 knots. If your deviation on this course is 3° west, at what time **should** you first see the Spa Rock Light? When **should** this light be abeam? (Caution: each time you measure the distance, **do it from the S.B. buoy**.) Suspicious of your DR position, nineteen minutes later you swing your bow to take a bearing on the Spa Rock Light. Psc, with deviation at 4° E. the light bears 281°. Swinging your bow again, you take a bearing on the Santa Barbara Light yielding 061° with 6° west deviation. With your new position clear, along with your set and drift, plot a new course to Carrington Point on Santa Rosa Island indicting your new course, adjusted speed calculation and ETA.

3) Setting a course for Santa Barbara Light from West Point Light at 1350 and making 10.2 knots with deviation at 5° E, you stop after 1h 10m to take a fix. Maintaining course, you sight on the West End which yields psc 175°. Coche Point bears psc 115°. In view of these new elements of the weather, what is your true course and ETA to the Santa Barbara Light?

4) On a true course of 290° with deviation at 6° E, Cavern Point Light bears psc 209° at 1330. Your speed is 11.6 knots. At 1410, you shoot the light again; this time the compass bearing is 109°. Indicate your 1410 position.

5) With deviation at 2° W and a speed of 9.3 knots and a compass course of 007°, the Bunny Isle light bears 037° psc at 1512. At 1624, the same light bears 105° true. Indicate your 1624 position.

6) Depart Cavern Point Light at 1647 making 10.3 knots on a compass course of 331° with deviation on this course 4° E. One hour twenty-nine minutes later you take a compass bearing on the Santa Barbara Light which indicates 316°. At the same time, Rincon Point bears psc 056°. Plot the set and drift so you can indicate your new course and ETA to Rincon Point. Keep in mind that since no one said "turning your bow to bear on the object" you must assume a pelorus bearing and **each deviation** used must conform to the heading of the vessel; in this case 4° east.

1) New course=180° true. New speed 15.6 knots. ETA 2036.

2) Light at 1917. Abeam at 2005. Set 087°-Drift 1.7. New course=198°-New speed 6.2 knots. ETA 2300.

3) New course=049° true. New speed=8.4 knots. Distance=11.0 Mi. ETA 1616.

4) 1410 position-latitude 34° 07.6' N & longitude 119° 39.8' W.

5) 1624 position-latitude 34° 14.7' N & longitude 119° 32.5' W.

6) New course=084° true. New speed=8.1 knots. ETA 1936.

⚓

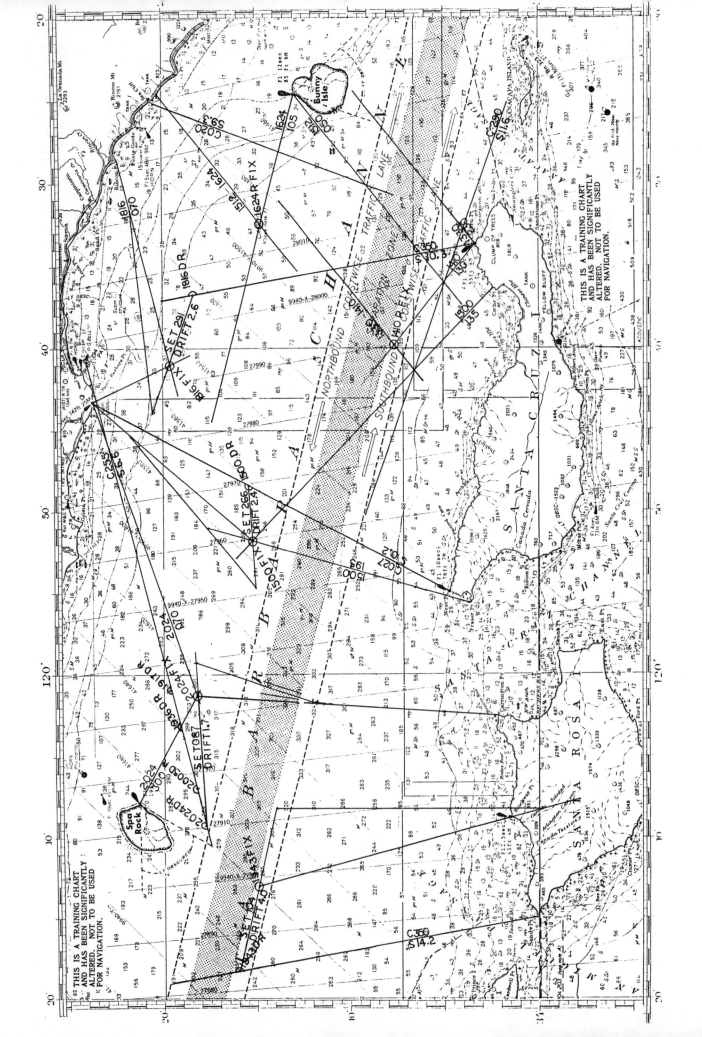

Complex leeway problems are not new on CG exams, but are, like the rest, multiple choice. These can show up on your Navigation/General quiz or the charting quiz itself. We will give you two solved examples then present five more for you to work. Do yourself a favor and sketch them before producing an answer.

Example #1
Your course to make good is 075⁰ but a southerly wind is causing a 4⁰ leeway. What should you steer to make your course?
The problem revolves around leeway caused by a southerly wind due to the deckhouse reach on that high cabin scow of yours. It is pushing you off course to the left, or counter-clockwise around the compass card. You're crabbing and it's blowing you off 4⁰ farther north (southly winds will do that) so you need to oversteer 4⁰ more to the south, 079⁰.

Example #2.
What would happen if you were steering something close to **westerly,** say, 265⁰ with 3 degree leeway caused by a southerly wind? You must subtract the leeway.
Do you see why? You're being blown too far north, or to the right, or clock-wise, or whatever you want to call it. You would have to steer more south to overcome the south wind. You would have to **subtract** to get back on course, wouldn't you? Try 262⁰

This leeway business has to be solved with a logical choice. There are too many variations to make up a bag of rules. Your bag would be too full. Let's try a few general questions and be humble-no one's watching. Sketch them as we go. You'll have a better chance of survival.

1) The wind is northerly (coming out of the north) and your leeway is 2 degrees on a course of 049⁰, what course should you steer?

2) A south wind is causing a 4 degree leeway on a desired course of 315⁰. What should you steer to compensate for the wind?

3) A howler out of the north is causing an 8 degree leeway on a required course of 265⁰. What do you steer to compensate?

4) A strong easterly causes a 3 degree leeway on a course of 358⁰. What should you steer?

5) A westerly current causes a 6 degree leeway on a desired course of 050⁰. What should you steer to compensate?

ANSWERS

1) 047⁰, 2) 311⁰, 3) 273⁰, 4) 001⁰, 5) 056⁰. Ah, you remembered currents are named by the direction they are **going** rather than the direction they are **coming from** as is the wind? Very good.

A DIRTY DOZEN FOR THE ROAD

Here's the big time. The following twelve problems are solved on two reduced charts found on pages 198 and 199 and explained on pages 196-7. These are very similar to the **type** of problems you will encounter on the real Coast Guard charting test. They encompass all prior concepts on our exercises with a few variations. You can use these examples repeatedly to hone your skills, but if it's rough you might consider our Second Dirty Dozen on the order form or better yet the Chartlets with CG data bank plotting problems and answers. Numerous subtle glitches are included to frustrate you like the CG exams frequently employ. Don't throw the book across the room when you miss. Study the solutions and discussions and learn **why** it works. Like I said before, better you screw it up here than with the CG.

Two things to remember. Assume all variations herein to be 15° east. A "radar mile" is considered as 2,000 yards.

1) Departing from a point 1.5 miles southwest of the Santa Barbara flashing green bell buoy at 0415 on a compass course of 253° making 11.6 knots and deviation on this course of 3° west, plot your 0532 DR. At this point a Spa Rock Light pelorus bearing yields 275° psc. At the same time, Goleta Point bears 041° psc. From this information determine what course you must steer against the prevailing current to arrive at the point 1/2 mile south of Spa Rock's southern-most point by 0619

2) Having departed the Santa Barbara flashing bell buoy at 1515 on a compass course of 131° making 12.5 knots and deviation at 4° east, you take bearings at 1627. Visibility is excellent so you take a compass bearing on the Bunny Isle lighthouse of 081°. Anacapa Island Light bears psc 123°. Utilizing this information

and maintaining your present course, state your ETA at the northern edge of the Separation Zone.

3) Depart Carrington Point at 2040 on course 331° true. Making 16.2 knots at what time should you first see the Spa Rock Light?

4) Depart the West Point Light at 2140 knowing your set and drift will be 090° and drift will be 4.5. Turning up engine rpm's to make your usual 10.5 knots, what will be your ETA at the Santa Barbara flashing green bell buoy?

5) Leaving the Santa Barbara flashing green bell buoy at 1230 making 15.6 knots, you are informed that the set, plotted previous to your departure, is 100° with a drift of 2.5 knots. Your destination is Cavern Point. After arriving at Cavern Point, you troll the area fishing for the day then return to Cavern Point. Departing Cavern at 1815, you are bound for Santa Barbara and your afternoon point of departure experiencing the same set and drift.

Give your afternoon ETA at Cavern Point and your evening ETA upon return to Santa Barbara.

6) Underway at 2130 on compass course 071° with deviation at 4° east. The Bunny Isle Light bearing is 131° psc four miles off. What is your position?

7) On a course of 076° psc with deviation at 6° west, the Brockway Point Light bears 126° psc at 2240. Ninety minutes later, making a constant speed of 5.8 knots, the same light shows a compass bearing of 231°. What is your position?

8) On a foggy night at 2035 the range on Goleta Point is 15,600 yards. At the same time Spa Rock Light shows a range of 18,000 yards while the West Point Light is 28,000 yards off. Indicate your position.

9) The following radar ranges are taken on the following three points at 0410. Plot these and indicate your position.

a) The end of the Punta Gorda Pier - near upper right corner of chart where the Fl 5 sec light is located- ranges 12,000 yards.
b) Bunny Isle Light - 14,000 yards.
c) Cavern Point - 27,000 yards.

10) The visibility is restricted at 2212. Your fathometer indicates you are on the forty fathom line. Swinging your bow to bear on Carrington Point your compass reads 199° and your deviation card shows deviation on this heading of 3° east. Setting a course for Spa Rock and making 9.2 knots, the meteorological visibility degenerates to "thin fog" with visibility at one-half mile. Under these conditions, what time would you see the Spa Rock Light. Hint: Go to the Luminous Range Diagram in the appendix.

11) At 1835 you set a course for Bunny Isle Light from West Point Light making 10.3 knots with deviation on this course of 2° west. At 1930 Cavern Point Light bears 107° psc. The Bunny Isle Light bears 047° compass. Plot your set and drift, indicate your new course and speed and give your ETA at Bunny Isle Light.

12) You are en route to the Santa Barbara Fl G bell buoy departing West Point Light at 1718, deviation 5° east making 13.2 knots. If the Santa Barbara radio beacon has a broadcasting range of 10 miles what time **should you** first hear its signal? At this time you take a radar bearing of 325° true to Goleta Point when the Santa Barbara Light bears 340° psc. Knowing your new position, what course would you steer while maintaining a speed of 12 knots to reach the Bunny Isle Light?

Still feel a little unsure? By now, you should have made your appointment with the Coast Guard to take your exam. Want some more practice plotting problems like those above? Something to work on the night before the exam? See the special order form in the back of the book.

‡

AIDS AND ANSWERS
TO THE DIRTY DOZEN

1) This is an example of the type #4 we Zenned out on as per page 191. First, find your DR and FIX. Your set/drift line will be three miles long yielding a 2.3 S&D. Extend the S&D line 2.3 miles just like always and label the end "W". Now, go back and draw your track line from your FIX through the point 1/2 mile south of Spa Rock's southern-most point. From "W" someone is telling you (indirectly) what speed to make by telling you when to arrive. From where to where? **From your FIX** to that point south of Spa Rock and it measures 9.4 miles and that's how far you have to travel. Problem is, you must *maintain* a speed which will take you there (against the prevailing S&D) in 47 minutes. (0532 {time of fix} to 0619). Okay, distance is 9.4 miles and time is 47 minutes which means you will have to make 12 knots and that's how far you draw the line (WP) until it intersects your track line; 12 miles. The question was, what course must you steer against the prevailing current? With the course plotter measure the course line WP. You should get 279^0.

2) Did you notice that your set is exactly the opposite of your course line? This means the current is working directly against you. You're bucking it straight on. In fact, over the 1h 12m you were underway you lost 3.7 miles of distance because of the current. Over a period of 72 minutes underway, that works out to a drift of 3.3. If you turned up rpm to make 12.5 knots and had a drift of 3.3 working **against** you, your speed was really 9.2 knots. (12.5 minus 3.3). At a speed of 9.2 knots with 7.5 miles to go, you would make the Separation Zone in another 49 minutes...or 1716 for an ETA. No fancy "W" "O" and "P" drawings were necessary.

3) This one was conceived to make you watch all around. Assume nothing. Maybe you thought those dotted lines emanating from Spa Rock Light indicated the six mile limit the light could be seen.

No way. If you come across one of these seemingly simple things, beware. You won't get in the range of the visibility of the light until you pass by the rock picking up the light on the other side. Note the six mile arc drawn on the solution chart. The light will show up at 2200, course 331^0

4) Isn't this sweet of some one? They gave you the set and drift before you departed West Point Light. Get that! **You don't have to plot set and drift.** Assume West Point Light is your **fix**. Well, O.K., call it point "O". Since the set is 090^0 and the drift is 4.5, draw this line **from** "O" before you head for the Santa Barbara buoy. On the east end of this 090^0 4.5 mile line is our old friend "W". And how fast were you expected to head for S.B? 10.5 knots? Then, from "W" spread a 10.5 mile space on your dividers and find "P" on the track line. You should get a new speed of 12.2 knots steering a course of 010^0. The distance to S.B.'s buoy is 22.8 miles. Your ETA would be 2332.

5) Same as above, but doubled. There are two separate and distinct problems here. Plot your set and drift from Santa Barbara by finding "W" which is 2.5 miles 100^0 from the buoy. The new speed to Cavern will be 16.5 knots on a course of 172^0 true. The distance from the buoy (point "O") to Cavern is 21.6 miles. ETA Cavern will be 1349. On the return trip the distance is the same from Cavern to the buoy. However, your set and drift must be plotted again before you depart. The new speed (OP) is 14.3. The distance is still 21.6 miles. Departing at 1815 on a course of 336^0, your ETA will be 91 minutes later, or 1946.

6) First draw the bearing line from Bunny Isle Light. This is 150^0 true. Four miles from the light -on 150^0- is your position. Latitude 34^0 16.4' N. & longitude 119^0 26.9' W.

7) This is a running fix. Plot the 2240 bearing line 135^0 true to the light. Next,

plot the 0010 bearing line of 240° true. Ninety minutes later is 8.7 miles for a 0010 DR. (Recall: your course line can pass through these two bearings from the light at any distance off the light.) Find 8.7 miles from your 2240 DR. Advance your 2240 135° bearing line to your 0010 DR. To make this advance, draw a 135° bearing line through your 0010 DR on your course line. Where the advanced (2240-0010) 135° line intersects the second bearing line from the light, (240°) is your 0010 position. Latitude 34° 05.2' N & longitude 120° 01.1' W.

8) Each range in yards should be divided by 2,000. For example, the range on Goleta Point was 15,600. Divided by 2,000 this yields a distance of 7.8 miles. Use your drafting compass to swing a 7.8 mile arc. Do the same with the other arcs from Spa Rock and West Point. Where the three intersect -or the center if there is a space in the middle- is your position. In this case: latitude 34° 18.7' N & longitude 119° 57.3' W.

9) Same technique as above. Position: latitude 34° 16.7' N & longitude 119° 31.7' W.

10) The purpose of this problem is to encourage the use of the luminous range diagram in the appendix. The true bearing from Carrington Point as 217°. The forty fathom line is marked on the answer chart. This is indicated by dots and dashes. See page 106, numbers 14 and 17. On your chart look for the string of four dots separated by dashes. Where your 217° bearing intersects this line there is a numeral "40" -for forty fathoms- just below and to the right of your position. Starting from here at 2212 you will travel 16.7 miles before sighting the Spa Rock Light. Why 16.7 miles? Because if the meteorological visibility is 1/2 mile on a light with a nominal range of 6 miles, the visibility is then reduced to **one mile.** This **one mile** is not indicated on the right side of the Luminous Range Diagram, but on the left side. Look carefully. You will reach this point at 0001.

11) The course to Bunny is 072° true. Set works out to 113° with drift at 4.9 because the set drift line is 4.5 miles long. The true bearing on Cavern Point was 120°, the one on Bunny was 060° true. New course will be 038° with a new speed of 12.4 knots. The distance to go is 14.0 miles which will take 68 minutes making it 2038 ETA.

12) The true course is 031° as indicated on the answer chart. Your bearing to the Santa Barbara Light at 1815 is 000°. Your set-drift line measures 3.1 miles, which over a 57 minute period of underway time should give you a drift of 3.3. The set is 086°. Since you are now heading for Bunny Isle Light, draw a course line from your fix (now called point "O") to the light. Go back to the end of your set-drift line. Extend the set-drift line 086° for the length of the drift which is 3.3 knots. That gives you point "W". The problem indicates you must maintain a speed of 12 knots. Draw a line from "W" towards the track line (the line from "O" to your destination) 12 miles long and maneuver this 12 mile line so it intersects your track line at exactly 12 miles from "W" and terminates at the track line. Where the 12 mile speed line intersects and stops at the track line label it "P". Using your course plotter, measure the course line from "W" to "P". You should get 103° which is the new course to steer to maintain a 12 knot speed against the prevailing current.

Thus, once again: If for any reason you are told a course to steer or a speed to make against any prevailing current, line "WP" becomes both course to steer and speed made good and they have to give you one or the other.

⚓

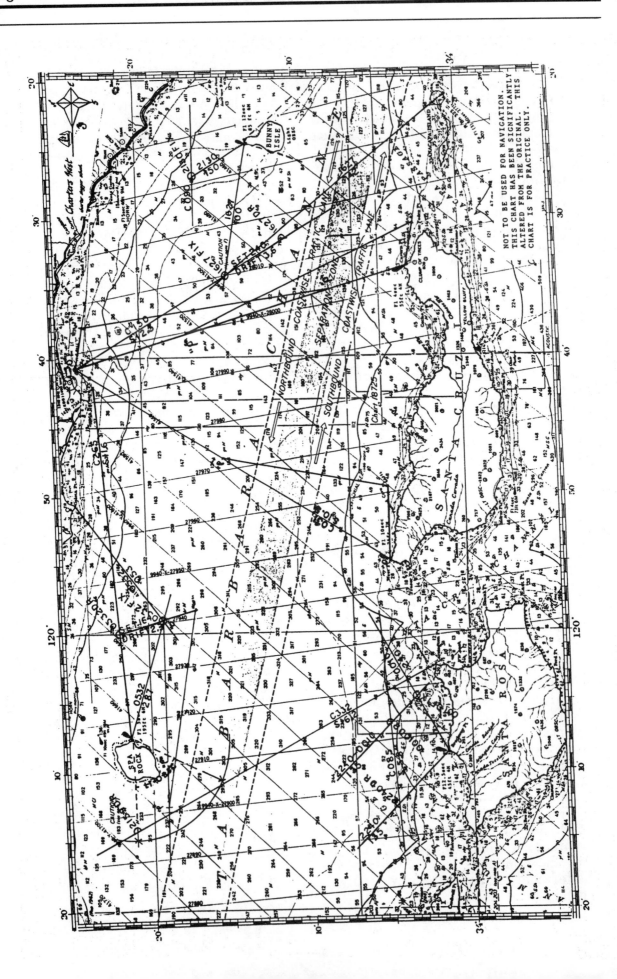

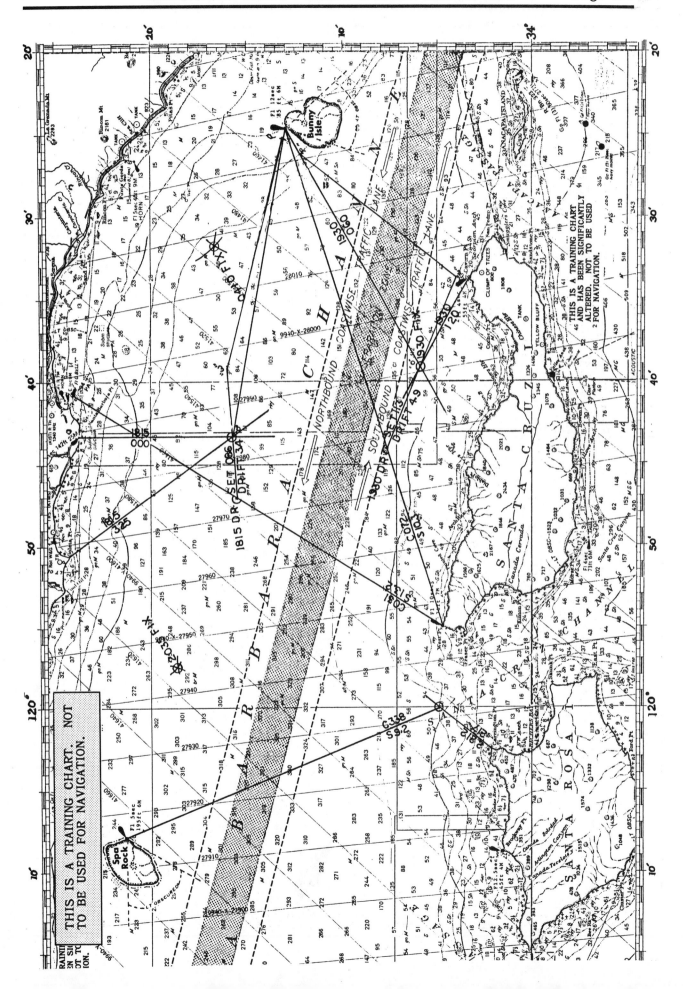

THIS IS A TRAINING CHART. NOT
TO BE USED FOR NAVIGATION.

THIS IS A TRAINING CHART
AND HAS BEEN SIGNIFICANTLY
ALTERED. NOT TO BE USED
FOR NAVIGATION.

APPENDIX

CONTENTS

LUMINOUS RANGE DIAGRAM

Meterorological Visibility is a term used to indicate the degree of restricted visibility of a given light in fog, haze, etc. This diagram, or one like it, is found in the Light List, generally on page vii. Sometimes there are no directions on its use! Just the diagram. Some offices include problems requiring candidates to find the meterological visibility of lights and how soon the light will be visible on a given course and speed track.

Assume a foggy night and you are approaching a light on some shoreline which has a **nominal range** of say, thirteen miles. This nominal range is found along the bottom of the chart. Pinpoint that number thirteen first.

Moving up this thirteen mile line one encounters circled numbers, each between two curved lines. Each of these numbered areas is defined and written right on these charts as follows. 1 = Light Fog-visibility .37 to .54 miles. 2 = Thin Fog-visibility .54 to 1.1 miles. 3 = Haze-visibility 1.1 to 2.2 miles. 4 = Light Haze-visibility 2.2 to 5.4 miles. 5 = Clear-visibility 5.4 to 11 miles. 6 = Very Clear-visibility 11 to 27 miles. Exceptionally Clear-visibility over 27 miles.

You are supposed to estimate your visibility. Let's pick one. Try Light Haze. Follow that thirteen mile nominal range line up and into the area bracketed by the two curved lines on the top and bottom of number 6 . Estimate, as closely as you can, the half-way point between those two curved lines marking the area encompassing the circled "6". Now, move to your left until you come to the edge of the chart. What number are you on? I get about 6.5 miles. What does all of this mean?

On a night with Light Haze and looking for a light showing a nominal range of 13 miles, you *probably* won't see the light until it's *about* 6.5 miles off. Remember that the "nominal range" of a light is that range which is printed directly on the **navigation chart** next to the light.

Try another. The nominal range of the light is 20 miles. What would the meterological visibility of the light be in Light Fog?

How about 0.8 miles. That's half-way between 0.1 (the bottom line) and 1.5,) the next line up inside the Light Fog area which is number 3 .

Again? Okay. Find the meterological visibility of a light with the nominal range of ten miles on a night sporting Haze.

Get 2.8 miles? Close enough. Now watch out. Sometimes they actually give you the meterological visibility and you won't need this chart. But, it makes you *think* you do and precious minutes are lost.

‡

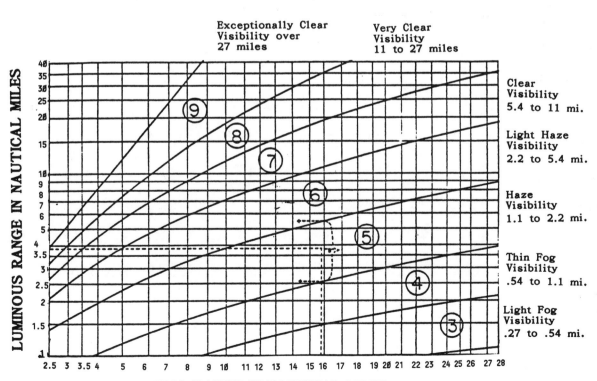

NOMINAL RANGE IN NAUTICAL MILES

Address REC's below as "U.S. Coast Guard Marine Safety Office." Also notice that cities are no repeated; be sure to insert properly when addressing envelopes. Some of these addresses an phone numbers are notorious for their frequent changes. To play it safe check your telephon directory white pages under U.S. Government - Dept. of Transportation - U.S. Coast Guard

Alaska, Anchorage - 701 C Street, Box 17 AK 95513-0065-(907) 271-3513

Alaska, Juneau - 2760 Sherwood Lane, AK 99801-8545 (907) 586-7309

California, Alameda - Building 14, Rm. 109, Coast Guard Island, CA 94501-5100 (415) 437-3092, 3 or 4.

California, Long Beach - 165 N. Pico Ave., CA. 90802-1096 (213) 499-5532

Florida, Miami - 155 S. Miami Ave., FL 33130-1609 (305) 536-6548 or 6549

Hawaii, Honolulu - Rm.1, 433 Ala Moana Blvd., HI 96813-4909 (808) 541-2072

Louisiana, New Orleans - 1440 Canal Street, 8th floor. LA. 70112. (504) 589-6183, 6184, 6185

Maryland, Baltimore - U.S. Custom House, 40 S. Gay St., MD 21202-4022 (301) 962-5133, 5134 5135.

Massachusetts, Boston - 447 Commercial St., MA 02109-1096 (617) 565-9040

Missouri, St. Louis - P.O. Box D-17, 210 N. Tucker Blvd., Rm 1130, MO 63188-0017 (314) 425-4657.

New York, New York - Battery Park Blvd., NY 10004-1466 (212) 668-7492

Ohio, Toledo - Rm. 501, Federal Blvd., 234 Summit Street, OH 43604-1590 (419) 259-6394, 6395 6396, 6397.

Oregon, Portland - 6767 N. Basin Ave., OR 97217-3992 (503) 240-9346

S. Carolina, Charleston - 196 Tradd St., SC 29401-1899 (803) 724-7693

Tennessee, Memphis - 200 Jefferson Ave., Suite 1302, TN 38103-2300 (901) 521-3297

Texas, Houston - 8876 Gulf Freeway, Suite 210, TX 77017-6595 (713) 229-3560

Washington, Seattle - 1519 Alaskan Way S., Bldg. 1, WA 98134-1192 (206) 286-5510

Puerto Rico, San Juan - P.O. Box S-3666, Old San Juan, PR 00904-3666 (809) 725-0857 and 772-2697

DEPARTMENT OF TRANSPORTATION U.S. COAST GUARD
CG-866 (Rev. 6-82)

APPLICATION FOR LICENSE AS OFFICER, OPERATOR OR STAFF OFFICER
(Print or Type Application)

FILING DATA *(C.G. USE ONLY)*

DATE SUBMITTED

TYPE OF ISSUANCE *(Check appropriate box)*

☐ 1 ORIGINAL ☐ 2 RENEWAL ☐ 3 RAISE OF GRADE ☐ 4 ENDORSEMENT ☐ 5 DUPLICATE **EXTENSION OF ROUTE/** ☐ 6 INCREASE IN SCOPE

I – APPLICANT DATA *(To be completed by all applicants.)*

1. NAME			2. MAILING ADDRESS *(Number and street) (City and state) (Zip code)*
(Last)	*(First)*	*(M.I.)*	

3. SOCIAL SECURITY NO.	4. TELEPHONE NUMBER	5. DATE OF BIRTH MO. DAY YR.	6. PLACE OF BIRTH *(City, state, country)*

7. APPLYING FOR *(State fully class, grade, type of license desired. Include route, tonnage, horsepower, propulsion and endorsements as applicable.)*

II – LICENSE RECORD *(Radio officers must present current FCC license with application)*

8. YES ☐ NO ☐	HAS ANY LICENSE, CERTIFICATE, OR MERCHANT MARINE DOCUMENT HELD BY YOU EVER BEEN SUSPENDED WITH PROBATION GRANTED? *(If "YES", complete Item 8a.)*	8a. DATE *(approximate)* AND PLACE

9. LICENSE NUMBER	10. DATE OF ISSUE	11. PORT OF ISSUE	12. ISSUE NUMBER

13. GRADE, CLASS, LIMITATIONS OF PRESENT LICENSE *(CG, FCC, or Foreign)*

14. QUALIFYING EXPERIENCE FOR ORIGINAL LICENSE *(To be completed by all applicants.)* ☐ SEA SERVICE SCHOOL *(Specify)* _____ ☐ UNLICENSED SERVICE ☐ OTHER *(Specify)* _____	15. YES ☐ NO ☐ ARE YOU PRESENTLY ON ACTIVE DUTY IN THE U.S. ARMED FORCES? *(If "YES", complete Item 15a.)*
	15a. Branch of Service

III – U.S. CITIZENSHIP AND MILITARY RECORD *(For Original Licenses and Certificates of Registry ONLY)*

Naturalized U.S. Citizens Complete Items 16 and 17 ▶	16. COURT NATURALIZED *(State location)*	17. DATE NATURALIZED

18. PROOF OF U.S. CITIZENSHIP SUBMITTED *(To be completed by Inspector)*

19. YES ☐ NO ☐	HAVE YOU EVER SERVED IN THE U.S. ARMED FORCES? *(If "YES", complete Items 19a through 19f.)*	19a. DATE ENTERED	19b. DATE SEPARATED
19c. SERVICE NUMBER	19d. FULL NAME *(If different from block 1.)*	19e. BRANCH OF SER.	19f. TYPE DISCHARGE

IV – EMPLOYMENT AND/OR TRAINING *(List employment other than sea duty for the last five years only. List all sea service related training since issuance of your last Coast Guard license.)* ☐ Check if continuation sheet attached.

NAME AND ADDRESS *(City and State)* OF SCHOOL OR EMPLOYER	POSITION HELD OR TYPE OF TRAINING	DATES *(Mo., Yr.)* FROM	TO

V – CHARACTER RECORD *(Information provided on previous applications need not be repeated)*

20. YES ☐ NO ☐	HAVE YOU BEEN CONVICTED BY ANY COURT—INCLUDING MILITARY COURT—FOR OTHER THAN A MINOR TRAFFIC VIOLATION? *(If "YES", complete Item 22. below.)*
21. YES ☐ NO ☐	HAVE YOU USED OR BEEN ADDICTED TO THE USE OF NARCOTICS? *(If "YES", complete Item 22. below.)*

22. PARTICULARS OF CONVICTION/USE OR ADDICTION *(State place, date, and particulars)*

VI – CHARACTER REFERENCES *(For Original Licenses and Certificates of Registry ONLY)*

We, the undersigned, Certify from personal knowledge of the above named applicant that he is a person of temperate habits and of good character, and recommend him as a suitable person to be entrusted with the duties of the station for which he makes application.

SIGNATURE	NAME AND ADDRESS	OCCUPATION

Previous Editions are obsolete.

7530-00-F01-0450

DEPARTMENT OF TRANSPORTATION U.S. COAST GUARD CG-866 (Rev. 6-82)	SEA SERVICE FORM (SMALL BOAT EXPERIENCE) See Privacy Act Statement on Instruction Sheet	

NAME

(Last)   (First)   Middle Init. (Suffix)   SOCIAL SECURITY NO.   FILING DATA (C.G. USE ONLY)

VESSEL NAME:_____ OFFICIAL NO. OR STATE REGISTRATION NO. _____ LENGTH OF VESSEL: _____

GROSS TONS:_____ PROPULSION:_____ SERVED AS:_____

VESSEL WAS OPERATED BY THE APPLICANT UPON THE WATERS OF: _____

_____ BETWEEN _____ TO _____
(Name body or bodies of water)   (Geographical Point)   (Geographical Point)

NAME OF OWNER OR OWNERS OF BOAT IF OTHER THAN APPLICANT:_____

WRITE IN THE BLOCK UNDER THE APPROPRIATE MONTH THE NUMBER OF DAYS THAT YOU OPERATED OR SERVED ON THE ABOVE NAMED BOAT.

JANUARY (Year)	FEBRUARY (Year)	MARCH (Year)	APRIL (Year)	MAY (Year)	JUNE (Year)
JULY (Year)	AUGUST (Year)	SEPTEMBER (Year)	OCTOBER (Year)	NOVEMBER (Year)	DECEMBER (Year)

VESSEL NAME: _____ OFFICIAL NO. OR STATE REGISTRATION NO. _____ LENGTH OF VESSEL: _____

GROSS TONS:_____ PROPULSION:_____ SERVED AS:_____

VESSEL WAS OPERATED BY THE APPLICANT UPON THE WATERS OF: _____

_____ BETWEEN _____ TO _____
(Name body or bodies of water)   (Geographical Point)   (Geographical Point)

NAME OF OWNER OR OWNERS OF BOAT IF OTHER THAN APPLICANT:_____

WRITE IN THE BLOCK UNDER THE APPROPRIATE MONTH THE NUMBER OF DAYS THAT YOU OPERATED OR SERVED ON THE ABOVE NAMED BOAT.

JANUARY (Year)	FEBRUARY (Year)	MARCH (Year)	APRIL (Year)	MAY (Year)	JUNE (Year)
JULY (Year)	AUGUST (Year)	SEPTEMBER (Year)	OCTOBER (Year)	NOVEMBER (Year)	DECEMBER (Year)

VII — CERTIFICATION — IMPORTANT, READ BEFORE SIGNING

Whoever, in any matter within the jurisdiction of any department or agency of the U.S. knowingly and willfully falsifies, conceals or covers up by any trick, scheme, or device a material fact, or makes any false, fictitious or fraudulent statements or representation, or makes or uses any false writing or document knowing the same to contain any false, fictitious or fraudulent statement or entry, shall be fined not more than $10,000 or imprisoned not more than 5 years, or both (18 USC 1001).

I CERTIFY that the information on this application, is true, and that I have not made application for a license of any type to the Officer in Charge, Marine Inspection in any other port and been rejected within 12 months of this application.	**23. SIGNATURE OF APPLICANT**

Certificate of Seaman's Service and/or Discharges sighted and service verified, then returned to licensee. Other supporting data attached.

24. DATE	25. SIGNATURE OF VERIFYING OFFICIAL	26. PORT OF

VIII — OATH *(To be completed by applicant when license is received.)*

I do solemnly swear or affirm that I am a citizen of the United States and that I will faithfully and honestly, according to my best skill and judgment, and without concealment or reservation, perform all the duties required of me by the laws of the United States. *I agree to have a thorough physical examination each year if I act as a pilot under authority of the License being issued.*	**27. DATE**

28. SIGNATURE OF LICENSEE	29. SIGNATURE AND TITLE OF WITNESSING OFFICIAL

VESSEL NAME: _____ OFFICIAL NO. OR STATE REGISTRATION NO. _____ LENGTH OF VESSEL: _____

GROSS TONS: _____ PROPULSION: _____ SERVED AS: _____

VESSEL WAS OPERATED BY THE APPLICANT UPON THE WATERS OF: _____

_____ BETWEEN _____ TO _____
(Name body or bodies of water)   (Geographical Point)   (Geographical Point)

NAME OF OWNER OR OWNERS OF BOAT IF OTHER THAN APPLICANT: _____

WRITE IN THE BLOCK UNDER THE APPROPRIATE MONTH THE NUMBER OF DAYS THAT YOU OPERATED OR SERVED ON THE ABOVE NAMED BOAT.

JANUARY (Year)	FEBRUARY (Year)	MARCH (Year)	APRIL (Year)	MAY (Year)	JUNE (Year)

JULY (Year)	AUGUST (Year)	SEPTEMBER (Year)	OCTOBER (Year)	NOVEMBER (Year)	DECEMBER (Year)

VESSEL NAME: _____ OFFICIAL NO. OR STATE REGISTRATION NO. _____ LENGTH OF VESSEL: _____

GROSS TONS: _____ PROPULSION: _____ SERVED AS: _____

VESSEL WAS OPERATED BY THE APPLICANT UPON THE WATERS OF: _____

_____ BETWEEN _____ TO _____
(Name body or bodies of water)   (Geographical Point)   (Geographical Point)

NAME OF OWNER OR OWNERS OF BOAT IF OTHER THAN APPLICANT:

WRITE IN THE BLOCK UNDER THE APPROPRIATE MONTH THE NUMBER OF DAYS THAT YOU OPERATED OR SERVED ON THE ABOVE NAMED BOAT.

JANUARY (Year)	FEBRUARY (Year)	MARCH (Year)	APRIL (Year)	MAY (Year)	JUNE (Year)

JULY (Year)	AUGUST (Year)	SEPTEMBER (Year)	OCTOBER (Year)	NOVEMBER (Year)	DECEMBER (Year)

DATE SUBMITTED	SIGNATURE OF APPLICANT	PAGE _____ of _____

Approved by OMB
2115-0006

| DEPARTMENT OF TRANSPORTATION U.S. COAST GUARD CG-866 (Rev. 6-82) | SEA SERVICE FORM (MERCHANT VESSEL SERVICE) See Privacy Act Statement on Instruction Sheet | FILING DATA (C.G. USE ONLY) |

| NAME (Last) | (First) | Middle Init. (Suffix) | SOCIAL SECURITY NO. | USMMD NUMBER |

Name of Vessel	Class of Vessel[1]	Tonnage or HP[2]	Steam or Motor[3]	Waters Nav.[4]	Served As	Date Shipped	Date Discharged	SERVICE		
								Yrs	Mos	Days

[1]Passenger, freight, towing, pleasure, fishing, yachts, uninspected, etc.
[2]If applying for deck officer's license, give gross tonnage; if applying for engineer's license, give horsepower.
[3]Engineer's ONLY — State whether S - Steam or M - Motor.
[4]O - Ocean; C - Coastwise; GL - Great Lakes; BSL - Bays, Sounds and Lakes other than Great Lakes; R - Rivers.

Name of Vessel	Class of Vessel[1]	Tonnage or HP[2]	Steam or Motor[3]	Waters Nav.[4]	Served As	Date Shipped	Date Discharged	SERVICE		
								Yrs	Mos	Days
							TOTAL			

DATE SUBMITTED   SIGNATURE OF APPLICANT   PAGE

_____ OF _____

DEPARTMENT OF TRANSPORTATION U.S. COAST GUARD CG-866 (Rev. 6-82)	SEA SERVICE FORM (MILITARY EXPERIENCE) *See Privacy Act Statement on Instruction Sheet*	FILING DATA *(C.G. USE ONLY)*

NAME *(Last)*	*(First)*	Middle Init. *(Suffix)*	SOCIAL SECURITY NO.	BRANCH OF SERVICE

VESSEL NAME:_____ CLASS:_____ TONNAGE OR HORSEPOWER[1]: _____

INCLUSIVE DATES OF SERVICE, FROM: Mo. | Day | Yr. _____ Mo. | Day | Hr. _____

RANK OR RATE:_____ PERCENTAGE OF UNDERWAY TIME_____ STEAM OR MOTOR[2]_____ WATERS NAV.[3]_____

LIST UNDERWAY WATCHSTANDING DUTIES: _____
_____
_____

LIST OTHER DUTIES:_____
_____
_____

DESCRIBE ANY OTHER QUALIFYING EXPERIENCE: _____
_____
_____
_____

VESSEL NAME:_____ CLASS:_____ TONNAGE OR HORSEPOWER[1]: _____

INCLUSIVE DATES OF SERVICE, FROM: Mo. | Day | Yr. _____ TO: Mo. | Day | Hr. _____

RANK OR RATE:_____ PERCENTAGE OF UNDERWAY TIME _____ STEAM OR MOTOR[2]_____ WATERS NAV.[3]_____

LIST UNDERWAY WATCHSTANDING DUTIES: _____
_____
_____

LIST OTHER DUTIES:_____
_____
_____

DESCRIBE ANY OTHER QUALIFYING EXPERIENCE: _____
_____
_____

VESSEL NAME:_____ CLASS:_____ TONNAGE OR HORSEPOWER[1]: _____

INCLUSIVE DATES OF SERVICE, FROM: Mo. | Day | Yr. _____ TO: Mo. | Day | Hr. _____

RANK OR RATE:_____ PERCENTAGE OF UNDERWAY TIME _____ STEAM OR MOTOR[2]_____ WATERS NAV.[3]_____

LIST UNDERWAY WATCHSTANDING DUTIES: _____
_____
_____

LIST OTHER DUTIES:_____
_____
_____

DESCRIBE ANY OTHER QUALIFYING EXPERIENCE:_____

VESSEL NAME: _____ CLASS: _____ TONNAGE OR HORSEPOWER[1]: _____

	Mo.	Day	Yr.			Mo.	Day	Hr.

INCLUSIVE DATES OF SERVICE, FROM: _____ TO: _____

RANK OR RATE: _____ PERCENTAGE OF UNDERWAY TIME _____ STEAM OR MOTOR[2] _____ WATERS NAV.[3] _____

LIST UNDERWAY WATCHSTANDING DUTIES: _____
_____
_____

LIST OTHER DUTIES: _____
_____
_____

DESCRIBE ANY OTHER QUALIFYING EXPERIENCE: _____
_____
_____

VESSEL NAME: _____ CLASS: _____ TONNAGE OR HORSEPOWER[1]: _____

	Mo.	Day	Yr.			Mo.	Day	Hr.

INCLUSIVE DATES OF SERVICE, FROM: _____ TO: _____

RANK OR RATE: _____ PERCENTAGE OF UNDERWAY TIME _____ STEAM OR MOTOR[2] _____ WATERS NAV.[3] _____

LIST UNDERWAY WATCHSTANDING DUTIES: _____
_____
_____

LIST OTHER DUTIES: _____
_____
_____

DESCRIBE ANY OTHER QUALIFYING EXPERIENCE: _____
_____
_____

VESSEL NAME: _____ CLASS: _____ TONNAGE OR HORSEPOWER[1]: _____

	Mo.	Day	Yr.			Mo.	Day	Hr.

INCLUSIVE DATES OF SERVICE, FROM: _____ TO: _____

RANK OR RATE: _____ PERCENTAGE OF UNDERWAY TIME _____ STEAM OR MOTOR[2] _____ WATERS NAV.[3] _____

LIST UNDERWAY WATCHSTANDING DUTIES: _____
_____
_____

LIST OTHER DUTIES: _____
_____
_____

DESCRIBE ANY OTHER QUALIFYING EXPERIENCE: _____
_____
_____

---

[1] If applying for deck officer's license, give gross tonnage; if applying for engineer's license, give horsepower.
[2] Engineer's ONLY — State whether S - Steam or M - Motor.
[3] O - Ocean; C - Coastwise; GL - Great Lakes; BSL - Bays, Sounds and Lakes other than Great Lakes; R - Rivers.

DATE SUBMITTED	SIGNATURE OF APPLICANT	PAGE
		_____ OF _____

REQUEST PERTAINING TO MILITARY RECORDS

Please read instructions on the reverse. If more space is needed, use plain paper.

DATE OF REQUEST

SECTION I—INFORMATION NEEDED TO LOCATE RECORDS (Furnish as much as possible)

1. NAME USED DURING SERVICE *(Last, first, and middle)*	2. SOCIAL SECURITY NO.	3. DATE OF BIRTH	4. PLACE OF BIRTH

5. ACTIVE SERVICE, PAST AND PRESENT   (For an effective records search, it is important that ALL service be shown below)

BRANCH OF SERVICE *(Also, show last organization, if known)*	DATES OF ACTIVE SERVICE — DATE ENTERED	DATE RELEASED	Check one — OFFICER	EN-LISTED	SERVICE NUMBER DURING THIS PERIOD

6. RESERVE SERVICE, PAST OR PRESENT   If "none," check here ▶ ☐

a. BRANCH OF SERVICE	b. DATES OF MEMBERSHIP — FROM	TO	c. Check one — OFFICER ☐ / EN-LISTED ☐	d. SERVICE NUMBER DURING THIS PERIOD

7. NATIONAL GUARD MEMBERSHIP   (Check one): a. ARMY ☐   b. AIR FORCE ☐   c. NONE ☐

d. STATE	e. ORGANIZATION	f. DATES OF MEMBERSHIP — FROM	TO	g. Check one — OFFICER ☐ / EN-LISTED ☐	h. SERVICE NUMBER DURING THIS PERIOD

8. IS SERVICE PERSON DECEASED   ☐ YES   ☐ NO   If "yes," enter date of death:

9. IS (WAS) INDIVIDUAL A MILITARY RETIREE OR FLEET RESERVIST   ☐ YES   ☐ NO

SECTION II—REQUEST

1. EXPLAIN WHAT INFORMATION OR DOCUMENTS YOU NEED; OR, CHECK ITEM 2; OR, COMPLETE ITEM 3

2. IF YOU ONLY NEED A STATEMENT OF SERVICE   check here ☐

3. LOST SEPARATION DOCUMENT REPLACEMENT REQUEST *(Complete a or b, and c)*

☐ a. REPORT OF SEPARATION (DD Form 214 or equivalent)   YEAR ISSUED — *This contains information normally needed to determine eligibility for benefits. It may be furnished only to the veteran, the surviving next of kin, or to a representative with veteran's signed release (item 5 of this form).*

☐ b. DISCHARGE CERTIFICATE   YEAR ISSUED — *This shows only the date and character at discharge. It is of little value in determining eligibility for benefits. It may be issued only to veterans discharged honorably or under honorable conditions; or, if deceased, to the surviving spouse.*

c. EXPLAIN HOW SEPARATION DOCUMENT WAS LOST

4. EXPLAIN PURPOSE FOR WHICH INFORMATION OR DOCUMENTS ARE NEEDED

6. REQUESTER

a. IDENTIFICATION : (check appropriate box)
☐ Same person identified in Section I   ☐ Surviving spouse
☐ Next of kin (relationship): _____
☐ Other (specify): _____

b. SIGNATURE (see instructions 3 and 4 on reverse side)

5. RELEASE AUTHORIZATION, IF REQUIRED (Read instruction 3 on reverse side)

I hereby authorize release of the requested information/documents to the person indicated at right (item 7).

VETERAN SIGN HERE ▶ _____

(If signed by other than veteran, show relationship to veteran)

7. Please type or print clearly —   COMPLETE RETURN ADDRESS

Name, number and street, city, State and ZIP code

TELEPHONE NO.   (Include area code) ▶

INSTRUCTIONS

1. Information needed to locate records. Certain identifying information is necessary to determine the location of an individual's record of military service. Please give careful consideration to and answer each item on this form. If you do not have and cannot obtain the information for an item, show "NA," meaning the information is "not available." Include as much of the requested information as you can. This will help us to give you the best possible service.

2. Charges for service. A nominal fee is charged for certain types of service. In most instances service fees cannot be determined in advance. If your request involves a service fee you will be notified as soon as that determination is made.

3. Restrictions on release of information. Information from records of military personnel is released subject to restrictions imposed by the military departments consistent with the provisions of the Freedom of Information Act of 1967 (as amended 1974) and the Privacy Act of 1974. A service person has access to almost any information contained in his own record. The next of kin (see item 4 of instructions) if the veteran is deceased and Federal officers for official purposes are authorized to receive information from a military service or medical record only as specified in the above cited Acts. Other requesters must have the release authorization, in item 5 of the form, signed by the veteran or, if deceased, by the next of kin. Employers and others needing proof of military services are expected to accept the information shown on documents issued by the Armed Forces at the time a service person is separated.

4. Precedence of next of kin. The order of precedence of the next of kin is: unremarried widow or widower, eldest son or daughter, father or mother, eldest brother or sister.

5. Location of military personnel records. The various categories of military personnel records are described in the chart below. For each category there is a code number which indicates the address at the bottom of the page to which this request should be sent. For each military service there is a note explaining approximately how long the records are held by the military service before they are transferred to the National Personnel Records Center, St. Louis. Please read these notes carefully and make sure you send your inquiry to the right address. (If the person has two or more periods of service within the same branch, send your request to the office having the record for the last period of service.)

6. Definitions for abbreviations used below:

NPRC—National Personnel Records Center   PERS—Personnel Records
TDRL—Temporary Disability Retirement List   MED—Medical Records

SERVICE	NOTE	CATEGORY OF RECORDS — WHERE TO WRITE		ADDRESS CODE ▼
AIR FORCE (USAF)	Air Force records are transferred to NPRC from Code 1, 90 days after separation and from Code 2, 30 days after separation.	Active members (includes National Guard on active duty in the Air Force), TDRL, and general officers retired with pay.		1
		Reserve, retired reservist in nonpay status, current National Guard officers not on active duty in Air Force, and National Guard released from active duty in Air Force.		2
		Current National Guard enlisted not on active duty in Air Force.		13
		Discharged, deceased, and retired with pay (except general officers retired with pay).		14
COAST GUARD (USCG)	Coast Guard officer and enlisted records are transferred to NPRC 3–6 months after separation	Active, reserve, and TDRL members.		3
		Discharged, deceased, and retired members (see next item).		14
		Officers separated before 1/1/29 and enlisted personnel separated before 1/1/15.		6
MARINE CORPS (USMC)	Marine Corps records are transferred to NPRC 4 months after separation	Active and TDRL members, reserve officers, and Class II enlisted reserve.		4
		Class III reservists and Fleet Marine Corps Reserve members.		5
		Discharged, deceased, and retired members (see next item).		14
		Officers and enlisted personnel separated before 1/1/1896.		6
ARMY (USA)	Army records are transferred to NPRC as soon as processed (about 30 days after separation)	Reserve, living retired members, retired general officers, and active duty records of current National Guard members who performed service in the U.S. Army before 7/1/72.*		7
		Active officers (including National Guard on active duty in the U.S. Army).		8
		Active enlisted (including National Guard on active duty in the U.S. Army) and enlisted TDRL.		9
		Current National Guard officers not on active duty in the U.S. Army.		12
		Current National Guard enlisted not on active duty in the U.S. Army.		13
		Discharged and deceased members (see next item).		14
		Officers separated before 7/1/17 and enlisted separated before 11/1/12.		6
		Officers and warrant officers TDRL.		8
NAVY (USN)	Navy records are transferred to NPRC 6 months after retirement or complete separation.	Active members (including reservists on active duty)---PERS and MED		10
		Discharged, deceased, retired (with and without pay) less than six months, TDRL, drilling and nondrilling reservists	PERS only	10
			MED only	11
		Discharged, deceased, retired (with and without pay) more than six months (see next item)---PERS & MED		14
		Officers separated before 1/1/03 and enlisted separated before 1/1/1886---PERS and MED		6

* Code 12 applies to active duty records of current National Guard officers who performed service in the U.S. Army after 6/30/72.
Code 13 applies to active duty records of current National Guard enlisted members who performed service in the U.S. Army after 6/30/72.

ADDRESS LIST OF CUSTODIANS (BY CODE NUMBERS SHOWN ABOVE)—Where to write/send this form for each category of records

1) USAF Military Personnel Center
Military Personnel Records Div.
Randolph AFB, TX 78148

2) Air Reserves Personnel Center
7300 East 1st Avenue
Denver, CO 80280

3) Commandant
U.S. Coast Guard
Washington, D.C. 20590

4) Commandant of the Marine Corps.
Headquarters, U.S. Marine Corps.
Washington, D.C. 20380

5) Marine Corps Reserve Forces
Administration Center
1500 E. Bannister Road
Kansas City, MO 64131

6) Military Archives Division
National Archives and Records
General Services Administration
Washington, D.C. 20408

7) Commander-
U.S. Army Reserve Components
Personnel & Administration Center
9700 Page Blvd
St. Louis, MO 63132

8) USA Milpercen
ATT: DAPC-PSR R
200 Stovall St.
Alexandria, VA 22332

9) Commandant
U.S. Army Enlisted Records
and Evaluation Center
Ft. Benjamin Harrison
Indiana 46249

10) Chief of Naval Personnel
Department of the Navy
Washington, D.C. 20370

11) Naval Reserve
Personnel Center
New Orleans, LA 70146

12) Army National Guard
Personnel Center
Colombia Pike Office Building
5600 Colombia Pike Blvd.
Falls Church, VA 22041

13) The Adjutant General
(of the appropriate State,
DC or Puerto Rico).

14) National Personnel Records Cntr.
(Military Personnel Records)
9700 Page Blvd.
St. Louis, MO 63132

Applicant's Name

Social Security Number

Type of Examination: (Check One)

1.) ☐ GENERAL PHYSICAL CONDITION, VISUAL ACUITY AND COLOR SENSE & HEARING.
(Required for Orig. license, Orig. AB, Tankerman, or QMED)

2.) ☐ GENERAL PHYSICAL CONDITION, VISUAL ACUITY AND HEARING. *(Required for license renewal.)*

3.) ☐ GENERAL PHYSICAL CONDITION ONLY. *(Required for raise of grade of license if applicant has not had an original or renewal physical in last three years.)*

EXAMINATION RESULTS - LICENSED PHYSICIAN OR PHYSICIAN ASSISTANT

Height	Weight	Color Eyes	Color Hair	Distinguishing Marks

COLOR SENSE	VISUAL ACUITY	HEARING	Audiometer req. for impaired hearing					Auditory Canals

COLOR SENSE
☐ NORMAL
☐ NOT NORMAL
TEST GIVEN:

VISUAL ACUITY
UNCORR. RIGHT: 20/   UNCORR. LEFT: 20/
CORRECTABLE TO
RIGHT: 20/   LEFT: 20/

HEARING
☐ NORMAL
☐ IMPAIRED
(Audiometer only req. if impaired is checked)

Hz	500°	1000°	2000°	3000°
L				
R				

*over 40 db hearing loss is considered impaired & requires a waiver

Auditory Canals
☐ NORMAL
☐ DISCHARGE

HEART & LUNGS

STIFF JOINTS, OLD FRACTURES, DEFORMITIES & OTHER MAJOR DEFECTS:

REMARKS & MEDICATION: *(DOSAGE, FREQUENCY, HISTORY WHILE ON MEDICATION, SIDE EFFECTS, ETC.)*

I HEREBY CERTIFY THAT I HAVE THIS DAY EXAMINED THE DESCRIBED APPLICANT AND MADE THE ABOVE FINDINGS. IN MY OPINION HE/SHE IS PHYSICALLY (CHECK ONE)

☐ COMPETENT
☐ INCOMPETENT

TO PERFORM DUTIES ABOARD A MERCHANT VESSEL OF THE UNITED STATES.

Printed/Typed Name of Physician/Physician Assistant	OFFICE ADDRESS (ZIP CODE)
State License No.	
Telephone	
Physician/Physician Assistant Signature	Date	Applicant's Signature (Observed by phys./phys. assistant)

Previous Edition Is Obsolete

SN 7530-00-F01-0110

PRIVACY ACT STATEMENT

As required by 5 USC 552a (e) (3), the following information is provided you when supplying personal information to the U.S. Coast Guard.

1. <u>Authority</u> which authorizes the solicitation of the information – 46 USC 2104 (a), 7101 (c) - (e), 7306 (a) (4), 7313 (c) (3), 7317 (a), 8703 (b), 9102 (a) (5). (See 46 CFR subparts and paragraphs 10.205 (d), 10.207 (e), 10.209 (d), 12.05-5, 12.15-5, 12.20-3)

2. <u>Principal purposes</u> for which information is intended to be used:
   (1) To determine if an applicant is physically capable of performing shipboard duties.
   (2) To ensure that the applicant's physical is conducted by a duly licensed physician/physician assistant and to verify information as needed.

3. The <u>routine uses</u> which may be made of this information:
   (1) This form becomes a part of the applicant's file as documentary evidence that the regulatory physical requirement has been satisfied and the applicant is physically competent to hold a merchant marine license or document.
   (2) This information becomes a part of the total license or document file and is subject to review by federal agency casualty investigators.

4. <u>Disclosure</u> of this information is voluntary, but failure to provide the information will result in non-issuance of a license or merchant mariner's document.

PHYSICAL STANDARDS

1. In general, epilepsy, insanity, acute venereal disease, neurosyphilis or badly impaired hearing, or other defect that would render the applicant incompetent to perform the ordinary duties of an officer or an unlicensed seaman at sea are causes for certification as incompetent.

2. VISUAL ACUITY:

A. For an original license as engineer, offshore installation manager, barge supervisor, ballast control officer, radio officer, or certificates as QMED or tankerman the applicant must have uncorrected vision of at least 20/200 in each eye correctible to 20/50 in each eye. Vision beyond these parameters requires a waiver.

B. For an original license as master, mate, pilot, operator, or certificate as able-seaman, the applicant must have uncorrected vision of at least 20/200 in each eye correctible to 20/40 in each eye. Vision beyond these parameters requires a waiver.

C. License renewals require the same standards as an original.

3. COLOR SENSE:

A. X-Chrom lenses may not be used during the test.

B. Applicants for an original license as engineer, radio officer, offshore installation manager, barge supervisor, ballast control operator, or QMED endorsement shall be examined only as to their ability to distinguish the colors red, blue, green, and yellow.

C. Applicants for original deck licenses (not including MODU licenses), or able seaman or tankerman endorsements must have normal color sense. The color sense must be tested by one of the following tests:

   (1) PSEUDOISOCHROMATIC PLATES (DVORINE, 2nd EDITION; AOC; REVISED EDITION OR ADC-HRR; ISHIHARA 16-, 24-, or 38- PLATE EDITIONS)
   (2) ELDRIDGE-GREEN COLOR PERCEPTION LANTERN
   (3) FARNSWORTH LANTERN
   (4) KEYSTONE ORTHOSCOPE
   (5) KEYSTONE TELEBINOCULAR
   (6) SAMCTT (SCHOOL OF AVIATION MEDICINE COLOR THRESHOLD TESTER)
   (7) TITMUS OPTICAL VISION TESTER
   (8) WILLIAMS LANTERN

4. HEARING:

A. An audiometer test is only required if the applicant has, or is suspected to have, impaired hearing. A hearing loss of over 40 db is considered impaired hearing and requires a waiver.

1) Alabama
O'Neil Bldg
2021 Third Ave., North
Birmingham, 35203
(205) 731-1056
0900 to 1700

2) California
ARCO Plaza-C-Level
505 So. Flower St.
Los Angeles, 90071
(213) 894-5841
0830 to 1630

Room 117, Federal Bldg.
450 Golden Gate Avenue
San Francisco, 94102
(415) 556-0643
0800 to 1600

3) Colorado
Room 117, Federal Bldg.
Denver, 80294
(303) 844-3963
0800 to 1600

World Savings Bldg.
720 North Main Street
Pueblo, 81003
(719) 544-3142
0900 to 1700

4) Dist. of Columbia
U.S. Gov't Printing Office
710 No. Capitol Street
Washington, D.C. 20401
(202) 275-2091
0800 to 1600

1510 H Street NW
Washington, D.C. 20401
(202) 653-5075
0900 to 1700

5) Florida
Room 158, Federal Bldg.
Jacksonville, 32203
(904) 791-3801
0800 to 1600

6) Georgia
Room 100, Federal Bldg.
Atlanta, 30343
(404) 331-6947

7) Illinois
Room 1365, Federal Bldg.
219 S. Dearborn Street
Chicago, 60604
(312) 353-5133
0800 to 1600

Maryland
See last address
this page.

8) Massachusetts
Room G25, Federal Bldg.
Sudbury Street
Boston, 02203
(617) 565-2488
0800 to 1600

9) Michigan
Suite 160, Federal Bldg.
477 Michigan Avenue
Detroit, 48226
(313) 226-7816
0800 to 1600

10) Missouri
120 Bannister Mall
5600 E. Bannister Rd.
Kansas City, 64137
Mon-Sat 1000 to 2130
Sun 1200 Noon to 1800

11) New York
Room 110
26 Federal Plaza
New York, 10278
(212) 264-3825
0800 to 1600

12) Ohio
1st Floor, Federal Bldg.
1240 E. 9th Street
Cleveland, 44199
(216) 522-4922
0900 to 1700

Room 207, Federal Bldg.
200 N. High Street
Columbus, 43215
(614) 469-6956
0900 to 1700

13) Oregon
1305 S.W. 1st Ave.
Portland, 97201-5801
(503) 221-6217
0900 to 1700

14) Pennsylvania
Robert Morris Bldg.
100 N. 17th Street
Philadelphia, 19103
(215) 597-0677
0800 to 1600

Room 118, Fed. Bldg.
1000 Liberty Avenue
Pittsburg, 15222
(412) 644-2721
0830 to 1630

15) Texas
Room 1C46, Fed. Bldg.
1100 Commerce St.
Dallas, 75242
(214) 767-0076
0800 to 1600

9319 Gulf Freeway
Houston, 77017
(713) 229-3515
Mon-Sat 1000 to 1800

16) Washington
Room 194, Fed. Bldg.
915 Second Avenue
Seattle, 98174
(206) 442-4270
0800 to 1600

17) Wisconsin
Room 190, Fed. Bldg.
517 E. Wisconsin Ave
Milwaukee, 53202
(414) 291-1304
0800 to 1600

18) Maryland
Retail Sales Outlet
8660 Cherry Lane
Laurel, 20707
(301) 953-7974
792-0262
0745 to 1545

A LIST OF QUESTIONS
I MUST ASK THE LOCAL REC

1) _____

2) _____

3) _____

4) _____

5) _____

6) _____

7) _____

8) _____

9) _____

10) _____

11) _____

12) _____

13) _____

14) _____

15) _____

16) _____

17) _____

18) _____

19) _____

20) _____

21) _____

22) _____

23) _____

24) _____

1)	28)	55)	82)	109)	136)	163)
2)	29)	56)	83)	110)	137)	164)
3)	30)	57)	84)	111)	138)	165)
4)	31)	58)	85)	112)	139)	166)
5)	32)	59)	86)	113)	140)	167)
6)	33)	60)	87)	114)	141)	168)
7)	34)	61)	88)	115)	142)	169)
8)	35)	62)	89)	116)	143)	170)
9)	36)	63)	90)	117)	144)	171)
10	37)	64)	91)	118)	145)	172)
11)	38)	65)	92)	119)	146)	173)
12)	39)	66)	93)	120)	147)	174)
13)	40)	67)	94)	121)	148)	175)
14)	41)	68)	95)	122)	149)	176)
15)	42)	69)	96)	123)	150)	177)
16)	43)	70)	97)	124)	151)	178)
17)	44)	71)	98)	125)	152)	179)
18)	45)	72)	99)	126)	153)	180)
19)	46)	73)	100)	127)	154)	181)
20)	47)	74)	101)	128)	155)	182)
21)	48)	75)	102)	129)	156)	183)
22)	49)	76)	103)	130)	157)	184)
23)	50)	77)	104)	131)	158)	185)
24)	51)	78)	105)	132)	159)	186)
25)	52)	79)	106)	133)	160)	187)
26)	53)	80)	107)	134)	161)	188)
27)	54)	81)	108)	135)	162)	189)

1)	28)	24)	21)	18)	15)	12)
2)	29)	25)	22)	19)	16)	13)
3)	30)	26)	23)	20)	17)	14)
4)		27)	24)	21)	18)	15)
5)	1)	28)	25)	22)	19)	16)
6)	2)	29)	26)	23)	20)	17)
7)	3)	30)	27)	24)	21)	18)
8)	4)		28)	25)	22)	19)
9)	5)	1)	29)	26)	23)	20)
10	6)	2)	30)	27)	24)	21)
11)	7)	3)		28)	25)	22)
12)	8)	4)	1)	29)	26)	23)
13)	9)	5)	2)	30)	27)	24)
14)	10	6)	3)		28)	25)
15)	11)	7)	4)	1)	29)	26)
16)	12)	8)	5)	2)	30	27)
17)	13)	9)	6)	3)		28)
18)	14)	10	7)	4)	1)	29)
19)	15)	11)	8)	5)	2)	30)
20)	16)	12)	9)	6)	3)	
21)	17)	13)	10)	7)	4)	
22)	18)	14)	11)	8)	5)	
23)	19)	15)	12)	9)	6)	
24)	20)	16)	13)	10	7)	
25)	21)	17)	14)	11)	8)	
26)	22)	18)	15)	12)	9)	
27)	23)	19)	16)	13)	10)	
		20)	17)	14)	11)	

A

Advection fog - Fog caused by warmer offshore air cooling rapidly over a cold sea and condensing into fog. See Weather section under Seamanship.

All-around light - A 360° light visible on all points of the horizon.

Arc - Part of a 360° circle.

Avast - Belay. Stop. Now on CG tests.

B

Backfire arrestor - A high density wire mesh covering carburetor air intake preventing flames emerging during a backfire. Required on all U.S. manufactured power craft burning gasoline.

Backing - The directional change or movement of wind counter-clockwise. Also called "hauling".

Barometer - A device for measuring atmospheric pressure.

Beam - At a right angle to the keel.

Bearing - A relative, magnetic or true direction of an object **from** one's location.

Bifurcation - Technical term denoting converging channels.

Bollard - A piling which sticks up through the dock to which mooring lines are tied.

Broach - To veer to windward and come broadside to the wind and/or waves.

Broad on the beam - At a right angle to the keel at the widest point of the vessel.

C

COLREGS - A term applying to the "Convention of the International Regulations for Preventing Collisions at Sea, 1972." Formalized in 1972, becoming effective July 15, 1977. Sometimes referred to as the '72 COLREGS and refer primarily to the International Rules of The Road. On June 1, 1983 fifty-five amendments were added to the '72 COLREGS.

Combustible (liquid) - One having a flashpoint at 100° F. or higher, *e.g.* vegetable and lubricating oils.

Compass error - The algebraic sum of the variation and deviation.

Cross signals - An old, now illegal, signal whereby one blast was answered with two blasts and vice versa.

Current - Movement of a body of water caused by any force.

D

Danger signal - At least five short blasts on ship's whistle. More appropriately, in maneuvering, a signal of **doubt**.

Demarcation line - A line across harbor entrances, or nearby, indicating the separation line between inland and international waters and the rules applying thereto. Indicated on most large scale harbor charts.

Deviation - Compass error caused by ferrous metals in close proximity to a compass on board ship.

Diabetes - A blood disease wherein victim is unable to burn normal amounts of sugar.

Diaphone - An out-of-date air pressure diaphram device which activated a fog horn ashore. Diaphram was pumped up mechanically, then released to activate fog horn.

Down-draft carburetor - Carburetor with air intake facing up. Air is pulled "down" the carburetor. Standard on today's gas powered craft.

Drift - Speed of the current.

Drip Pan - Small pan placed beneath old fashioned up-draft carburetors with air intakes facing down. To catch dripping fuel.

Drogue - A sea-anchor trailing from the stern to keep stern into oncoming sea and prevent yawing.

E

Ebb current - A current flowing away from shore following high tide.

ETA - Estimated time of arrival.

Extremis - Term used to imply collision is imminent

F

Fairway - A navigable channel or traffic pattern, generally within a harbor.

Fix - A known location found by bearings; visual, radar, loran or SatNav.

Flammable (liquid) - One having a flashpoint below 100° F. with a vapor pressure less than 40 psi, e.g. gasoline, alcohol, and acetone.

Flashing - Referring to a buoy light which flashes about 30 times per minute.

Flood current - A current flowing towards land following a low tide.

Fog horn - A warning of foul ground generated by a horn buoy or lighthouse ashore. Term is no longer used in Rules of The Road as regards ships.

Fog Signal - One of many whistle, bell or gong soundings when underway or at anchor in or near an area of restricted visibility. Generally, the deeper the whistle the larger the vessel.

G

Give-way craft - The burdened vessel in a meeting, crossing or overtaking situation. Does not have the right-of-way.

H

Hauling - See backing.

Hogging line - A line strung beneath the ship from one side to the other. Used to support collision matting (canvas or similar) to prevent taking on water when a hull is stoved.

I

I.A.L.A. - International Association of Lighthouse Authorities. Refers to the new buoyage system which started in 1983 to be finished by 1989. See "Buoys" under Seamanship chapter in this volume.

Inland - Referring to any navigable bodies of water shoreward from a demarcation line. Western rivers, Great Lakes and Pudget Sound are examples of inland bodies considered separate as regards **some cases** in the Inland Rules of The Road. See VTC below.

Inspected vessels - Vessels inspected by the U.S. Coast Guard and granted a Certificate of Inspection to carry passengers for hire. Certificate denotes maximum number of passengers vessel may carry and other conditions of operation.

Insulin - An injection given to diabetic victim to aid in balancing of body sugar.

Insulin shock - A reaction from having been administered too much insulin.

Isolgonic lines - Lines connecting points of equal magnetic variation.

K

Knot - A measurement of speed over the water, i.e. how many nautical miles are covered each hour underway.

L

"L" Vessel - Certificated passenger carrying vessel sixty-five feet or greater in length.

LPG gas - Liquid petroleum gas. Examples are butane and propane. Not allowed on passenger carrying vessels.

LOP - Line of Position. A plotting line on a chart derived from a bearing for the purpose of finding one's position at sea.

M

Master Near Coastal Waters, Great Lakes and Inland - License granted to operate passenger carrying vessels, *et. al.* Replaces Ocean Operator to 100 gross tons.

Masthead light - A 225º white light high on a mast.

Mayday - Verbal radio distress call.

N

Nautical mile - Approximately 6076 feet, (6076.1155')

NFPA - The National Fire Prevention Association.

Not under command - "Exceptional circumstances" prevent maneuvering. Adrift.

O

Occluded - Weather term referring to the coming together of air masses with dissimilar temperatures.

Occulting - A light which is on more than it is off.

Ocean Operator - See Master Near Coastal Waters

OinC - Officer in Charge.

OCMI - Officer in Charge, Marine Inspection.

Operator Uninspected Passenger Vessels, (OUPV) - Denotes license to carry six or less passengers for hire on Coastal, Great Lakes or Inland. Six Pac.

P

Parcelling - The taping of a cable, generally after it has been wormed.

PFD - Personal flotation device. A life jacket, cushion or ring/horseshoe buoy.

Piledikes - Poles driven into a riverbed adjacent to the riverbank to prevent erosion by passing current.

Pitchpole - Term applied to any vessel when bow digs into wave and oncoming stern wave forces stern up and over the bow.

Port - To the left. The left side of a vessel facing forward.

Psc - Short for "per steering compass".

Pgc - Short for "per gyro compass."

Q

Quick flashing – A buoy light which flashes 60 fpm.

R

Radio beacon – A radio shoreline transmission signalling device with frequency and identifying morse code signal indicated on a chart. Range is generally limited to about ten miles.

RDF – Radio direction finder – A radio signal receiving device equipped with a loop antenna capable of pinpointing direction of any given incoming broadcast.

REC – Regional Examination Center. Where marine exams are given by the U.S. Coast Guard. See appendix this volume for locations and phone numbers.

Relative bearing – The direction of some object from the boat's position irrespective of vessel's heading. As a comparison: Bearing 3:00 O'clock would be bearing 090°. Bearing 9:00 O'clock would be bearing 270°. See page 104.

Restricted in ability to maneuver – Special nature of vessel's work severely hampers maneuverability.

Restricted visibility – Vision hampered by fog, mist, falling snow, heavy rain, sandstorm or similar causes.

Rode – Anchor line.

Running fix – A fix by taking two bearings at different times on the same object.

Running lights – An all-inclusive term referring to lights required on any vessel when underway at night or in restricted visibility. Frequently mis-used to indicate sidelights.

S

"S" vessel – Certificated passenger carrying vessel less than sixty-five feet in length.

Scope – Ratio of anchor rode to depth of water including freeboard.

Separation zone – A buffer zone between two opposite bound traffic lanes.

Serving – the wrapping of a cable,

stanchion or fitting with a preservative type of lanyard or line, (generally marlin).

Set – Direction of current flow.

Sidelights – Lights of a vessel shinning from dead ahead to 22.5° abaft the beam on their respective sides of red to port, green to starboard.

SIP – Senior Inspector Personnel in a REC.

Six-Pac – A slang term for Operator of Uninspected Passenger Vessel for hire. Also referring to a "six-pac boat" meaning a small passenger carrying vessel, less than 100 gross tons, permitted to carry six or less passengers for hire without a Coast Guard Inspection or certificate of inspection.

Small passenger vessel – A vessel equipped to carry passengers for hire and conforming to the requirements of the U.S. Coast Guard. Less than 100 gross tons.

Spar – A boom to which lifeboats are secured. Any long boom, generally wood or aluminum. From the Coast Guard motto (s)emper (par)atus. A World War II female Coast (sic) Guardsman.

Stability - Anti-capsizing forces of gravity and buoyancy held in control to maintain ship's upright position.

Stand-on craft - The vessel with the right-of-way in a meeting, crossing or overtaking situation.

Starboard - The right side of a vessel facing forward.

Stern light - A white light shown from stern of craft underway. Shows in an arc of 135°.

T

Torch - A British term for flashlight.

Towing lights - Yellow lights shown from the stern light of any tug towing a tow from behind. Also used inland when pushing ahead or alongside in inland waters. 135° of arc.

Trolling - Trailing a fishing line behind a boat.

U

Up-draft carburetor - An out-of-date version on which the air intake pointed downwards, towards the bilge or nearly so.

Underway - Any craft is underway when not made fast to shore, at anchor or aground.

Underway with way on - Underway and making way through the water.

Unified - Referring to inland waters' rules and their close proximity to those applying in international waters. Enacted into law Dec. 24, 1980, becoming effective Dec. 24, 1981 (effective Great Lakes March 1, 1983).

Uninspected vessels - Those vessels not inspected by U.S. Coast Guard to carry passengers for hire, e.g. six-pac small passenger carrying vessels.

V

Variation - Part of compass error. Geographic difference between magnetic and true north.

Veering - The changing of the direction of wind in a clockwise direction; to let out more anchor chain.

Veering anchor - Method by which a large vessel at anchor on a river can move from side-to-side by turning the rudder hard over. Current reacting against the rudder moves the vessel to one side. Also letting out more anchor chain.

VTC - Vessel traffic control. Special area rules applying to various sections in the Western Rivers. Sometimes called VTM-meaning vessel traffic management.

W

Way on - The action of being underway.

Western Rivers - Those rivers which empty into the Mississippi River. Exception: Red River of The North.

Williamson Turn - see p. 140.

Worming - The weaving of treated line into cable grooves to make it flush.

PLEASE READ THE ORDERING DIRECTIONS
ON THE REVERSE SIDE BEFORE ORDERING.

1) The Coast Guard License Book   14th edition $29.95-$_____
   Six Pac to Masters - 100 tons.

2) The VHS Videos - See accompanying sheet before ordering.
   The Coast Guard License/Exam Room Open Book Refs. $21.95-$ _21.95_
   Rules of The Road $21.95-$ _21.95_
   Piloting-For Coast Guard Exams $21.95-$ _21.95_

3) The Chartlets. Circle those desired: 12221-Chesapeake, $21.95-$ _21.95_
   12354-Long Is., 13205-Block Is. $7.95 ea. or $21.95
   for complete set. Includes plotting questions and answers
   from CG data banks.

4) The Supplement. Over 800 additional quiz questions $12.95-$ _12.95_
   in all modules.

5) Gonder's Rules of The Road $12.95-$ _12.95_
   With facing pages explaining CG test approach.

6) 237 Rules. Hot off the Coast Guard Data Banks. 237 of $9.95-$ _9.95_
   their most recent Rules of The Road Questions.

7) Course Plotter. No frills. $8.95-$ _8.95_
   Similar to one in text. Sturdy-accurate.

8) Flashcards-Uncut to save $$ - on 8 1/2" x 11" cardstock. $8.95-$ _8.95_

9) Dividers. For measuring distances & plotting lat/long $6.95-$ _6.95_
   on charts. With plastic envelope.

10) The Second Dirty Dozen-Charting problems with detailed $4.95-$ __
    answers and chart solutions as in text.

California Residents must add 7 3/4% sales tax $_____
Multiply total (before shipping costs) by .0775

For all shipping costs plus specials to Alaska or Hawaii please
see reverse for descriptions and shipping.   Shipping $_____

TOTAL-$ _150.55_

PLEASE RUSH THIS ORDER TO:

Name_____

Street-(No P.O. Boxes for UPS)_____

City_____   State_____   Zip_____

The order form with this sheet consists of items of considerable use to CG license candidates. Each is less than similar items available in most retail stores. Some are not available in any form. This is a description and cost of each item. All are shipped on a one working day turnaround basis.

1) The Coast Guard License - From Six Pac to Masters 100 tons - **Revised.** This book is now published once every six months with applicable updates. First published in 1972 the book has enjoyed an enduring tenure. Our files are resplendent with letters from those who acquired their license using only this book. $29.95

2-THE THREE VHS VIDEOS

a) The Coast Guard License Video.
License application and sea time tips. Overview of the test modules for Six Pac to Master 100 tons. Requirements for the license. Reference books in the exam room and how to use them on the open book exams. Applicable Codes of Federal Regulations, *Light List, Coast Pilot, American Practical Navigator,* and use of relevant indexes. $21.95

b) Rules of The Road video.
Lots of animation. Lights and day-shapes. Arcs of visibility. Maneuvering signals & whistle signals plus those in restricted visibility, at anchor and aground. The elusive pecking order-the various rights-of-way of all vessels afloat. Heavy on quiz tips. $21.95.

c) Piloting As Required For Coast Guard Licenses.
Navigation for the Six Pac to Master 100 Tons. Made for simple hands-on and step-by-step procedures from latitude and longitude to set and drift. No flash, splash and big production scenes. All down-to-earth on how to do it, learn it and spit it back at them. Slow and easy. From simplifying variation and deviation to computations on speed-distance-time, course plotter how-to, dead reckoning, running fixes, bearings and set and drift. $21.95

3) The Chartlets. Black and white quality **full size** facsimiles of the three charts currently used in the REC's. With CG questions & answers. Better to become acquainted with these charts now rather than in the REC exam room where time counts. $7.95 each, or $21.95 for all three. Not for on-board navigation.

4) The Supplement-Over 800 **additional** quiz questions & answers on all modules direct from CG data banks. Cheap reassurance before your big day at the REC. Most questions not contained in other pubs on this page. $12.95.

5) Gonder's Rules of The Road. A copy of the official Rules with facing pages explaining how the CG uses the rules in their tests. Heavy editing for candidates use. Contains illustrations also found in our textbook. $12.95

6) 237 Rules of The Road questions & answers hot off the CG data banks. These are the current ones used on exams as of October 1992 and should be applicable for years. $9.95

7) Course Plotter. Thick, sturdy simple type hard to find. Shown in text. Measures about 4" x 15" for both small and standard chart work. $8.95.

8) Flashcards-**uncut**, nine to a page. Lights, dayshapes, fog signals and visibility of lights memory crutch. Fits in shirt pocket to carry and study anywhere during free time. Color coded and printed on 8 1/2" x 11" #67 cardstock ready to color if you like. Eighty-eight separate situations. Not a stack of inappropriate repeats like so many expensive glossy sets. $8.95.

9) Dividers. Small, simple and compact with plastic envelope-case. $6.95.

10) A dozen charting problems similar to those found in the text. Backed up by written **and** charted solutions using the text chart. The Second Dirty Dozen. **These are a waste of money if you ordered the Chartlets above.** $4.95

11) Updates and errata, as we acquire them, go out with all orders. **FREE** upon request if you send a self-addressed stamped envelope.

SHIPPING

All orders are shipped United Parcel Service so please -no P.O. boxes if avoidable.

Forty-Eight States

If order is less than $20, shipping cost is $4.25

If order is $20 or more, shipping cost $5.35

Hawaii/Alaska

All orders are shipped UPS 2nd Day Air.

All UPS shipments. Add $10.75 for orders less than $20, add $12.75 for orders $20 and more.